# Zero Trust Overview and Playbook Introduction

Guidance for business, security, and technology leaders and practitioners

**Mark Simos**

**Nikhil Kumar**

BIRMINGHAM—MUMBAI

# Zero Trust Overview and Playbook Introduction

**Group Product Manager**: Pavan Ramchandani
**Publishing Product Manager**: Rahul Nair
**Senior Editor**: Isha Singh
**Technical Editor**: Nithik Cheruvakodan
**Copy Editor**: Safis Editing
**Book Project Manager**: Neil D'Mello
**Proofreader**: Safis Editing
**Indexer**: Rekha Nair
**Production Designer**: Gokul Raj S.T
**Marketing Coordinators**: MaryLou De Mello and Shruthi Shetty

First published: October 2023

Production reference: 1231023

www.zerotrustplaybook.com

Published by
Packt Publishing Ltd.
Grosvenor House
11 St. Paul 's Square
Birmingham
B3 1RB, UK.

ISBN 978-1-80056-866-2

www.packtpub.com

*I dedicate this book to my wonderful and beautiful wife and children. Thank you for your patience, support, and love – I couldn't have done it without you. Thank you!*

*– Mark Simos*


*To my wife, Peelu, and children, Nitin and Laya, whose immeasurable love, patience, and support helped me through the long journey of getting this book done.*

*– Nikhil Kumar*

# Foreword

As global threats continue to compound, accelerate, and grow exponentially, there has never been a greater need for a change in thinking about cybersecurity. As a security practitioner since 2000, I have witnessed the ever-changing threat landscape and the evolution of industry solutions – as great innovation has attempted to keep pace with well-funded, well-orchestrated, and sophisticated attacks. Global organizations of all sizes and sectors have been impacted by the rampant pace of cyber-attacks – ransomware, DDoS, phishing, business email compromise, intellectual property theft, data theft, and cyber espionage, just to name a few of the types of attacks that exist today. Business has also become more digital, elevating security to an all-encompassing concern across business and technology. As we have witnessed this landscape changing, the industry also recognized it needed to evolve and change. With this recognition for change well understood, adopting a Zero Trust philosophy, architecture, and strategy became the rallying cry for cyber professionals.

What is lost in the race for a better solution to the growing cyber threats is a unified definition and set of capabilities for the successful implementation of Zero Trust in an organization's environment. Through their series of books, the authors of *The Zero Trust Playbook Series*, Nikhil Kumar and Mark Simos, attempt to answer questions surrounding Zero Trust – including the core defining capabilities and characteristics and how to successfully implement a Zero Trust architecture.

Nikhil and Mark both have extensive professional experience on the front lines of cyber defense, advising global organizations on architecture and best practices. As they delve into the topic of Zero Trust, they not only define the topic but also provide answers to the why, as well as detailed guidance on the how.

There has never been a greater need for a change in the cybersecurity defense methodology, and Zero Trust will bring the industry a long way toward maturity. Grounding this topic in pragmatic guidance while also clarifying why the purpose is a worthy task, I commend Nikhil and Mark for embarking on this journey.

Ann Johnson

*Corporate Vice President – Microsoft*

# Contributors

## About the authors

**Mark Simos** helps individuals and organizations meet cybersecurity, cloud, and digital transformation goals. Mark is the lead cybersecurity architect for Microsoft, where he leads the development of cybersecurity reference architectures, strategies, prescriptive planning roadmaps, best practices, and other guidance. Mark is active in The Open Group where he contributes to Zero Trust standards and other publications.

Mark is constantly gathering, analyzing, and refining insights, lessons, and best practices to help rapidly secure organizations in the digital age.

Mark has presented at numerous conferences, including Black Hat, RSA Conference, Gartner Security & Risk Management, Microsoft Ignite and BlueHat, and Financial Executives International.

You can find Mark on LinkedIn (`https://www.linkedin.com/in/marksimos`).


**Nikhil Kumar** is the founder of ApTSi with prior leadership roles at PricewaterhouseCoopers and other firms. He has led the strategy and implementation of digital transformation, enterprise architecture, Zero Trust, and security, and security architecture initiatives from start-ups through to Fortune 5 companies, translating vision to execution.

An engineer and computer scientist with a passion for biology, Nikhil is known for communicating with boards and implementing with engineers and architects.

Nikhil is an MIT mentor, board member, innovator, and pioneer who has authored numerous books, standards, and articles and presented at conferences globally. He co-chairs The Open Group's Zero Trust Working Group, a global standards initiative.

You can find Nikhil on LinkedIn (`https://www.linkedin.com/in/nikhilkumar/`).

*Thank you to our many mentors and teachers over the years.*

*Special thanks to Jon Shectman, Elizabeth Stephens, John Flores, Tom Quinn, Carmichael Patton, Steve White, Wes Malaby, Brent Holliman, Michele Simos, Neb Brankovic, Dinakar Sosale, and Paul Weisman for excellent and thoughtful feedback on early drafts. You made this so much better!*

*We also want to thank the security and IT professionals on the front lines sacrificing to keep our organizations, society, and economy safe. Your work is deeply appreciated, and we hope this book helps you on your journey!*

## About the reviewer

Thomas Plunkett wrote his first computer program in 1981. He has industry experience with Oracle and IBM. He is the author of several books and a frequent public speaker. Thomas has a Master of Science degree in blockchain and digital currency from the University of Nicosia. He also has a Master of Science degree in computer science and applications from Virginia Polytechnic Institute and State University. He has taken graduate courses from Stanford University on blockchain and cryptocurrency, computer security, cryptography, and other topics. He has a Bachelor of Arts degree in government and politics from George Mason University. He has a Juris Doctor degree from George Mason University Antonin Scalia Law School.

# Table of Contents

# 6

## How to Scope, Size, and Start Zero Trust                                      75

# 7

## What Zero Trust Success Looks Like                                            93

# Preface

This is the first book in a series that makes the complex topic of cybersecurity as simple, clear, and actionable as possible (and hopefully a little more fun, too ☺).

In today's continuously changing world, people face overwhelming complexity while trying to protect business assets from cybersecurity attacks.

**Zero Trust** enables business, technical, and security teams to work together to reduce risk in the face of continuously evolving attackers and threats, business models, cloud technology platforms, **Artificial Intelligence** (**AI**) innovations, and more.

*The Zero Trust Playbook Series helps demystify cybersecurity* and Zero Trust by breaking them down into discrete, actionable components to guide you through the *strategy, planning, and execution of a Zero Trust transformation.*

These books provide *clear and actionable* role-specific guidance for everyone from board members and CEOs to technical and security practitioners. They will help you understand Zero Trust, why it is important, what it means to each role, and how to execute it successfully. *The series integrates 0* best practices and guidance to avoid common mistakes (antipatterns) that slow you down and drive up risk.

*These books enable individuals and organizations to do the following:*

- **Modernize security programs** *to increase effectiveness and reduce daily toil, suffering, and wasted effort resulting from classic security approaches*
- **Securely enable digital business models** *to increase agility and reduce friction and business risk*
- **Successfully execute** *individual role tasks to grow your skills, knowledge, and career*

These books are designed to help you thrive in the security aspects of your role (and career) while helping your organization prosper and stay safe in today's world.

## Who this book is for

*This first book serves as both a standalone overview of Zero Trust for anyone and an introduction to the playbooks in Zero Trust Overview and Playbook Introduction.* with a part to play in Zero Trust to understand what Zero Trust is, why it's important to you, and what success looks like.

This table provides a list of roles that will benefit from this book:

| Role Type | Roles |
| --- | --- |
| Organizational senior leaders | Member of board of directors |
| | Chief Executive Officer (CEO) |
| | Chief Financial Officer (CFO) |
| | Chief Operating Officer (COO) |
| | Chief Legal Officer (CLO) |
| | Chief Privacy Officer (CPO) |
| | Chief Risk Officer (CRO) |
| | Chief Compliance Officer (CCO) |
| | Product and business line leaders |
| | Communications/public relations director |
| Adjacent/ancillary roles | Human resources |
| | Business analysts |
| | Internal readiness/training |
| | Internal and external communications |
| Risk and compliance roles | Risk team |
| | Compliance and audit team |
| Technology senior leaders | Chief Digital Officer (CDO) |
| | Chief Information Officer (CIO) |
| | Chief Technology Officer (CTO) |
| | Chief Information Security Officer (CISO) |
| | Enterprise security integration (deputy CISOs and staff, security [business] analysts) |
| | Technology directors |
| | Software delivery Vice President (VP) |
| | Security directors |

| Role Type | Roles |
|---|---|
| Architects | Enterprise architects |
| | Security architects |
| | Infrastructure architects |
| | Business architects |
| | Information architects |
| | Access architects |
| | Solution architects |
| | Software/application architects |
| Managers | Technology managers |
| | Security managers |
| | Security Operations (SecOps) managers |
| | Product line managers/directors |
| | Product owners |
| | Software development directors |
| | Technology delivery managers |
| | Software testing/quality managers |
| Security posture management | Security posture management |
| | Security governance and compliance management |
| | People security (user education and insider risk) |
| Technical engineering and operations | Cloud engineering and operations |
| | Endpoint/productivity |
| | Identity |
| | Infrastructure |
| | CI/CD infrastructure |
| | Network |
| | Data security |
| | Operational Technology (OT) security |
| | Security posture engineering and operations |

| Role Type | Roles |
|---|---|
| Application and product security | Software security engineers |
| | Software developers |
| | Software testers |
| | Supply chain security |
| | Internet of Things (IoT) security |
| Security operations | Triage analysts |
| | Investigation analysts |
| | Threat hunting |
| | Detection engineering |
| | Attack simulation (red and purple teaming) |
| | Incident management |
| | Threat intelligence |

**Figure Preface.1 - Illustrative list of roles that enable Zero Trust**

The book is written for people who are currently in these roles (and similar roles) as well as those who aspire to work in these roles, work with people in the roles, and provide consulting and advice to these roles.

## What this book covers

This first book kicks off *The Zero Trust Playbook Series* with an overview of Zero Trust and an introduction to the playbooks in the series. This book sets up the context of all that follows and introduces the common context everyone should know.

The chapters in this book are as follows:

- *Chapter 1, Zero Trust – This Is the Way*, gets us started by introducing Zero Trust and *The Zero Trust Playbook Series* and answering common questions about Zero Trust.

- *Chapter 2, Reading the Zero Trust Playbook Series*, introduces us to the structure and layout of the playbook series and suggested strategies to get what you need from these books quickly.

- *Chapter 3, Zero Trust Is Security for Today's World*, shows us how Zero Trust is designed for the digital age of continuous change that we live in, and why it's critically important to get right. This chapter also clears up some common points of confusion around security and Zero Trust.

- *Chapter 4, Standard Zero Trust Capabilities*, describes the standard Zero Trust capabilities in the *Zero Trust Reference Model* from The Open Group that are referenced throughout the playbooks. These are the key elements that will stay constant as we continuously improve on Zero Trust.

- *Chapter 5, Artificial Intelligence (AI) and Zero Trust*, teaches us about AI and how this technology is disrupting business, technology, security, and society at large. It describes AI's impacts, limitations, and relationship to Zero Trust that will be managed through the guidance for each role in the playbooks.

- *Chapter 6, How to Scope, Size, and Start Zero Trust*, answers the top questions about planning and getting started with a Zero Trust transformation. This also describes key terminology changes and common points of confusion about terminology that is used differently by different teams in an organization.

- *Chapter 7, What Zero Trust Success Looks Like*, covers the three key success factors for Zero Trust that are embedded into the playbooks: having a clear strategy and plan, managing mindset and culture shifts, and integrating human empathy.

- *Chapter 8, Adoption with the Three-Pillar Model*, lays out the three pillars of the playbook (strategic, operational, and operating model) and shows how the elements in that model work together to integrate business, technology, and security to create Zero Trust.

- *Chapter 9, The Zero Trust Six-Stage Plan*, describes the six stages used by the playbook, including a detailed summary of "who does what." This shows us how the playbook brings everyone together to make Zero Trust real.

- *Chapter 10, Zero Trust Playbook Roles*, describes the role-based approach and per-role guidance in the playbooks. This sets us up for success as we move on to the playbook for our role.

The remaining playbooks in the series provide actionable role-by-role guidance for each affected role.

## To get the most out of this book

You don't need anything except a desire to learn to get a clear picture of Zero Trust and how to execute it from this book.

You will get more out of this book if you have experience working in business, technology, or security for an organization (or an aspiration to do so). *This experience is not required* to understand the concepts as we explain those throughout the book to ensure clarity.

Follow the guidance in *Chapter 2, Reading the Zero Trust Playbook Series*, to identify the best reading strategy for your needs.

## Conventions used

Text conventions throughout this book include:

> **Tips or important notes**
>
> That appear like this.

## Get in touch

Feedback from our readers is always welcome.

**General feedback**: If you have questions about any aspect of this book, email us at `customercare@packtpub.com` and mention the book title in the subject of your message.

**Contacting the authors**: If you wish to contact the authors, you may reach out via LinkedIn: `https://www.linkedin.com/in/marksimos` | `https://www.linkedin.com/in/nikhilkumar/`

**Errata**: Although we have taken every care to ensure the accuracy of our content, mistakes do happen. If you have found a mistake in this book, we would be grateful if you would report this to us. Please visit `www.packtpub.com/support/errata` and fill in the form.

**Piracy**: If you come across any illegal copies of our works in any form on the internet, we would be grateful if you would provide us with the location address or website name. Please contact us at `copyright@packt.com` with a link to the material.

**If you are interested in becoming an author**: If there is a topic that you have expertise in and you are interested in either writing or contributing to a book, please visit `authors.packtpub.com`.

## Share Your Thoughts

Once you've read *Zero Trust Overview and Playbook Introduction*, we'd love to hear your thoughts! Scan the QR code below to go straight to the Amazon review page for this book and share your feedback.

https://packt.link/r/1800568665

Your review is important to us and the tech community and will help us make sure we're delivering excellent quality content.

# Download a free PDF copy of this book

Thanks for purchasing this book!

Do you like to read on the go but are unable to carry your print books everywhere?

Is your eBook purchase not compatible with the device of your choice?

Don't worry, now with every Packt book you get a DRM-free PDF version of that book at no cost.

Read anywhere, any place, on any device. Search, copy, and paste code from your favorite technical books directly into your application.

The perks don't stop there, you can get exclusive access to discounts, newsletters, and great free content in your inbox daily

Follow these simple steps to get the benefits:

1.  Scan the QR code or visit the link below

https://packt.link/free-ebook/978-1-80056-866-2

2.  Submit your proof of purchase
3.  That's it! We'll send your free PDF and other benefits to your email directly

# 1

# Zero Trust – This Is the Way

*Zero Trust secures business assets everywhere they go.*

Zero Trust is a modern security approach that aligns security with business priorities and risks. Zero Trust enables organizations to manage increased risk from rapidly evolving security threats (including ransomware) and to manage a fundamental shift in security assumptions (the organization's private network isn't enough to keep business assets safe). Zero Trust also gives you the ability to manage risk and opportunities from new technologies such as the cloud, **artificial intelligence** (**AI**), and more.

This chapter will cover the following topics:

- Introducing Zero Trust
- Introducing the *Zero Trust Playbook Series*

## Introducing Zero Trust

*Zero Trust affects anyone working in any organization* that uses any kind of computer, device, or internet technology—which is nearly everyone in business, government, and other organizations today. Zero Trust makes security a business enabler and drives an organization-wide transformation to effectively protect digital business assets.

*Earlier is better!* Nearly all organizations are already starting on a Zero Trust journey (whether they call it Zero Trust or not). Organizations that start the transformation early and integrate security into cloud technology and digital business practices earlier will experience lower risk and a smoother experience.

*The Zero Trust Playbook Series provides detailed role-by-role guidance on the strategy, planning, and execution of Zero Trust to guide you through this journey.*

This book kicks off the series and lays the foundation for everything that follows, providing a summary of Zero Trust, how it affects each role in an organization, and how the playbooks guide you through this transformation. The context of this book is critical to ensure all stakeholders work toward the same goals, hence this book is recommended for all readers.

> **Note**
>
> Think of this first book like you would a big kickoff meeting for a large program. This gets everyone the context they need before each team goes off into its own follow-up meetings to plan and execute its projects or workstreams using the playbooks in the series.

This first book includes a definition of Zero Trust, how it relates to risk and conflict in the physical world, how it addresses security threats such as ransomware and data breaches, a summary of key Zero Trust principles, and what changes to expect in your organization across technology, processes, and human experiences on this journey.

This first book also introduces the role-based approach in the Zero Trust playbooks, showing how Zero Trust is put into practice for each affected role. We encourage you to use these playbooks and the six-stage plan in them as a reference template for your own organization's Zero Trust transformation.

> **Agile or waterfall? The best of both!**
>
> The playbooks blend the best of agile approaches with well-established best practices for strategic planning and top-down executive sponsorship for large transformations.
>
> This blended approach enables flexibility and speed without losing focus on the long-term end-to-end Zero Trust transformation. As a result, these playbooks are compatible with any organizational style, from well-established organizations following traditional program management methodologies to boundary-pushing digital-native organizations that have widely adopted agile approaches.
>
> **You can go big or go small**: Smaller Zero Trust initiatives can deliver value faster but have a limited impact compared to a full transformation. To get the full value and benefits of a Zero Trust transformation, you will need to coordinate across the organization with an intentional plan and supporting cultural elements.
>
> The playbook series enables you to start anywhere with Zero Trust and get quick wins to reduce security risk and enable the mission. See *Chapter 6*, *How to Scope, Size, and Start Zero Trust*, for more details on how to choose quick wins and how to adapt the playbooks to different organizational styles.

Now, let's get started with how to read this book and this series to quickly get the information you need the most!

# Introducing the Zero Trust Playbook Series

*"The future is already here—it's just not evenly distributed."*

*– William Gibson*

This book serves as both a standalone overview of Zero Trust for anyone (without reading anything else) as well as an introduction to the *Zero Trust Playbook Series*.

This *Zero Trust Overview and Playbook Introduction* book helps you understand the **what**, **why**, and **how** of Zero Trust and cybersecurity—*what* it means to you, *why* it is important to you, and *how* you benefit by implementing Zero Trust.

The playbook series also helps *filter out unneeded details for each role while still providing the context of "why"* people are being asked to do things differently than before. We did our best to streamline things that don't matter to people while still providing a clear picture of the whole plan and how Zero Trust changes the organization around you.

Regardless of your role in an organization, this book provides insights that will help guide your Zero Trust journey and overcome the challenges you will likely face.

Before we dive into the details, let's go through some quick answers to some common questions.

## Common Zero Trust questions

Some important questions come up often, and we'll start by answering those. These are short answers, and more details are coming in this book and the series, but we'll start with some simple clarity.

### Who should use the Zero Trust Playbook Series?

This series benefits nearly everyone in an organization, particularly business leaders, technology leaders, security leaders, and practitioners in **Information Technology** (**IT**) and security teams.

> **Note**
>
> The book series also helps people in organizations that support these roles, such as advisory/consulting services, **managed service providers** (**MSPs**), educational institutions, and other organizations.

Information security is a complex topic and changes fast, with risks and priorities shifting as fast as daily or hourly. The *Zero Trust Playbook Series* provides clear guidance to consistently manage this complexity and tailors that guidance for each role, from CEOs to individual employees.

This guidance covers everything, from cultural change and board-level business risk to changes that security, business, technical, and compliance professionals will execute in daily operations.

The *Zero Trust Playbook Series* is an ideal resource for anyone doing the following:

- **Planning or supporting a full Zero Trust transformation** in any role
- Evaluating, optimizing, and refining **existing Zero Trust security capabilities**
- **Planning Zero Trust quick wins** to validate or prove the value of the approach
- **Forming or updating individual career and skills** learning paths for yourself, your team, or your department
- **Planning team re-organization or growth** as a manager, director, or senior leader
- **Improving inter-team processes** and collaboration related to security as a manager, director, or senior leader
- **Developing cybersecurity curricula** as an educational institution or instructor
- **Advising organizations** as a consultant or other advisory role
- **Learning about cybersecurity** as a student or as someone preparing for a career change
- **And more!**

## What is Zero Trust?

Zero Trust is simply security for today's world of continuous change—securing digital business assets over their lifetime and anywhere they go. This security approach is based on *zero assumed trust*, which forces everyone to make informed decisions using data, not assumptions.

Zero Trust is a foundational shift in security philosophy from implicit (assumed) trust to explicit validation of trust. Instead of trusting any computer on your corporate network, you would explicitly validate that it is trustworthy before allowing access to valuable business assets.

The Open Group, a global standards organization, defines Zero Trust as follows:

> *"An information security approach that focuses on the entire technical estate – including data/information, APIs, and Operational Technology/Industrial Control Systems – throughout their lifecycle and on any platform or network."*

The US **National Institute of Standards and Technology** (**NIST**) *SP 800-207 Zero Trust Architecture* standard states the following:

> *"Zero trust assumes there is no implicit trust granted to assets or user accounts based solely on their physical or network location (that is, local area networks versus the internet) or based on asset ownership (enterprise or personally owned)."*

**Global consensus on Zero Trust**

Documentation on Zero Trust and its importance has been published by many organizations globally, including the US NIST, the UK **National Cyber Security Centre (NCSC)**, The Open Group, the **Cloud Security Alliance (CSA)**, the **World Economic Forum (WEF)**, the US **Cybersecurity and Infrastructure Security Agency (CISA)**, the US **National Security Agency (NSA)**, the US **Department of Defense (DOD)**, and others.

Many commercial organizations have adopted and advocated for the use of Zero Trust, including Microsoft, Google, leading global solution integrators, and countless security technology vendors.

This playbook guidance will help you align your security program with this growing consensus on Zero Trust and execute it.

*Zero Trust is not a silver bullet!* No single action or technology product can provide an easy miracle cure for security risks (despite any marketing claims you may have heard ☺). *Zero Trust is a journey* of incremental progress that aligns the time, energy, and money you spend on information security to three things:

- Your business goals and organizational mission
- The cloud technology you are adopting
- The actual security threats and risks you face

The Zero Trust journey is similar in many ways to paying down a long-term debt or working through a backlog of tasks. This is because the Zero Trust journey requires discovering and removing false assumption of trust that have influenced people, processes, and technologies in your organization for years (or even decades).

**Zero trust integrates a mature risk management approach**

Organizations differ widely in how well security is aligned with and integrated with business risk.

For organizations that haven't integrated security into risk management, Zero Trust will introduce this. For organizations that have already started the journey of aligning security risk with business opportunities and risk, Zero Trust will accelerate and refine this with increased agility and improved security outcomes.

The playbooks help your organization adopt Zero Trust and mature risk management practices regardless of where you are on this journey.

## What does Zero Trust mean to me?

Zero Trust can look different depending on your role in an organization. Let's take a closer look at this:

- **To a business leader**, Zero Trust is the security component of a digital business strategy.

- **To a technical leader**, Zero Trust is the security component of IT strategy and cloud transformation initiatives.

- **To security leaders and architects**, Zero Trust is the central strategy that aligns security with business priorities and makes security agile to keep up with a continuously changing world.

- **To security professionals**, Zero Trust is the way to keep up with continuously evolving threats, continuous changes from cloud platforms, and continuous changes in security technology. Zero Trust includes classic network security perimeter approaches but goes far beyond them to protect assets on any network or cloud.

- **To individual users**, Zero Trust enables you to do the work you need wherever you are, with less friction and workflow interruptions from security processes and technology. Zero Trust educates you on how to think about your role in security to protect your organization.

*These books help you to see Zero Trust from your perspective ("How does it impact me?") and provide an actionable playbook for you—and your organization—to navigate these changes.*

The term *Zero Trust* was originally coined by an industry analyst at Forrester, John Kindervag, to describe a concept for rethinking computer network security. This name comes from the fact that the network itself provides no inherent trust ("Zero Trust") for business assets on it. This concept has since evolved over the past decade or so to become a broader **strategic security paradigm** that aligns with and empowers **digital transformation**.

One simple way to think about it is that *Zero Trust is cybersecurity (information security) without the flawed assumption a private network can magically keep business assets secure.* Traditional information security approaches often rely on a pervasive and wrong assumption that an organization can keep assets secure by simply keeping them connected to a private network managed by the organization.

---

### Is Zero Trust new?

Partially. The formalization of Zero Trust as an industry-standard approach is relatively recent, but Zero Trust builds on concepts that were formally documented by The Jericho Forum™, which was founded in 2004. Additionally, many aspects of Zero Trust are adaptations of concepts from earlier work and other disciplines such as military doctrine, economics, psychology, and more. As with business and cloud technology, Zero Trust details will continually evolve with external requirements, but this core will stay as a consistent foundation.

## Why is Zero Trust important?

Zero Trust enables *security to operate at the speed of business*, providing safety and security for today's world. Zero Trust helps organizations to operate and grow while managing continuous changes in markets, technology platforms, and cybersecurity threats. Organizational risk has increased, and existing static perimeter-centric security approaches simply can't keep up with these changes.

Business-critical systems and data are constantly evolving and moving around networks and cloud providers around the globe. Security threats are increasing from ruthless criminal gangs (often using extortion/ransomware) and nation-state attackers.

We need security that is agile and can keep up with these changes—hence Zero Trust.

## What is the scope of Zero Trust?

Zero Trust affects everything in cybersecurity (information security) today and also expands security's scope in business and technology disciplines. This is because nearly every part of a modern business, government agency, or other organization relies on technology and data and needs that technology and data to be safe from attacks.

The term *Zero Trust* can also refer to more than one *thing*, so you can expect this term will be used in multiple ways throughout the series. Zero Trust can refer to an overall approach (or paradigm) for security, a security strategy, or can refer to specific architectures and technologies that support the Zero Trust approach and strategy.

---

**Don't panic!**

While this transformation can seem big and overwhelming, *the good news is that there are already plenty of successes to learn from*. Organizations are already implementing Zero Trust, and we have incorporated the lessons learned here to guide your transformation. These lessons learned by other organizations are directly integrated into this actionable playbook to help illuminate your path.

*Chapter 6, How to Scope, Size, and Start Zero Trust*, discusses how to size, scope, and get started on Zero Trust.

---

## Why is Zero Trust confusing?

We have seen a lot of confusion about what Zero Trust is (and even cynicism that it isn't real or new). We have learned that this confusion arises primarily for three reasons:

- Zero Trust looks different to different roles in an organization, as described earlier

- Zero Trust *changes fundamental existing assumptions* of information security, requiring a change in mindset (focusing on outcomes rather than existing methods)
- Some cybersecurity marketing and sales approaches use Zero Trust overzealously and inaccurately

This book directly addresses the first two factors, and we sincerely hope it helps with the third one as well.

### What does a Zero Trust transformation look like? How long does it take?

*Zero Trust doesn't happen overnight; it requires focusing on quick wins and incremental progress.*

Zero Trust is an ongoing journey of continuous changes to keep up with attacker innovation, changing markets, and changing technology platforms. Zero Trust provides the core principles and framework that guide you along the modernization journey and stay agile to meet continuously changing demands. It also provides the architectural structure and governance guardrails to enable that journey.

Zero Trust is not a static discipline and does not exist in an independent silo; it is a living, breathing part of a modern business that is continuously adapting to the world. For more information on planning quick wins and incremental progress, see *Chapter 6, How to Scope, Size, and Start Zero Trust*.

### Why should you read these books?

Read these books for clarity on what Zero Trust is, what implementing it means, why you do it, and how to do it.

The authors led the development of the first industry-wide definition of Zero Trust (The Open Group Zero Trust Core Principles), which has found its way into commercial and national cybersecurity initiatives. They are now leading the definition of global standards for Zero Trust to create interoperable Zero Trust solutions and define what Zero Trust means.

In addition to leading standards initiatives, the authors have experience working with multiple organizations to lead, plan, and implement Zero Trust initiatives. The series captures their experience and integrates lessons learned and best practices into an actionable six-stage plan for Zero Trust. This plan will support any digital transformation or cloud migration initiative—regardless of the organization's size or industry. Let's take a closer look at what the series provides:

- **A reference guide for the whole Zero Trust journey**: The books include a six-stage reference plan to guide the whole organization on the journey of implementing Zero Trust. As with an orchestral musical composition, a sports team playbook, or a movie script, these playbooks orchestrate how different people work together on this common goal.

- **Bite-size pieces**: The playbooks break it up into smaller, bite-sized chunks focused on different roles to enable you to *focus on what you need*. They also include different examples of fictitious Acme corporations throughout the series to illustrate how to apply this to different industries and organizations.

- **Role-based guidance**: The playbooks explain what Zero Trust means for each affected role (including best practices) so that you don't have to figure this out yourself. This role-based approach of the playbooks allows you to plan for your individual part of adopting Zero Trust while also seeing how you fit into the overall picture.

- **Complete view through multiple perspectives**: The playbooks provide a complete view of Zero Trust from all relevant perspectives. This allows you to switch lenses and see how Zero Trust looks at other roles in the organization, providing increased clarity on the topic.

## Summary

We have seen many instances of how Zero Trust approaches make life better at organizations for business, technology, and security teams alike. We look forward to seeing your success on this journey using this book series!

Now that we have a general sense of Zero Trust and the *Zero Trust Playbook Series*, let's move on to how to get the most out of these books with *Chapter 2, Reading the Zero Trust Playbook Series*.

# 2

# Reading the Zero Trust Playbook Series

*A journey without direction is just wandering.*

Now that we have clarity on some of the most important questions from *Chapter 1, Zero Trust – This Is the Way*, it's time to plan how to get the most out of these books for you.

Everyone should read this first book to understand what Zero Trust means and develop a shared understanding of Zero Trust. *Read it closely, as it's foundational to the rest of the series and to Zero Trust at large.* These chapters provide an overview of Zero Trust, including the core definition of Zero Trust, how it relates to business and digital transformation, the guiding principles, a view of what success looks like, and the six-stage playbook to create and implement a Zero Trust initiative.

This chapter covers the following topics:

- **Reading strategies**, which compares focusing only on your role (without missing critical context) with a full reading for complete context
- **How we structured the playbooks**, to help you navigate this full set of integrated guidance

## Reading strategies

While you can read the playbook series any way you want, we recommend one of two approaches:

- **Method 1 – Focus only on my role**

  The most efficient way to get actionable guidance is to read the playbook for your role (or the role you aspire to). This will quickly get you relevant information for your current role immediately that you can act on without delay.

  *How do I focus only on my role?* Read this first book and then proceed to the playbook for your role. Ensure to read the introductory chapters in your playbook before reading the chapter dedicated to your role.

*Who should focus only on their role?* People with an urgent need to learn and execute on Zero Trust will often read the playbooks this way to get to their role guidance fastest. This includes people assigned to support an existing Zero Trust project and is particularly useful when you have to meet deadlines for an executive-sponsored project. Senior organizational leaders often have extremely limited time for reading and may also use this method.

---

### Notes on this method

**You may need to read about multiple roles**: Some roles interact very closely with other roles as part of their core job. Roles whose success depends on closely working with other roles will be instructed to read about those roles in the introduction chapter(s) of their playbook. For example, technical and security managers should read about the roles of team members they manage to help them plan daily processes, career development, learning/training activities, and performance measurement.

**Skipping context has risks**: While it's possible (and tempting ☺) to jump ahead to read only the chapter for your role, we don't recommend this for most readers unless you have an extremely urgent need to execute immediately.

It is faster to jump ahead, but skipping the context could cause confusion or misinterpretation of the guidance. Each role chapter assumes people have read and understand the context of this book and the playbook introductory chapter(s). For example, the chapters for **security operations (SecOps)** roles such as triage analyst (Tier 1), investigation analyst (Tier 2), threat hunter, and **threat intelligence (TI)** analyst all assume you understand the terminology and concepts in the introductory chapters of the playbook. If you must jump ahead, we recommend going back to read the common context as soon as you can. As with many things in life, context matters!

---

- **Method 2 – Read all the playbooks in the series**

  Reading each playbook will give you a full end-to-end perspective on the Zero Trust journey from all relevant perspectives. The series covers the organizational vision, continues through strategy and plans, and then looks at how those translate to a practitioner's hands-on view.

  Reading about all of the roles will allow you to understand Zero Trust completely from a business/organizational leadership perspective, how that translates to technical leaders, and how practitioners experience this and get the job done on the ground. This full context helps you understand each role in the organization and its individual Zero Trust transformation experiences. This will help you be more effective and successful in your current role, plan your career path, and prepare you for your next career steps.

  *Who should read the whole series?* Roles who interact with most or all other roles in the playbook will need to understand the full journey for all of them (even if just reading playbook introduction chapters and skimming the role chapters). This is particularly valuable for external consultants and internal architect roles who interact with and advise many roles in an organization. This is also a valuable method for people new to cybersecurity and trying to identify which role best fits their skills and interests.

Anyone who wants to learn more about cybersecurity can read all the playbooks to broaden their understanding of cybersecurity, grow their skills and knowledge, and prepare for a role that they aspire to. This method of looking at other roles can be especially useful if you are puzzled or frustrated with why and how other roles make decisions in your organization. ☺

> **Note**
>
> Zero Trust will look slightly different depending on an organization's size, industry, culture, past investments into security, and other factors.
>
> Zero Trust applies to all organizations, from large well-established global organizations to smaller digital-native "born in the cloud" agile organizations, and everything in between.
>
> The guidance in the playbooks is both prescriptive and flexible to meet the needs of any organization. See *Chapter 6, How to Scope, Size, and Start Zero Trust*, for details on how to use the playbook guidance for large global organizations, digital-native agile organizations, and more. Each playbook also includes many Acme examples that span industries and sizes to show how to apply the playbook guidance in different situations.

## How we structured the playbooks

Because the Zero Trust experience is different for each type of role (business leaders, technology leaders, IT and security managers, and practitioners), we broke the series into different books focusing on groupings of related roles. Each playbook uses examples to illustrate how to apply Zero Trust to different scenarios.

*Figure 2.1* shows how different roles can quickly find the information relevant to them:

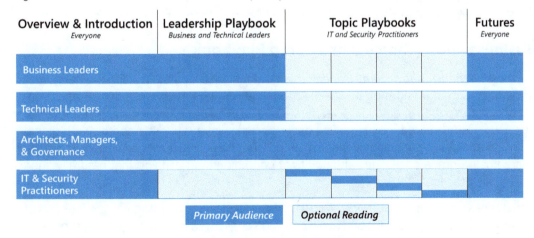

Figure 2.1 – Playbook series structure

Each book focuses on the needs of specific roles, as outlined here:

- The *Zero Trust Overview and Playbook Introduction* provides *all roles* with the shared context you need to understand and navigate Zero Trust.

- The *Business and Technical Leadership Playbook* provides *role-by-role guidance* for *business, technical, and security leadership* roles to successfully integrate security and align security with business priorities and risk management. This also guides the integration of security and technology teams, processes, and tooling.

- The *Topic Playbooks* provide *role-by-role guidance* for *practitioners and managers across security, technology, and business teams* to navigate, lead, and execute the Zero Trust transformation.

- The *Zero Trust Futures* provides *all roles* with insight into what changes are coming around the corner that will continue to disrupt and shape Zero Trust so that you can anticipate and manage the next stage of continuous changes.

The playbooks follow a three-pillar structure frequently used in business strategy and planning (strategic, operational, and operating models). This is described in detail in *Chapter 8, Adoption with the Three-Pillar Model*.

Now, let's take a look at the approach and content of each type of book in the series.

## Zero Trust Overview and Playbook Introduction

*Everyone*—all roles need the critical common context on Zero Trust in this book, *Zero Trust Overview and Playbook Introduction*. This book defines what Zero Trust is and puts it into the context of digital transformation, information security, business risk and impact, and security strategy. It also provides an overview of the Zero Trust reference model and architecture, busts some common myths and misconceptions, and introduces the six-stage playbook, three-pillar model, role-based approach, Acme corporation examples, and more.

## Business and Technical Leadership Playbook

*Business, technical, and security leadership* roles each have a part in leading the Zero Trust transformation or integrating it with the organization's business and risk management. This book describes in detail how leaders ensure Zero Trust delivers the full benefits of business agility and reduced organizational risk (while integrating it smoothly with digital business and cloud technology transformations). The book enables these leaders to quickly overcome common challenges and points of confusion (and conflict) that naturally arise during this process.

The *Business and Technical Leadership Playbook* provides *role-by-role guidance* for each of these leaders to drive success and avoid common challenges in this integration process.

This playbook includes guidance for these roles:

- **Business executives**, including CEOs, CFOs, COOs, CLOs, CPOs, CROs, and **line-of-business (LOB)** leaders, have relatively small but critical parts in the success of Zero Trust. These roles ensure Zero Trust is aligned with the priorities and risks of the organization and provide executive sponsorship to overcome common obstacles. This playbook guides these executives on how to best sponsor, support, guide, and measure Zero Trust to ensure it delivers on promised outcomes.

- **Technology leaders**, such as CIOs, CTOs, CDOs, and senior directors within those teams, typically support the Zero Trust strategy and initiatives within it. These roles ensure that the technical strategy aligns with the business goals, risk framework, and security strategy. This alignment helps build productive relationships with business and security leaders, driving the measurable success of the Zero Trust implementation.

- **Security leaders**, such as CISOs and senior directors within those teams, typically lead the Zero Trust strategy and sponsor initiatives within it. These roles ensure that the security strategy aligns with the business goals, risk framework, and technical strategy. This alignment helps build productive relationships with business and technology leaders, driving the measurable success of the Zero Trust implementation.

This playbook helps leaders build and execute a modern Zero Trust security strategy that minimizes business, technical, and security friction while aligning it to the organization's goals, culture, and unique business model. The playbook includes guidance on prioritization, success criteria, common pitfalls and antipatterns, technology strategy/direction, and how to measvure progress and ongoing success in a quantifiable manner.

## Technical Topic Playbooks

*The Topic Playbooks focus on groups of roles with related goals, skills, or responsibilities in the organization. These provide a common context for related roles and role-by-role guidance* for *practitioner and manager roles* to enable them to lead and execute their specific part of Zero Trust.

> **Note**
> Small organizations may not have dedicated roles for all of these functions, but someone should perform these functions at a basic level in every organization, whether a part of a job for an existing role, by an outsourced provider, or by another means.

These playbooks focus on topics including the following:

- **SecOps/SOC**: These roles reduce risk to the organization by rapidly finding attackers with access to your business assets and removing them quickly and completely (analogous to firefighters who put out active fires). This playbook provides guidance for SecOps roles that triage inbound detections (Tier 1), investigate and remediate them (Tier 2), hunt for hidden threats, inform others of learnings (TI), manage incidents, manage SecOps teams, and more. The playbook guides these critically important roles through how to do this in today's world. This playbook enables SecOps roles to successfully reduce organizational risk using asset-centric Zero Trust approaches, tools, processes, and more (which supplement or replace existing approaches of detecting and blocking attacks at a network perimeter).

- **Architecture, posture, and compliance**: These roles work across teams to ensure that the strategy is executed and operated consistently across teams and over time. *Architecture* roles provide critical support for directors and managers who translate strategy into specific plans, priorities, and requirements for their individual teams. *Security posture and compliance* roles ensure that the organization is consistently satisfying regulatory requirements while also keeping up with attackers who are continuously changing attack techniques. This playbook enables these roles to keep all the specialized teams working together toward a common Zero Trust vision.

---

**Architects are critical to the  successful integration of silos**

It is strongly recommended to assign architect role(s) with an explicit goal of building an end-to-end vision to help identify and resolve gaps in cross-team processes and cross-cutting capabilities. Integrating teams is critical as these transformations disrupt the norms of past responsibilities and team structures. Whether using an architect title or not, having a role focused on this end-to-end view is a key enabler for the success of digital, cloud, and Zero Trust transformations.

Without role(s) focused on finding and solving these problems, transformations can slow down or fail with different teams blaming each other—an outcome that benefits nobody. The playbook's design, including a six-stage execution plan, includes mitigations for these challenges. See *Chapter 9, The Zero Trust Six-Stage Plan*, for more details.

Architects also work in many other roles across the organization and often need to familiarize themselves with those roles (and how Zero Trust is changing those roles) by reading their playbooks. The guidance for each role in the playbooks includes more detail on these interactions between architects and other teams.

---

- **Technical engineering and operations**: These roles put Zero Trust into action by integrating security into the design, implementation, and operation of technology that the organization relies on every day. *Technical managers* translate strategic goals into specific technical plans and priorities for their teams, *engineers* design it for scale across the technical estate, and *operations* professionals implement, configure, and sustain it. The playbook provides *role-by-role guidance* for technical practitioners and managers to guide you through how Zero Trust affects each aspect of daily practices and processes. The playbook includes guidance on solution and technology selection, design patterns to embrace and avoid, technical process design, technical configurations, operational best practices, how to integrate with security teams and DevOps/DevSecOps teams on security, how to plan to rapidly recover from attacks, and more.

- **Product and application security**: These roles integrate security into the design, implementation, and operation of custom applications, websites, services, and APIs. These workloads are required to digitally transform the organization, spanning internal business processes as well as the products and services used by the organization's customers. Integrating security into these teams is critical to reduce organizational risk from compromise of these systems, the data in them, and the access they have to other systems and data.

  In the modern agile delivery model that most digital enterprises operate in, *product managers* are responsible for integrating security into the product strategy they build to support business goals and steward business and customer data. These roles also work with product owners to translate the product strategy into product business requirements that meet security, business risk, and regulatory obligations. *Solution and enterprise architects* will often work with product managers to keep the product strategy and product requirements aligned with the organization's over-arching strategy, methods, and compliance requirements. *Security architects* provide security oversight and governance, helping establish or update security architectures for these solutions. *Application architects* design technical solutions that meet the requirements and plan how to build applications and components, while *developers* implement these applications and components using security best practices and standards. *DevOps/ DevSecOps teams* or *technical operations* teams enable this process by instrumenting and automating the development and operations, ensuring that security governance checks and best practices are automated, built in, and as frictionless as possible. *Software security engineers* provide security expertise for all roles along all the phases. The playbook guides these teams through the process of blending security expertise with product and application expertise as these roles build custom capabilities for the application and product portfolio(s).

**Notes about the content in the playbooks**

**Security-focused**: The playbooks focus on the security aspects of each role and only cover non-security aspects of the roles when that context is required for security.

**Outcome-focused**: The playbooks focus on the security outcomes that may be performed by technology teams, DevOps/DevSecOps teams, security teams, or outsourced providers. The playbooks also describe who performs the tasks when the specialization doesn't exist so that you can quickly adapt the guidance to smaller organizations; see *Chapter 10*, *Zero Trust Playbook Roles*, for more details.

**Durability-focused**: The playbooks do not include step-by-step technical configuration instructions. Product technical details change too fast today for any written guidance to stay current for more than a few months. The playbooks include clear technical guidance and criteria that are immediately actionable and can drive decisions, but will also endure for years as technical roles and the technical estate transform with Zero Trust.

**Real-world examples**: These playbooks include many examples of how to apply this guidance in a real-world setting using Acme examples from multiple industries.

## Futures

*Everyone*—all roles need clarity on the future trends that will shape and influence their role and Zero Trust so that they can anticipate changes coming around the corner.

This *Zero Trust Futures* book is for everyone and describes how to apply the Zero Trust approach to emerging technologies that are rapidly evolving and growing. This includes a discussion on the **Internet of Things** (**IoT**), **artificial intelligence** (**AI**), affective computing, the metaverse(s), and more.

The *Zero Trust Playbook Series* cuts through noise, connects people together, reduces conflict, and accelerates the benefits of Zero Trust. This format and structure set you and your organization up for success by providing a complete set of implications and perspectives, enabling teams to coordinate effectively, transform successfully, and execute rapidly.

## Summary

In this chapter, we reviewed how the series is structured and the best strategies for getting to the information you need.

Next up, in *Chapter 3*, *Zero Trust Is Security for Today's World*, we will take a deeper look at the importance and implications of Zero Trust, including dispelling common myths and misconceptions.

# 3
# Zero Trust Is Security for Today's World

*Zero Trust aligns security strategy and teams with today's world.*

In this chapter, you will learn about **Zero Trust** and why this agile security approach is critical in today's high-speed, high-complexity world. You will get a baseline understanding of the powerful forces at work that are shaping business, technology, and cybersecurity and how Zero Trust is designed to address them.

This chapter will cover the following topics:

- Continuous change and why we need Zero Trust
- Changes come faster in the digital age
- Defining success in the digital age
- Technology accelerates change and complexity
- Implications and imperatives of Zero Trust
- Dispelling confusion—frequently asked questions on Zero Trust

## Continuous change and why we need Zero Trust

*We are living in an age of continuous change in our lives and our work.*

Everyone's life has been changed by the technological breakthroughs of our time. The internet and computer technology have changed communication, work, and entertainment in our society. *These changes aren't letting up, and the rate of change is accelerating, promising to continuously change our lives for the foreseeable future.*

A recent example is the COVID-19 pandemic, where many people quickly found themselves working from home instead of commuting to an office. This shift drove new business models, new technologies to support those models, new societal norms, and new evolutions in threats to business assets. Zero Trust security is designed for this world of continuous change.

## Changes come faster in the digital age

*Massive change is not new, but today's speed and scale of change are new.* There are plenty of historical precedents for this level of change—the printing press spread new ideas that challenged long-established structures of power and religion, the advent of the scientific method transformed how we see (and control) the physical world around us, the rise of democracies transformed the role of governments around the world, and the Industrial Revolution and the assembly line transformed business models, products, cities, lifestyles, careers, and more. The digital age is a similar disruptive trend that has introduced both instant global access to information and the ability to change business models globally (and create new ones) in a matter of weeks, days, and sometimes even hours. *Constant change defines the digital age.*

We now live in a world where a lot of work can be done anywhere, and our top challenges are information overload and misinformation, not the lack of information we faced throughout human history. *This gives an advantage to organizations that embrace the data-centric aspects of this new world—* organizations gain a powerful competitive edge if they use data and analytics to generate business insights and support decisions, adopt **machine learning** (**ML**) and **artificial intelligence** (**AI**) technologies to automate analysis of data and routine tasks, and seek out new data sources from **Internet of Things** (**IoT**) devices and other sources.

*This proliferation of technology and data-centric thinking creates opportunities that are rapidly becoming mandates for organizations to stay relevant.* While this started out as a nice-to-have benefit of increased agility and cost-effectiveness, the new generation of customers and citizens are now demanding this type of agility, and they will go elsewhere if they don't get it from your organization.

> **Important note**
> Nowhere is the rate of change more evident than in the way the world reacted to the COVID-19 pandemic. For example, some drug discovery processes happened in a matter of two days when they would have taken four to five years previously (Richard et al.). This was enabled and propelled by new technologies and new science at the boundaries of biology, mathematics, computing, as well as data-centric approaches.

# Defining success in the digital age

**What does success look like in the digital age?** Success translates to a fresh set of requirements for modern data-centric organizations and the information systems and security of their digital assets. These requirements include meeting the following criteria:

- **Agile and responsive**: It take forever to modify systems or stand up new ones. They can change quickly and easily to meet market demands (of both existing markets and expanding into new markets).

- **Resilient**: The business must operate wherever customers and citizens demand, even if that is a public or an open network. *The business must assume the failure of controls and build in fail-safe mechanisms to provide a defense-in-depth (DoD) approach.*

- **Data-driven**: Quantifiable data is sought out and used for technology and security decisions rather than relying on pure qualitative data and how things have always been done.

- **Empowering**: Technology and information security are focused on enabling the business and identifying opportunities, not just managing/mitigating downside risk.

Zero Trust helps organizations meet these requirements and makes them *more competitive and compelling to customers*. Organizations adopting Zero Trust will also experience *less internal friction*.

# Technology accelerates change and complexity

While businesses and markets have always been a world of constant change and innovation, technology has dramatically accelerated the pace and scale of change in business. *Business models are rapidly evolving to match pace with the rapid growth and normalization of technological change*—be it internet access, mobile devices, cloud services, AI, digitization of processes and capabilities; the list goes on. As an illustration, modifying a website or mobile app today can change how every customer interacts with an organization in a matter of hours—reaching thousands, millions, or billions of people.

A changing business model drives changes in people, processes, and the underlying technology. It may also instantly invalidate generations of institutional knowledge. Business model changes often result in new threats and an extreme need for organizational agility to capture the opportunity before it passes. Time and money are usually in short supply, so a clear strategy to drive the right focus and ruthless prioritization are critical for success.

Cloud technology and AI are the largest technology change agents today. The scale and speed of cloud technology enables and drives rapid change to business models and the creation of new ones. This then creates new requirements for technology changes, creating a feedback loop that makes everything move even faster. AI builds on the foundation of cloud technology (including **large language models** (**LLMs**) such as **ChatGPT**) to disrupt how data and technology are discovered and used. More on this in *Chapter 10: Zero Trust Playbook Roles*.

Add disruptive events such as the COVID-19 pandemic, 9/11, the financial crash of 2008, shifts in world politics, and the rise of ransomware and extortion attacks, and this rate of change becomes even more disruptive.

These nonstop high-speed changes are reshaping the underlying assumptions of business executives, technology executives, IT practitioners, security practitioners, and everyday citizens alike.

As professionals, we are responsible for capturing the opportunities of these changes and navigating the risks and threats posed by them. A Zero Trust approach helps us by taking a pragmatic view of security that isn't bound by the assumptions of classic security (we must restrict business assets to our own networks to keep them safe).

## A darker trend – the growth of cybercrime

Largely, these technological changes have been beneficial to society, but there is also a parallel darker trend. Criminals, activists, and spies (aka intelligence agencies) have also been going through a transformation in how to achieve their goals in this world.

Organizations and individuals now face a rising tide of criminals, nation-states, hacktivists, and other actors using this technological transformation for their ends, at the expense of private citizens, businesses, government agencies, and other organizations.

Success in this world requires learning how to grow, adapt, and get more productive in this world while simultaneously managing threats that are constantly growing in volume and sophistication. A Zero Trust security approach provides the agility required to keep up with these threats.

> **Important note**
> As cybercrime grows in profitability and volume, it also evolves to become more effective, more creative, and more pervasive. Many criminals reinvest profits into improving their operations and tooling, fueling a continuous increase in potential risk to legitimate organizations.

The list of threats keeps growing—attackers regularly operate from compromised assets within our organizations, sophisticated social engineering attacks regularly trick people, and more keep emerging, such as supply chain attacks and insider threats. Dark markets are also being used by bad actors to buy and sell stolen data, stolen passwords, attack tools, access to specific organizations, and so on.

We have also seen the use of sophisticated affiliate business models drive up attack volume and impact. The affiliate model is commonly seen in ransomware/extortion attacks, such as the Colonial Pipeline attack where authors of attack kits share profits with independent attack operators using those kits to conduct attacks.

The Zero Trust approach helps security teams keep up with these threats with a combination of durable security fundamentals and an agile approach to security that allows teams to rapidly adapt to growing threats.

## Staying balanced – assume failure and assume success

A new approach is needed that assumes attackers will sometimes be successful and focuses on what you can do about it. This idea of **assuming failure** is often expressed as *assume breach* or *assume compromise*. Attackers often have access to a compromised network for weeks or months before being detected.

In this world of assumed compromise, you must focus on **protecting what is important to the organization and reducing the blast radius** of any given attack, similar to how watertight compartments in a ship contain a leak, thereby preventing the sinking of the ship.

> **What is the blast radius?**
>
> The blast radius is a reference to the damage caused by an attack. This is analogous to the area damaged by physical explosives.

An assumption of failure can sometimes seem overwhelming, but it's simply a risk to be managed. Just as people don't abandon living on tropical islands because hurricanes sometimes come, we won't abandon the benefits of the internet because it comes with some inherent risks. *We will learn to adapt to those risks and manage them*, returning the organization to normal operations. This is what we call **assuming success**.

This practical approach of Zero Trust that assumes both successes and failures will enable your organization to better manage risk in today's messy world of constant change.

While every organization runs similar technology architectures, each organization is also unique in some ways. As with anything else, Zero Trust should start from a strong, consistent foundation (outlined in this book) and then be tailored to your organization's size, industry, IT and security process maturity, and other factors (noted throughout the book).

## Cybersecurity or information security?

While some people have strong opinions on which term is better, the book series uses "cybersecurity" and "information security" interchangeably. We define them as *"managing risk to the organization from abuse of technical systems by either external actors or insiders."*

# Implications and imperatives of Zero Trust

Now that we understand the strategic importance of Zero Trust, let's explore some of the most pervasive implications and a bit more of the background.

## It's a team sport

*One of the most critical requirements of success is for different stakeholders within the organization to work together as a team.* Business, IT, and security teams are going through their version of a transformation to a new normal of continuous change. Teams cannot rely on static processes and blamestorming to get through this transformation successfully. Teams must work together to tap into the knowledge, expertise, and creativity of other teams to successfully navigate the dynamic challenges they face.

This diagram captures this imperative to work together:

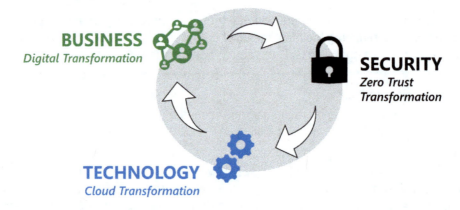

**Figure 3.1 – Simultaneous digital, cloud, and Zero Trust transformations**

Digital transformation, cloud transformation, and Zero Trust are not ivory tower solutions that are developed once, handed down, and followed exactly forever. These are continuously evolving, living strategies that must work together to manage a constant flow of market demands and attacker evolution. Any or all stakeholders may offer an insight that influences the architecture, plans, and strategy of the others as the organization rapidly evolves and learns from the environment.

This *Zero Trust playbook* includes details for each team and stakeholder to rapidly collaborate with colleagues across business, technology, and security teams.

## Security must be agile

The first impact felt by security teams will be the pace of change and the need to adapt to changing situations. While many information security teams value consistency and risk reduction above all else, this often results in extreme resistance to change where security becomes an obstacle.

**Security teams must be agile.** Security teams must adapt to continuous changes in a digital business strategy, rapidly evolving cloud platforms, and threats. Security must see itself as empowering and enabling digital execution *while* keeping the organization safe from threats.

Keeping organizations and their customers safe today requires revisiting long-held assumptions as you build a new modern Zero Trust security strategy. A fundamental difference from past information security practices at many organizations is that Zero Trust *both addresses risk and enables business opportunity*. Traditional security models focused first on compliance regimes and network perimeter models that simply don't work anymore. Critical business resources now live outside traditional network perimeters, and attackers regularly get into corporate networks using phishing emails, credential theft, and other attacks. Security must adapt to today's world.

Security must protect business assets wherever they are and wherever they go, assuming attackers will sometimes succeed and adapting to that. This shift in assumptions requires security to be agile and flexible in a way that can be unfamiliar to many security teams that have relied heavily on a "secure network" paradigm.

This agile approach of Zero Trust helps you find and fix problems quickly when they are small, allowing teams to rapidly learn, adapt, and get back on track. The playbooks include specific guidance to help teams transform to an agile security approach and embrace continuous change.

## Failure is not an option

**We must not fail**. It's hard to overstate the ramifications of failing to protect computer systems well. Over the past decades, we have come to depend on digital technology far more than most people realize. Just as we only notice how important power or water infrastructure is when it fails, we typically only notice how much we depend on computers when they go down.

Digital technology drives every aspect of our lives—from communications for first responders to the machines that plant, harvest, and cook our food, to machines that keep us alive in hospital; the list goes on and on.

Because of how pervasive and important digital technology is, *we need it to work as it's supposed to, not as some criminal or foreign government wants it to work (or stop working)*. Stealing secrets, altering official data and records in these systems, or taking these systems offline is much more than a small annoyance. Attacks lead to millions of dollars in business losses, drive societal dysfunction, kill people, and so on. The cost of responding to these attacks can bleed away organizational value and negatively impact the daily lives of everyday citizens.

Sticking with the current reactive approach is like playing a game of *whack-a-mole* where the attackers have the advantage. Attackers often have millions of dollars of profits from previous attacks to reinvest into the next generation of attacks. Organizations must shift to a proactive approach with Zero Trust and work to get ahead of these attacks.

Just as the power grid and running water are both *invisible and essential* to our daily lives, computer technology is now an integral part of nearly every part of society. We probably don't know how to live without it.

This makes Zero Trust transformation critical because classic approaches to security (where it is treated as an independent "silo solving a technical problem") simply won't work anymore. We need an approach where security is integral to technology and business—Zero Trust.

Zero Trust naturally aligns with business priorities and risk, which helps avoid failures to protect the most important assets. Classic security approaches often take a technical "bottom-up" approach that often spreads security resources thin and leaves business-critical assets with relatively little protection.

Additionally, Zero Trust is a full strategic approach that includes multiple security tactics that are applied via processes, people, and many different technologies. This broad approach contrasts with narrow classic security approaches that depend on a single tactic (perimeter protection) applied via a single technology (network). The narrow classic approaches lead to many security failures because they create defender blind spots that attackers exploit. Zero Trust still includes networks and perimeters but also includes other technologies and tactics so that you can apply the right tool to the right problem (rather than treating every problem the same).

To further help you avoid failure, the playbook series integrates many lessons learned and bright spots from organizations that have successfully navigated Zero Trust transformations.

Next, let's clarify some common points of confusion that come up often.

# Dispelling confusion – frequently asked questions on Zero Trust

These are some questions that address some common points of confusion around cybersecurity and Zero Trust.

## Aren't attackers just kids in their basements playing on computers?

The short answer is no. Cybersecurity attacks have evolved far beyond their origins of amateur experimentation. They have become a high-profit criminal industry and a preferred method of conducting nation-state espionage.

The easiest way to see the impact of security attacks is to simply scan the cybersecurity headlines of the past decade or so. Attackers have inflicted millions of dollars' worth of damage to organizations as they pursue their illicit goals (typically criminal, espionage, and/or activist objectives). This costs organizations money to clean up after these attackers, pay a ransom (which we don't recommend in most circumstances), write off lost business productivity, and recover reputational damages.

Now that we understand that this is a serious problem, we might ask why it hasn't been solved.

## Shouldn't security have solved this simple technical problem by now?

Unfortunately, that isn't possible. These aren't simple or static problems that we can solve once and move on. Attackers, or bad actors, are intelligent humans who adapt and evolve as they attack highly complex computer environments that grew organically and inconsistently over decades.

Organizations today depend on technology that was developed and implemented at different times over the past 30-50 years. Most organizations' technology estates are a hodgepodge of different generations of technologies wired together in ways that nobody fully remembers or understands. *Additionally, technology decisions reflect how technology and security were viewed at that time.* Security was often a low priority, and our understanding of security was much less sophisticated than today. This means complex technology estates we currently depend on are a rich hunting ground for attackers to quickly find openings they can abuse.

> **Note**
>
> **Technology estate** refers to the sum total of all technology used by an organization to get work done. We discuss why we use this term in more depth in *Chapter 6, How to Scope, Size, and Start Zero Trust*.

The term **technical debt** is sometimes used to describe this accumulation of past technical decisions that don't meet today's standards. This is because it requires a lot of money to fix problems, and problems get worse if they are left unfixed (just as with interest on financial debt).

All of this results in organizations having a massive amount of complexity that often includes gaps, cracks, and overlaps that attackers can discover and exploit. *Applying half measures and layers of security Band-Aids often does not lead to more security but makes those problems worse by adding more complexity.*

Solving this problem takes people working together as a team to bring their skills, perspectives, and ideas. Because it's a moving target (technology keeps evolving) and extremely complex, new approaches are needed. That is where Zero Trust comes in.

While Zero Trust isn't a magic wand you can wave to solve all of your security problems, it closely aligns security with the business and mission so that you can fix security problems that matter first. The Zero Trust approach gets everyone in the organization on the same page, ensures new assets are created with modern security, and pays down that technical debt in priority order.

Now that we understand the complexity of solving security problems, let's focus on the root cause of them—the attackers.

# Who are the attackers?

Today's attackers are smart humans who continually adjust how they attack and how they make money from attacks, making it challenging to defend technical systems. They often work as part of an organization and are very good at finding new ways to use modern technology for attacks. Tomorrow's attackers are likely to use AI and other cutting-edge technology to continuously evolve to evade new defenses in a vicious cycle.

We face attackers whose motivations (darkly) mirror those of legitimate organizations, which is illustrated in *Figure 3.2*:

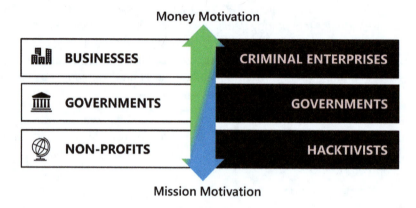

**Figure 3.2 – Attack groups are mirrors of legitimate organizations**

Criminals make money by attacking these systems and using stolen data for their benefit, selling it to others, selling access to your systems, or extorting you by making you pay to regain access to your systems and data (for example, ransomware).

Governments attack computer systems to achieve their military and economic development goals, ranging from espionage techniques to active destruction of data and systems.

Lastly, there are occasionally activist groups (hacktivists) that use some of the same techniques to advance a cause they believe in.

Now that we know who these attackers are, one might wonder why they aren't already in jail.

# Can't we just arrest these criminals and put them in jail?

Arrests do occasionally happen, but they are a rarity compared to the number of attacks and attackers. Criminal prosecution across borders for high-tech crimes is still very difficult, so it's not a reliable deterrent. Furthermore, high-tech crimes are often difficult to prosecute in any circumstance because prosecution requires police, judges, and others in the system to possess skills and have an understanding of these attacks.

Evolving geopolitics and the nature of the internet make this even more difficult—criminals can and do operate anywhere in the world where there is an internet connection. This means that effectively deterring this criminal behavior requires that all governments agree the problem is important enough to solve (voluntarily through consensus or through diplomatic pressure, sanctions, and so on) and work to solve it. In some cases, countries are not equipped to investigate and prosecute a high volume of these crimes; some aren't motivated or sufficiently funded to solve them; in some cases, governments are complicit in the crime.

While laws are evolving, it will take a long time to have a meaningful impact on our defenses. For the moment, *we need to focus on what we can do*, which is to use Zero Trust strategies to protect organizations.

## Is this just a matter of spending more money?

Simply throwing money at the problem doesn't solve it. Just as running fast in the wrong direction won't get you where you want to go, buying the wrong things can be equally unproductive. Remember—there is no silver bullet!

More investment into security is almost always necessary, but it must be directed at a proactive, clear, and coherent outcome. We frequently see resources wasted on outdated security models that attempt to force everything onto a *trusted* internal network (which isn't feasible), on technology-only solutions (without consideration for people and processes), and on efforts that aren't aligned with business priorities. This is not money well spent.

Far too many times, we also see massive *post-crisis spending* after an incident, with organizational energy and resources getting wasted in a panic. After a big incident, there is often a knee-jerk reaction to spending a large amount on security products just to "do something" (which often creates an unrealistic expectation that the money spent somehow magically solved the problem).

Unfortunately, this spending is almost universally ineffective as it is frequently directed at a futile effort to make the internal network fully secure and trusted. The most heartbreaking part of this pattern is that in many cases, *the security technology never actually gets implemented or operationalized, and the business processes that create risk don't get fixed*. This is often because the organization didn't consider resource availability, schedules, dependencies, and other due diligence in the heat of the moment.

Zero Trust helps us avoid these traps by focusing on a proactive approach that both addresses known past attacks and sets up defenses that mitigate future risks from adaptive attackers. This naturally brings us to the next common question.

### If I have a Zero Trust strategy and funding, can I make this go away quickly?

Strategy and funding are critical ingredients, but so too is patience—*this is a journey that will take time and persistence.*

We will see quick wins and incremental progress along this journey, but we must recognize that this will be a long-term journey. We will be continuously executing changes and continuously improving how we address this. We must expect that new models, technologies, and other drivers will constantly change the operating landscape and update our plans accordingly.

Just as a digital business strategy requires a clear vision, executive sponsorship, coordination across business groups, and ongoing focus, Zero Trust requires the same. Organizations must commit to changing technology, people, culture, and processes if they want to be competitive and successful in this new world.

Security must be proactively integrated into business processes and digital transformation, rather than security being an ad hoc or after-the-fact set of tasks. Zero Trust is inseparable from digital evolution strategies (the names may change—digital transformation, legacy modernization, and so on) as it is the only practical way to keep these new assets safe. In some rare instances, security threats may be a driving force for justifying investment into a digital transformation strategy, but this is extremely rare as of the time of writing this book.

Now that we understand this journey will take time and persistence, we may wonder if it will ever end.

### Can we ever be completely safe? What should I do about it?

*There can be no guarantee of complete safety.* The goal we should aim for is to make the systems resilient against security risks. We can and should get good at limiting the likelihood and impact of a bad thing happening (called *reducing the blast radius* by infosec folks), reducing exposure of what we must protect (so that we don't waste energy on unneeded tasks), and accepting that bad things can and eventually will happen. Our goal should be to bring security risk down to an acceptable level by normalizing the ongoing management of security risk and attacks.

We should make sure that successful attacks are stopped as fast as possible, containing them to ensure they don't get worse, and get business operations back to normal as fast as possible. We should always learn from attacks to know how we can respond better next time (as attackers will always try again).

We can never be completely safe with computers, just as we can never be completely safe in the physical world. We can protect against big and common risks, but we can't ever guarantee someone's safety in the real world (or on computers on the internet).

Zero Trust gives us the best chance to keep people and systems safe with a practical and resilient approach that integrates resources, perspectives, and talents from across the organization.

Now, let's take a moment to address a common question on the relationship between cybersecurity and war.

## Is this cyberwar?

No—in almost all cases, cyberwar isn't an accurate term. While the term *cyberwar* is often used to quickly garner attention and headlines, *what we see covers the full range of human conflict types played out digitally.*

It's not limited to war, and more often includes criminal activity, such as theft and extortion (including ransomware), corporate espionage, activism, bullying/harassment, and a nearly endless variety of other human conflict types. There are some documented cases where cyberattacks are used to support a physical invasion that clearly fits a *war* definition, but these are still relatively rare events as of the time of writing this book.

While most activity is not war, nation-states are active participants as both defenders and attackers. Most nation-state attack activity fits the definition of espionage, with attackers focused on stealing sensitive information, influencing elections, or conducting limited targeted disruptive action.

Because the internet connects all types of systems (civilian, government, military, and so on) in near real time, nation-state conflicts can spill over into the civilian population (whether intentionally or accidentally). This was seen with the Stuxnet worm that infected many civilian systems that were not intended targets. The Petya/NotPetya destructive worm also affected many systems around the world that were outside of the (assumed) original intended target of Ukraine.

> **Note**
>
> There is a wide spectrum of how much the government of a nation-state may be responsible for attacks originating within its borders.
>
> Governments may do the following:
>
> • Directly conduct an attack on government employees (and choose to acknowledge it or not)
>
> • Directly hire or ask for an attack by private individuals (some of whom may be retired from government service or active employees acting privately)
>
> • Have a written or unwritten policy to not crack down on local criminals because of the economic benefit (for example, ransom payments bring money into the local economy)
>
> • Simply be unaware or incapable of investigating and prosecuting criminals in their country

Now that we know it really isn't about war, it's worth asking what kinds of attacks we should focus on.

## What are the most damaging attacks?

Ransomware/extortion is the one to worry about. While organizations face many attack types (including nation-state espionage), by far the most damaging attacks are based on an extortion monetization model and are usually referred to as **ransomware**.

These ransomware attacks started out as simple ransom demands (pay me or you don't get access to your data), but in recent years have grown to become a full and flexible extortion model where criminals extract payments in any way that they can (threaten you with disclosure of data, threaten your customers or medical patients, and so on).

These groups have become extremely sophisticated at researching their victims. They learn about your financial records, cyber insurance policies, potential regulatory fines you may have to pay, your business models, and so on to identify how much you would be willing to pay and how to exploit your weaknesses. They can successfully extort tens of millions of dollars from organizations, shut down critical infrastructure operations entirely until paid, and then reinvest those profits into research and development for newer and bigger attacks.

We expect this alarming ransomware/extortion trend to continue growing in volume, damage, and sophistication. By the time you read this text, the problem will likely have gotten worse than when we wrote it.

*But wait—there's more.* Unfortunately, ransomware/extortion isn't the only attack modern organizations face. Attackers also monetize their activity with stolen data that can be sold to your competitors, nation-states, or anyone else who is willing to buy it. Attackers also monetize attacks by using your computers and systems to attack other organizations that trust you (suppliers, vendors, customers, and so on), or simply use your resources to mine cryptocurrency or send phishing emails. These attackers are willing and able to increase the chances of payment by sending personalized messages to people (including business executives and their family members). We have even seen destructive variations of ransomware emerge that have the sole intent of disrupting your business operations (often pretending to be ransomware and using similar attacker tools).

---

**Focusing on ransomware/extortion helps with other attacks**

Focusing on ransomware/extortion defenses will also prepare you well for other attacks because the attackers use similar attack techniques regardless of their goal.

The defenses for destructive attacks are identical to ransomware attacks, and the defenses for targeted data theft are extremely similar as well. For example, protecting your privileged accounts is a top priority, whether your goal is to prevent attackers from erasing all systems or prevent them from stealing sensitive data from all systems.

---

We classify attacks by the attacker business models instead of technology because most attackers are flexible and willing to use any technical attack technique that achieves their objective. New techniques seem to emerge all the time, and when they do, they get added to the attacker's playbooks. Most attacker groups have developed skills and automation that allow them to send phishing emails to trick someone into delivering malicious programs to control the computer (malware). They can directly attack a website or online application and research or buy a zero-day vulnerability (undisclosed vulnerability in software), as well as many other technical means of attacks.

*Zero Trust helps with all attacks.* Ultimately, Zero Trust provides a resilient and flexible approach to security that addresses multiple types of attacks and adapts to new ones as they emerge. Adopting Zero Trust makes your organization resilient to ransomware and whatever else comes along.

You may be wondering where this ends and what success looks like.

## What does success look like for security and Zero Trust?

Success for security is simply the failure of attackers. While this is a simple statement, it is quite challenging to do and to measure. Attackers are intelligent, creative, and adaptive humans who are motivated to attack you and benefit from it in some way. The playbooks describe success for the various roles in your organization in detail, but a few key themes that should guide your thinking and security investments are set out here:

- **Increase attacker cost and friction**: Increase the cost and friction required for attackers to operate and succeed (especially on proven techniques that have worked in the past).

- **Limit attacker return**: Limit or completely block attackers' ability to get value from an attack by limiting their access to your assets (in terms of time, volume, asset value, and more).

**Cybersecurity success is a team sport** that requires *everyone in the organization* to help out. Attackers have many opportunities to attack the people, processes, and technology of an organization. Because of this, everyone must be vigilant, and cybersecurity basics should be as normal as the basics of food safety or fire safety.

**Zero Trust eventually becomes the new normal**. What Zero Trust looks like will change through the transformation as it becomes normalized as "this is the way we do security." While Zero Trust starts as a new concept, it eventually becomes normal and invisible, just like the oxygen in the air around us. The old way of security will eventually fade into the past, like passenger travel on stagecoaches or cargo shipping on sailing vessels.

## Why is Zero Trust so confusing?

We often see common points of confusion as people learn about Zero Trust. Some of these are because the information security discipline is still in its early days. This discipline has only been around for a few decades compared to centuries or millennia of study of business, physical security and war, building architecture, psychology, and other human disciplines.

We will cover these in more detail in coming chapters (particularly *Chapter 7, What Zero Trust Success Looks Like*), but this is a quick summary of common misperceptions that cause the most confusion:

- **Not just the network**: Technology experts often think the job of information security is to "protect the network", rather than the Zero Trust approach of *protecting business assets across any network*. While this shift is extremely simple in concept, it requires changing many instincts and habits that people have built up over years or decades of their careers.

- **A risk, not a technical problem**: Another common point of confusion comes from viewing information security as a technical problem that should simply be "solved." Just as there is no simple single solution for crime or spying, there is no single solution for the computer versions of them. *It's critical to view security as an ongoing risk from a live, intelligent human planning and executing attacks rather than a simple error or flaw.*

- **Security is not an island**: While security and business professionals often speak different languages and operate as independent units with minimal interactions, this approach is no longer viable. To be successful with security, roles throughout the organization must work together and influence each other's work. Business, IT, and security leaders and professionals must work together to manage constant change from business and market dynamics, technology platforms, and attacker evolution. If these roles don't constantly communicate and provide feedback to each other, they will be working against each other as they try to keep up.

ast misconception is very much a cornerstone in clearing up confusion. Putting security into the context of business priorities and risks will quickly shift perspectives and help clear up other points of confusion. These playbooks provide a blueprint to do exactly that.

> **Important note**
> Zero Trust is not a static solution or a single master plan that is developed once, handed down, and followed exactly forever. Zero Trust must be a living strategy that adapts to the fluid nature of the real world and adjusts constantly. Everyone should expect that any or all stakeholders may actively influence the architecture, plans, and sometimes the strategy as the organization learns to shift from a static to a dynamic approach.

## How do I know if something is Zero Trust?

The best source of clarity on what is and isn't Zero Trust is the *Zero Trust Commandments* from The Open Group. If something enables one or more commandments, then it supports Zero Trust. If it violates any, it isn't Zero Trust.

The full detailed commandments are available at `https://pubs.opengroup.org/security/zero-trust-commandments/`.

*Table 3.1 contains a summary of the Zero Trust Commandments:*

| Practice Deliberate Security | |
| --- | --- |
| **Secure Assets by Organizational Risk** | Security controls shall be designed to protect business assets appropriate to required security posture, business value, and associated risk. |
| **Validate Trust Explicitly** | Security assurance shall rely on explicitly validating trust decisions using all relevant available information and telemetry. |
| **Support Business Objectives** | |
| **Enable Modern Work** | Security discipline shall enable productivity and manage risk as the organizational capabilities, goals, environment, and infrastructure continuously evolve. |
| **Implement Asset-Centric Controls** | Asset-specific security controls shall be implemented whenever available to minimize disruption of productivity, increase precision of security/business visibility, and improve data used to drive security compliance metrics. |
| **Enable Sustainable Security** | Security controls shall be sustainable across the full life cycle of the business asset. |
| **Develop a Security-Centric Culture** | |
| **Practice Accountability** | The entities responsible for accessing and handling assets shall be responsible for their protection and survival throughout their lifetime. |
| **Enable Pervasive Security** | Security discipline shall be explicitly included in the culture, norms, and processes throughout the organization. |
| **Utilize Least Privilege** | Access to systems and data shall be provided only as required, and access shall be removed when no longer required. |
| **Deploy Simple Security** | Security mechanisms shall be as simple as possible while retaining functionality and remaining pervasive, practicable, and scalable. |

| Practice Deliberate Security | |
|---|---|
| **Deploy Agile and Adaptive Security** | |
| **Make Informed Decision** | Security teams shall make decisions based on the best available information |
| **Improve and Evolve Security Controls** | Security teams shall continuously evolve and improve to remain successful in an environment that constantly changes. |
| **Utilize Defense in Depth** | Security mechanisms and controls shall be layered to enhance resilience and preserve integrity. |
| **Enable Resiliency** | Security systems shall ensure the organization can operate normally under adverse conditions. |

Table 3.1 – Zero Trust Commandments

## Summary

In this chapter, we learned how to think about Zero Trust and how it fits into today's digital age. We discussed what Zero Trust is, what problems it solves, and why it is critical to manage risk and opportunity from continuous changes in business models, technology estates, and security threats. We cleared up some common points of confusion, debunked some common myths, and can now relate cybersecurity and Zero Trust problems to their real-world impact.

In the next chapter, we will start to make it real by defining success criteria and a reference model for Zero Trust.

# 4

# Standard Zero Trust Capabilities

*We all need to be on the same sheet of music.*

Now that we understand why Zero Trust is so important and how it's different from previous approaches to security, let's take a deeper look at what is in Zero Trust. This chapter defines Zero Trust in a simple, clear way using *The Open Group's* reference model. It also introduces key Zero Trust capabilities enabled by this model.

This chapter covers the following topics:

- *Consistency via a simple model and durable capabilities*
- *The Open Group Zero Trust Reference Model*, including an explanation for each key element of this central diagram
- *Security disciplines* defined in the reference model
- *Key Zero Trust capabilities*, including important context on each
- *Does Zero Trust include network security?* (Spoiler: yes!)

Before we get into the model itself, let's take a moment to discuss why it's important to define a simple model and its capabilities.

## Consistency via a simple model and durable capabilities

A modern organization is complex and composed of many different specialized roles—business strategy, technology deployment and operation, financial performance, regulatory requirements, and so on. To keep everyone working in the same direction, it's critical to provide a simple model that everyone can quickly understand, including a set of durable capabilities we can count on to stay consistent over time.

Creating this consistency early accelerates Zero Trust adoption and the value it brings—increased business agility and resilience to cyberattacks. This consistency reduces internal friction between teams, which holds back both business agility and security integration.

Because a Zero Trust transformation affects all aspects of security, it's worthwhile to take a fresh look at security and revisit the core basic outcomes of the discipline. Information security is very similar to other security and safety disciplines as they all focus on these key outcomes:

- *Prevent* bad things from happening as much as possible
- *Respond*: Manage when bad things do happen to minimize damage and rapidly get back to normal
- *Learn* from those experiences to improve prevention and response

For information security, these outcomes are expanded into a more detailed life cycle in the **National Institute of Standards and Technology (NIST)** Cybersecurity Framework of **Identify**, **Protect**, **Detect**, **Respond**, **Recover**, and **Govern**. This life cycle provides an excellent guide on the outcomes of security but still needs to be translated into the capabilities that security teams use to make those happen. Establishing a clear set of durable capabilities from security that stay consistent across technology and other changes is important both to guide security teams and to create a common language that allows technology, business, and security teams to work together.

We chose to use *The Open Group*'s initial **Zero Trust Reference Model** because it is a well-vetted, industry standard-driven approach that meets this need. This model is both simple and comprehensive, providing a clear picture of what to expect that makes sense to everyone, from business leaders to technologists and security practitioners.

---

**Operations – a word with many meanings**

You may note that the word *operations* and its variations are used in different ways in this series. This is because these similar terms are used across business, technology, and security teams in these different ways. See the *Disambiguation – operations, operational, operating model, and so on* section in *Chapter 6, How to Scope, Size, and Start Zero Trust* for a full reference of these terms and how they are used.

---

Now that we understand how critically important it is to have a simple model that is understood throughout the organization, let's discuss this Zero Trust model.

## The Open Group Zero Trust Reference Model

For people to work together, everyone needs a shared understanding of *what* they are building, operating, and assessing. This isn't a full set of technical details (that comes later), but a simple diagram and plain language that gives everyone a clear picture of where they are headed is required—that is, a clear picture of Zero Trust. This common point of reference is often called a *reference model* by technologists and technical leaders.

The following diagram is from the Zero Trust Reference Model from *The Open Group*. This model provides a consistent view of the definition that will be used throughout the playbooks. In this chapter, we will quickly summarize each part of the Zero Trust Reference Model and define what all the words mean so that we all have a consistent understanding:

## Zero Trust Components
Enable flexible business workflows for the digitized world

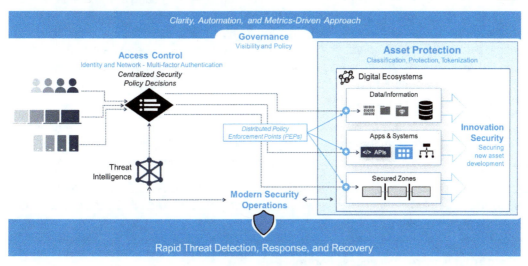

**Figure 4.1 – The Open Group Zero Trust diagram**

We will revisit this model many times throughout the playbooks to show it from the perspective of different roles and how each will use it.

It's also important to know that everyone isn't deeply interested or involved in every element of the reference model, and that's okay. Even if you don't interact with them directly, each element is essential for enabling Zero Trust outcomes (agility, adaptability, and so on), so we will briefly define all of them. The guidance for each role will highlight and explain which aspects of this are important for that role.

The reference model illustrates three kinds of elements:

- *Security disciplines*: These form the components of a full security program and strategy (bold blue text in the diagram)
- *Digital ecosystems*: The environment we live and operate in, including *business assets* and resources of value
- *Security capabilities*: These keep business assets safe in these environments

## Security disciplines

At its simplest, Zero Trust security makes sure that the right people have access to the right assets at the right time (*access control*), responds when things go wrong (*security operations*), makes sure there are clear security standards that are monitored (*governance*), and applies those standards to the organization's assets (*asset protection*). Because of how fast new capabilities are being built for the digital age, it's also critical to integrate security into the design process (*innovation security*).

These are all directly analogous to physical situations such as protecting a warehouse where you would erect fences and gates (*asset protection*), installing badge readers and checking ID badges at the gatehouse (*access control*), monitoring security cameras and responding to unusual behavior (*security operations*), and periodically inspecting to ensure processes are being followed and identifying areas for improvement (*governance*). As new buildings are built, bringing in security experts to integrate security within the design also reduces future security issues (*innovation security*).

Decisions should be informed by the context of the kinds of attacks that frequently happen to you and other organizations (*threat intelligence*, or *TI*). They should also reflect a current accurate picture of the technical environment to be protected, which is continuously evolving.

Because each of these disciplines means something different to a business leader, a technology leader, or a technology practitioner, we will dive deeper into their meaning and implications in the role-specific guidance.

> **Zero Trust is more than access control**
>
> Access control modernization is often the first and most visible initiative for Zero Trust, which can cause people to think Zero Trust is just about access control. Access control may come first, but the same forces driving access control modernization are also driving changes across all security disciplines.

Now that we understand the disciplines of security, let's look at what we are keeping safe.

## Digital ecosystems and business assets

Digital ecosystems host digital business assets and are composed of data, applications, and security ones. Let's take a deeper look at what each of these means:

- *Data* (*information*) is *the* most critical technical asset for most organizations. Data is the lifeblood of modern enterprises. If attackers cut off access to it, destroy it, or share it, they can cause (often incalculable) loss to the enterprise.

*Applications* (*systems*) and *application programming interfaces* (*APIs*, also known as *microservices*) are other critical business assets that are often required to "deliver" the goods and services your organization provides. Applications and APIs transform, modify, create, and delete the data your organization works with every day. For example, a retail website conducts transactions and creates financial records. A manufacturer can provide a product-ordering API that distributors and retailers use to automatically order more goods without manual steps.

- *Security zones* are the borders and boundaries around groups of similar assets. These allow the organization to apply similar controls to similar profiles of assets (high value, high-risk exposure, and so on) for scale and consistency.

Add these three together and you get the digital ecosystems we live in.

### Business assets

The word "asset" means different things to different stakeholders in the organization. Just as a truck delivers goods, a truck is also a mechanical device that needs inventory tracking, maintenance, parking spaces, and so on.

To a business leader, an asset is something with intrinsic value that the organization owns and can use to create more value. To a technology practitioner, an asset is often an item to be discovered and managed throughout its life cycle (for example, a laptop, server, application, website, file, database entry, and so on).

You should think about assets using *both* perspectives. A business, civilian agency, or military force won't be successful in getting the expected value from a fleet of delivery trucks if those trucks aren't maintained properly and regularly break down.

Unless otherwise noted, the term *asset* means a business asset—something that has intrinsic business value.

> **Note**
> The nature of a business asset can vary greatly, including monetary and financial instruments, *intellectual property* (*IP*), tangible physical equipment and buildings, customer-facing retail or banking websites, unique business processes, regulatory approval to operate in a market, brand perception, and many other tangible and intangible asset types.

High-level business assets need to be translated into or mapped to technical artifacts (documents, files, databases, applications, websites, servers, and so on) in order to plan and apply technical protections.

This leads to two imperatives:

- Ensure that all stakeholders are aware of which assets provide critical business value (competitive differentiation, enablement to enter new markets, and so on).

  *If teams don't know what's important (sensitive classifications), they can't provide the right level of protection and monitoring.*

- Ensure that the asset is managed and maintained well throughout its life cycle.

  *If you don't schedule and budget downtime on critical assets to perform security maintenance (for example, applying patches/updates), these critical assets are much more likely to be compromised in a cyberattack.*

We will discuss how to apply both of these imperatives in detail throughout the playbooks.

### Data (information)

Let's start with the **data** building block. From a security perspective, we care about data from the moment it is created until the moment it is destroyed, in any form it takes along that life cycle. That is, we care about data when it is stored somewhere (say, digitally or as a scrap of paper), when it's in an application, and when it's being sent somewhere (say, to your business partner).

Now, think about what goes into securing that data as we use it and share it to get business done. What happens if your trading partner is compromised? What happens if you are compromised? Can you protect all of it?

From a security perspective, we must always **assume compromise** to keep ourselves vigilant and thinking as attackers think. You should always assume that you will have bad actors on your systems at some point in time. Ask yourself what that means for low-value data (for example, a cafeteria menu) versus high-value data (pre-release product announcements or earnings reports).

*How would a compromise impact your business processes? How much should you invest in finding and securing important data?*

Focusing on the data itself (**data centricity**) allows you to be pragmatic and use your time and resources wisely. This allows you to focus closely on a smaller number of applications and systems with high-value data, protecting business-critical data better without wasting time and effort on things that don't matter as much.

This pragmatism extends to removing unneeded copies of high-value data to reduce the impact of any given incident. Just as you wouldn't want to have hundreds of photocopies of a secret project document running around, you shouldn't have unneeded extra copies of sensitive and regulated data spread willy-nilly across the environment.

*Figure 4.2* illustrates the data life cycle and the changes it undergoes:

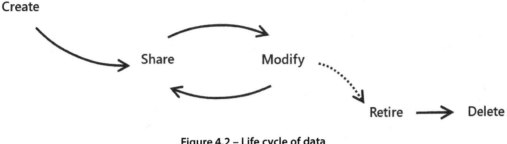

**Figure 4.2 – Life cycle of data**

## Protecting data for the life cycle

As your data goes through its life cycle, it will take many forms and likely will move and be used many times. You need to make sure that the data is appropriately protected during the full life cycle of its existence—through creation, modification, sharing, retirement, and deletion.

You also need to ensure that data is protected, especially high-value data, regardless of its location or current state (usually through some form of encryption). This is often referred to as protecting it while *in use* (when an application has it open), *at rest* (stored on a computer, USB "thumb drive," cloud service, and so on), or *in transit* (when it's being sent from one place to another).

Additionally, an organization's data has rapidly increased in value recently (to both the organization and potential attackers) because of how much **artificial intelligence** (**AI**) models and applications depend on good-quality data. This is discussed more in *Chapter 5, Artificial Intelligence (AI) and Zero Trust.*

## Applications and systems

The second building block, **applications and systems**, makes data and other services available to employees, partners, customers, and so on. Application and system downtime can have a significant impact on an organization. Imagine the impact of a banking or retail website going offline, a pipeline that can't pump oil, gas, or petrol because the computer controls (or billing systems) are offline, or a factory that can't produce goods because the controls are offline.

In the cloud-centric, service-oriented world of today, we add a third block—APIs (aka microservices, web services, and so on), which are how applications connect to each other. From a capability perspective, these are similar to applications (at a high level), and we will mostly talk about them together (though they are broken out for technical teams later).

Applications and APIs also make data useful by operating on it, updating it, and connecting it across different systems. Protecting these systems (or applications) as an individual discrete asset (rather than as part of a network) allows us to be more agile. For example, we can quickly allow a partner to access a single system or API rather than sharing access to all our internal systems on a network-wide basis. While this may seem like common sense, this is not possible with classic architectures and represents a fundamental shift to enable business agility with Zero Trust.

### Security zones

Security zones are groupings of similar assets with similar security requirements. Grouping assets this way allows us to focus resources based on how much protection is needed, spending the most time and effort on the most valuable assets (aka the *crown jewels*) rather than on the cafeteria menu. This concept is not new to security but is updated with Zero Trust.

Security zones also provide agility to the business by making business decisions simpler. Instead of having to work through a long, confusing list of technical assets for every business process, you can simply reference the zone name.

You can think about security zones like physical spaces in a retail bank:

- Outside the bank is fully public and there is limited control of the physical space, but you can install lights and cameras to increase the visibility and capture a record of suspicious behavior
- The bank lobby is open to the public but is a much more controlled space (via door locks and so on) and allows for even more monitoring
- Behind the counter is a restricted employee-only area where social and physical barriers (up to and including bulletproof glass) can protect employees and money
- In the vault is a highly guarded and protected zone where only select employees are allowed to interact with the highest-value items (and the highest density of valuable items)

Classic computer security often focused on trying to secure the whole bank building as if it were a vault. This attempt at simplification avoided identifying and analyzing individual business assets and their many (often undocumented) interdependencies but was impractical and often increased security risk. Everything was in this single vault (sometimes called a *flat network*), so all employees and partners had to be let into it, meaning any single mistake put everything in the vault at risk.

The strategy in the playbooks focuses on a security zone strategy that builds a general baseline for all assets and then establishes higher-level security zones for the highest-impact assets (aka the *crown jewels*).

The following diagram illustrates this concept:

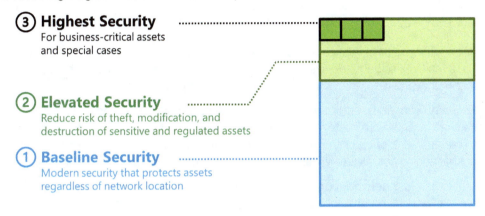

**Figure 4.3 – Asset protection levels**

Highly restricted security zones are expensive and aren't practical for most assets, but they are very valuable for the right special cases. These are discussed in more detail later, but some examples of where this approach makes sense include the following:

- *Business resources*: Maximum security restrictions are often required for certain (often small) sets of controlled data and systems, such as pharmaceutical research data, unpatented trade secrets, and the development of blockbuster products, such as video games that could be worth billions of dollars per year in future revenue.

- *Fragile resources*: Place protective zones around fragile resources that can't be protected with modern security controls and tools. This is often seen with **operational technology** (*OT*) that controls physical machines and processes using electronics that date back 30-50 years (ancient history in computer technology).

- *Protecting life and safety*: Isolate devices and systems that control physical processes that could lead to a loss of life or safety.

- *Isolating low-trust resources*: Isolate devices and systems that are difficult to protect to lower the risk of infection from these devices to other resources in the environment. This dynamic is similar to fragile resources, but often reflects devices whose function relies on a network or the internet (conference room phones, printers, and the like) and therefore can't be isolated.

- *Overlaps can happen*: Note that several of these may overlap, requiring some design work to reconcile them. For example, some systems are both life/safety impacting and fragile; while not an ideal combination, this does happen quite often in the real world.

### Learnings on security zones

These are some key learnings on the use of security zones:

- *Know what you have*: As you may imagine, creating these zones requires understanding the sensitivity of data and systems. This requires a joint effort between business and technology stakeholders, which is addressed throughout the playbook guidance.

- *Focus on simplicity*: Limit the number of zones you have to manage. Every time you separate assets, you create overhead for many people and systems across the company to maintain and support that. Use these when necessary, but always consider the high cost of adding complexity (which continues for the lifetime of the assets, often decades).

- *More than just network controls*: The controls for security zones should include all types of access control, including network, identity, application, data, and others. This is addressed in more detail in the playbook for engineering and operations.

- *People are critical*: While security zones often involve many controls, one of the most important is to ensure you trust the people who have access to the assets (background checks, audits, and so on).

- *Don't firewall and forget!*: It's critical to avoid a common antipattern where the security zone boundaries are configured once using network controls such as firewalls and then largely ignored. Illustratively, a globally impacting organization experienced a major security incident that forced shutdowns of multiple factories for a critical business line because of a lack of controls to securely handle exceptions to a security zone.

It's critical to take a full people/process/technology approach for security zones. You must define policy and secure processes for exceptions (for example, OT vendors that must connect maintenance laptops to maintain equipment), you must monitor the security zone for attacks and configuration changes, and you must regularly test and validate all of these.

So, now that we have defined the security disciplines and the digital ecosystems that we operate in, let's connect the Zero Trust model to business processes using a concept familiar to business leaders—*capabilities*.

## Key Zero Trust capabilities

To enable Zero Trust to integrate into business processes, we will describe the Zero Trust *capabilities* that this reference model enables. These capabilities make this model real by defining consistent outcomes that Zero Trust delivers to the organization over the years to come.

*What are capabilities?* Most organizations provide goods or services that are valuable to their customers (or clients, citizens, constituents, community, and so on). To provide these goods or services consistently over time, they need to define durable *capabilities*. Examples of capabilities include being able to price a product, deliver a product or service, log people in securely, or respond to a cybersecurity attack.

Capabilities capture *what* we are doing and abstract away from *how* things are done (which changes over time and varies between organizations). Many details of Zero Trust implementation will evolve over time as new ideas emerge and new components and technologies become available. However, Zero Trust's core capabilities are unlikely to change as they represent desired outcomes regardless of which technology is enabling them.

These capabilities become a collection of building blocks that you can use in business and technology processes.

## Capabilities as a common language of security

These key capabilities must become a basic vocabulary to describe security for leaders and team members across business, technology, and security teams. This common language is critical for all teams to effectively communicate about security and plan how to integrate security into the models and detailed processes across business and technology teams. These capabilities also often involve stakeholders from across business, technology, and security to varying degrees.

**Learning about other teams is a two-way street**

This is similar to how technology and security stakeholders must be familiar with a basic vocabulary of business terms.

For example, security and technology teams in a manufacturing organization must be familiar with the terminology used by business teams to describe business capabilities for acquiring raw materials, processing and assembling those into products, packaging the products and shipping them to retailers, getting paid by the retailers, and so on.

This section contains only a high-level description to introduce the concepts. The role-specific guidance in the playbooks provides much more detail on how to plan, build, operate, and improve them as part of a Zero Trust roadmap.

## Zero Trust capabilities reference

The following diagram from *The Open Group* shows the key Zero Trust capabilities that enable better security outcomes while also enabling business agility. These capabilities represent the basic components of security that all roles should be familiar with across the organization:

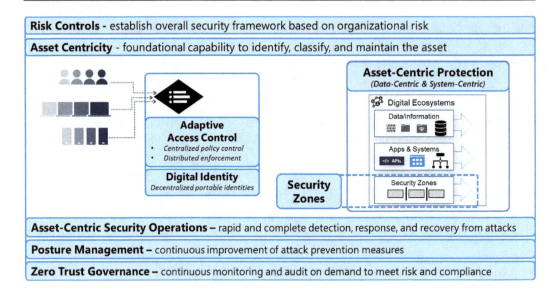

**Figure 4.4 – Depiction of key Zero Trust capabilities**

These Zero Trust capabilities collectively enable organizational *resilience* with an agile security approach that secures assets through their life cycle, continuously adapts to changes, and continuously improves.

The capabilities enhance the agility of an organization—increasing the ease of adding new partners, evolving into new channels, creating new *lines of business* (*LOBs*), and adapting to new market or technical conditions. These stand in contrast to traditional security approaches that slow down an organization's ability to innovate or adapt, which creates the risk of competitors gaining a competitive advantage.

Zero Trust capabilities can be grouped into three categories, as follows:

- *Foundational identification and life-cycle management*
- *Protecting business assets through their life cycle*
- *Operational functions to continuously prevent and respond to attacks*

Let's start with the foundational elements first.

### Foundational identification and life-cycle management

As with other disciplines, security has basic foundational capabilities that are required to enable more complex and high-value capabilities. *Figure 4.5* illustrates the foundational capabilities of security:

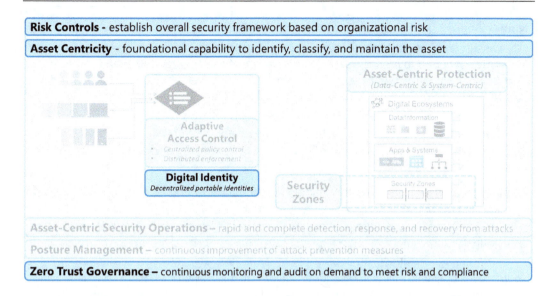

Figure 4.5 – Foundational identification and life-cycle management capabilities

The foundational security capabilities enable basic functions such as establishing a risk control framework so that teams can align security outcomes to business risk and priorities, consistently apply security policy and best practices to the organization, and effectively prioritize security resources. These also enable assigning digital identities to people and assets that are required to link them together, apply policy, and more.

The foundational capabilities are set out here:

- *Control management*: This capability establishes a risk control framework that enables the organization to establish, document, and manage regulatory and security controls. This enables the organization to align with business priorities and risks, and to consistently execute on security.

  *Without control management, the organization will have an inconsistent approach to security that results in more risk of organizational damage from security incidents and noncompliance with regulatory requirements.*

- *Asset centricity*: This capability provides the ability to identify, classify, and maintain system assets. This foundational capability enables the organization to discover, classify, label, and perform critical security maintenance on system assets. This includes activities such as vulnerability and configuration management, security configuration baselines and benchmarks, securing servers/*virtual machines* (*VMs*)/containers, securing user endpoints and devices, securing applications and development/DevOps, supply chain integrity/*software bill of materials* (*SBOM*), digital identity binding, and more.

> **Note**
>
> While asset centricity may appear to be a purely technical activity on its surface, *business leaders are required to identify business-critical assets* so that technical and security teams can use that to identify specific system and data assets that support those and secure them appropriately.

*Without asset centricity, organizations will be reliant on protecting arbitrary technical groupings of assets such as "anything on the corporate network" that are ineffective against modern attacks.*

- *Digital identity*: This capability enables the assignment and management of digital identities for people and technical assets such as applications, services, and data. The identities for people are increasingly becoming portable as people bring their own identity (in some cases, a sovereign identity). This relieves organizations of the burden of managing identities and accounts and simplifies mergers and acquisitions. This improves business agility and security but introduces new processes for evaluating and integrating external identity sources. This requires securing technologies and scenarios including identity directories, synchronization and federation services, **business-to-business (B2B)**, **business-to-consumer (B2C)**, decentralized external identities, identity governance, and more.

*Without digital identity capability, organizations often face massive barriers to business agility (complicating and slowing progress on the integration of mergers and acquisitions) and increased impact plus the likelihood of security issues (caused by inconsistent or incomplete identity and access management (IAM).*

> **Security zones can provide limited digital identities**
>
> Some assets don't natively support or can't be assigned a digital identity such as legacy OT devices, legacy IT systems, **Internet of Things (IoT)** devices with limited functionality, short-lived assets such as containers, and some assets managed by other organizations. We still need to protect that asset and protect other assets from it so that we can classify it into a group and assign it to a security zone.
>
> For example, a power utility can assign a proxy identity to a security zone (or segments of it) that contains sensitive legacy OT devices monitoring and controlling physical processes. This allows the devices to be identified and allowed to interact more securely with other systems in the organization.

- *Zero Trust governance*: This capability provides a *framework* to establish organizational structure, processes, and decision rights across people, processes, and cultural aspects of the transformation and ongoing operations. This provides clarity and consistency to the execution of security and Zero Trust. A Zero Trust governance capability is different from traditional security governance approaches at many organizations in a few respects, including the following:

*Zero Trust governance includes security intelligence and TI functions* that drive informed security decisions across the organization in an asset-centric manner.

*Without this, decisions throughout the organization are made without understanding the actual current threats to the organization, resulting in more preventable incidents and higher potential impacts from each.*

- *Zero Trust governance is continuously evolving* to meet changes in business, security, regulatory, and technology environments. Zero Trust governance also plays a critical role in driving *continuous learning* across organizations. As in many other fields (medical, technology, financial services, and others), continuous learning is required to keep people's skills and knowledge current with changes in the world.

  *Without this, meeting the business, security, and technical goals of today will be slowed or stopped by skills, policies, and architectures that were built for yesterday's technology, threats, and business requirements.*

- *Zero Trust governance defines a proactive and intentional approach* to managing security and risk with common goals, principles, and policies. In addition to a deliberate and intentional security strategy, Zero Trust includes an organization-wide *Privacy by Design* (*PbD*) capability to replace the typical organizational approach of reactive ad hoc efforts. Additionally, Zero Trust governance provides a continuous *audit-on-demand* capability that shifts organizational audit schedules from months to days or less. This approach to governance enables organizations to keep up with the rapidly changing regulatory landscape that includes different laws in the *European Union* (*EU*), UK, India, China, and individual states in the US.

  *Without this intentional approach, meeting compliance requirements will consist of a series of ad hoc efforts that slow business processes, waste effort, and may even result in fines for noncompliance.*

Now, let's talk about how Zero Trust builds on this foundation to protect assets anywhere in their life cycle.

### Protecting business assets through their life cycle

These capabilities build on the foundational capabilities in the previous section to secure business assets throughout their life cycle. *Figure 4.6* illustrates these key capabilities:

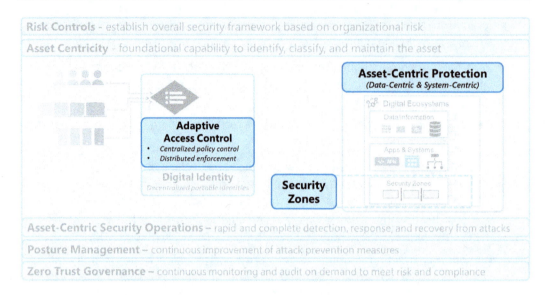

**Figure 4.6 – Capabilities to protect business assets across their life cycle**

*These capabilities enable users to get work done securely without being "on the network."* They enable organizational security, agility, and productivity by protecting business assets individually regardless of their internet or geographic location.

These capabilities include the following:

- *Adaptive access control*: This capability controls access to business assets by enforcing a consistent policy that automatically adapts to real-time threats and dynamic business changes (new attack techniques, a change in employment, unusual geolocations, and more). Adaptive access ensures that organizational policy is enforced based on risk rather than technical factors such as the network location of users or assets. This capability builds on traditional *single sign-on* (*SSO*) by integrating a policy engine, policy enforcement points, security operations tools such as *Endpoint Detection and Response* (*EDR*), TI context, and other business and security contexts.

This capability benefits all stakeholders because it does the following:

- *Improves user experience*: Users accessing assets no longer have to go through additional manual steps such as connecting to a *virtual private network* (*VPN*).

- *Increases business agility*: The policy-driven approach allows for rapid and simple changing of access rights as roles change—for example, a person who starts at a partner, who then gets hired at a competitor, who then becomes an employee when that competitor is acquired.

- *Strengthens security*: Adaptive access integrates real-time risk information (TI) into access decisions and can automatically reduce or revoke access to business assets in response to an attack. This rapid containment of a breach limits potential damage to the organization without waiting for human intervention (reducing the blast radius of the breach).

- *Simplifies management and administration*: Managing adaptive access policies is much simpler as they focus on assets, users, and risk factors, rather than complex technical configurations such as network locations. This enables administrators to focus on more productive and valuable tasks such as managing account life cycles and privileged access (which are often neglected and frequently exploited by attackers).

While it doesn't rely on geographic or network location, adaptive access allows restrictions based on those factors. For example, some organizations may have assets that should not be accessed by residents or citizens of certain countries or regions.

*Without adaptive access, organizations rely on complex and inflexible technical elements to control access (for example, users must connect to the network or VPN) instead of actual security risk factors. This frequently results in users bypassing security requirements to be productive, generating more security incidents that have larger likely impacts.*

- *Asset-centric protections*: This capability establishes protections for business assets in the technical environment. These capabilities are a direct complement to adaptive access controls—*adaptive access provides a secure way to access and use assets* while *asset-centric protections secure the assets themselves*. This is very similar to protecting a car from being stolen by physical break-ins (asset-centric protections) versus protecting the keys from being stolen (adaptive access).

Digital business assets are composed of one or both of these technical component types:

- *Data assets* are electronic information in the form of documents, databases, spreadsheets, pictures, design diagrams, and more. These assets may contain trade secrets, IP, customer data, or sensitive or other valuable information. Data assets require different controls to protect all copies over the course of their life cycle— including while in use, at rest, and in transit.

- *System assets* are services, applications, and other technical systems that execute business processes. These can take many forms, such as websites, mobile applications, **enterprise resource planning** (**ERP**) systems, **customer relationship management** (**CRM**) systems that control physical equipment, and many others. Protecting system assets varies by the nature and design of the system, but some universally important considerations include the following:

  - *Internet exposure*: Many systems today have interfaces available over the internet (websites, APIs, chatbots, and so on) that must be secured against attacks.

  - *Full application life cycle*: Attackers can exploit security introduced during any stage of their life cycle, including planning, design, deployment, and operations.

- *System assets must be protected from each other*: Systems today are interconnected, and attackers often perform lateral traversal attacks to exploit that. For example, attackers often compromise one system (such as an internet website or application) to use that as a platform to attack other systems and data in the organization's environment (by stealing credentials, scanning for, and exploiting software vulnerabilities, and so on).

Asset-centric protections include data classification and protection through its life cycle including while it is at rest, in transit, and being used. They also include tracking the data provenance (critical for AI, as noted in the next chapter) and various techniques to reduce risk such as data elimination, tokenization, obfuscation, and anonymization. Asset-centric protection also includes API gateways, technical protections for **denial-of-service (DoS)** attacks and more.

*Without asset-centric protections, organizations will be unable to identify and protect their most important data (trade secrets, IP, customer data, and more) against compromise by attackers.*

*This leads to increased frequency and impact of breaches that undermine customer trust, competitive differentiators, and revenue.*

- *Security zones* simplify the assignment of controls and policy to a group of assets with similar business criticality, security risk, or other common attributes. This can simplify security policy management and can improve security for legacy or limited-function technology that doesn't support modern security capabilities, as described earlier in this chapter.

While this concept has been around for a long time to describe network segments protected by firewalls, it's critical to reinforce that security zones aren't just network controls such as firewall rules that are configured once. In the era of cloud and Zero Trust, this concept has been expanded to include identity, application, endpoint, and other controls that enable the isolation of assets and applying a common policy to them.

While business and technology leaders may not be involved in the technical design and implementation of security zones, these stakeholders need to be involved in the processes. Business teams are responsible for the determination of what is sensitive enough (potential impact on the organization) to warrant the cost and effort of building and maintaining a security zone (and any potential impact on business agility for these assets).

Now that we have covered the capabilities to identify business assets, access them, and protect them through their life cycles, let's cover the capabilities that sustain and improve security assurances in the face of a continuous flow of attacks.

### Operational functions to continuously prevent and respond to attacks

Operational teams must continuously sustain and monitor security to keep up with risk and other changes in real time. *Figure 4.7* illustrates capabilities related to operational security functions:

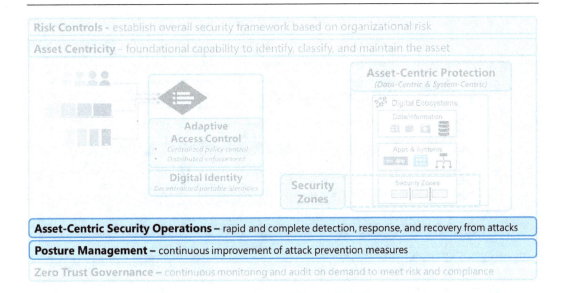

Figure 4.7 – Capabilities related to operational security functions

These capabilities enable the operational functions of security that manage and mitigate potential security risks (vulnerabilities) and realized risks (incidents or attacks).

*Security posture management* focuses on operational aspects of preventing attacks while *security operations* focuses on responding to and managing the incidents that happen. These complementary capabilities should be integrated with each other, IT operations, and business operations. Tightly integrating these with the organization's business and technical operations provides clear visibility into security risks and ensures that these risks are mitigated quickly and effectively.

Key operational security capabilities are set out here:

- *Security posture management* enables the organization to monitor and mitigate the countless ways that hostile actors can attack the organization's assets, often referred to as the "attack surface" of the organization. This is similar to protecting a car by ensuring that the car door locks are strong and are locked when nobody is using it, the keys aren't easy to forge and don't get left where they are easy to steal, the windows aren't left open while the owner is away, and so on.

  *Posture management is broad!* The attack surface of an organization in today's world is very large and complex, requiring posture management to work with many teams across the organization that operate and maintain different resources. *Figure 4.8* illustrates key technical areas that compose the technical attack surface of an organization and the teams that are involved in posture management:

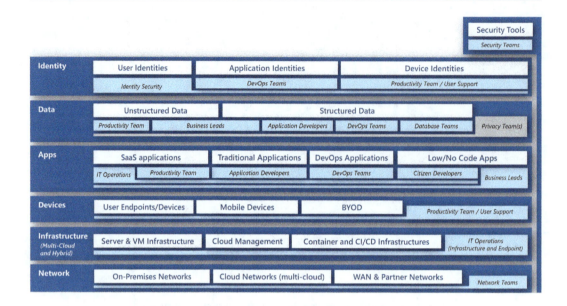

**Figure 4.8 – Security posture management is large and complex**

As the preceding diagram shows, preventing potential attacks requires monitoring and mitigating risk across a broad range of asset types. Getting visibility into this breadth of technology, processes, people, and policy requires a lot of work and time. It is critical to set expectations on the scale of this work and involve each of these teams to apply security to the assets that they maintain and know best. This work will never be done completely, but it is critical to make swift and steady progress to burn down the backlog of technical debt (similar to paying a high-interest financial debt). Posture management should focus on *continuous prioritization* and *continuous improvement*.

In today's world, security threats and vulnerabilities evolve a lot faster than most regulatory requirements, so organizations need to focus on a combination of compliance requirements and organizational security risk. The organizational security risk is informed by security intelligence that accounts for which assets are of the greatest value to the organization, TI on trends and likely attacks, relative strengths and weaknesses in the organization's security posture, and more.

Getting a full picture of security posture requires combining an outside-in view of your organization (**external attack surface management** or *EASM*) with an inside-out view to get a holistic view of strong and weak points in the posture. Technologies that enable the inside-out view include traditional configuration management tools, vulnerability management tools, as well as specialized security posture management tools such as **cloud security posture management** (*CSPM*) tools, **cloud-native application protection platform** (*CNAPP*) tools, and more (which often fuse together a lot of the diverse data sources for you).

*Without security posture management, an organization's approach to preventing attacks will be ad hoc, disconnected, and ineffective.*

*This leads to increased business damage from many incidents that would be prevented by posture management (or would have a less serious impact).*

- **Asset-centric security operations** (**ACSOs**) enable the organization to find and remove attackers who have successfully gained unauthorized access to the organization's business assets. **Security operations** (sometimes called **SecOps**, **Security Operations Center**, or **SOC**) reduce organizational risk by limiting the time that adversaries have access to business assets, which is sometimes referred to as attacker "dwell time."

As with security posture management, Security Operations is a large and complex discipline. SecOps must detect, respond, and help recover from attacks across the breadth of the technical estate described in the previous posture management section. ASCOs include capabilities for incident management (sometimes broken into *Triage/Tier 1* and *Investigation/Tier 2* capabilities), incident management, threat hunting, detection engineering, TI, red and purple teaming, and more. Security operations also partners closely with technology operations teams to continuously improve detections and rapidly restore affected services to full capacity (for example, during recovery from a ransomware or other destructive attack).

*Focus on assets, not networks.* The asset-centric approach to SecOps in Zero Trust uses asset-specific technical detections and is aware of higher-value business assets to prioritize detections and responses on those assets. This contrasts with traditional detection and response approaches that focus on defending a *network* perimeter primarily (or solely) using *network* technology. As *NIST SP 800-207* states, "*Perimeter-based network security has also been shown to be insufficient since once attackers breach the perimeter, further lateral movement is unhindered.*"

Some organizations are already moving beyond this (largely ineffective) network-centric approach by adopting advanced identity, cloud, and endpoint capabilities—ASCOs continue that change and build on it.

ASCOs prioritize the use of asset-specific threat detection such as EDR and **extended detection and response** (**XDR**) tools that provide high-quality (low false-positive) detections of common attacks. **Security orchestration automation and response** (**SOAR**) technology that automates common tasks is also a critical enabler to reduce wasted repetitive effort and errors. ASCO includes traditional **security information and event management** (**SIEM**) and related security data lake capabilities, but these are enhanced by technologies that help process massive amounts of data, including **machine learning** (**ML**, a form of AI) and behavior analytics (often called **user and entity behavior analytics** or **UEBA**).

The Zero Trust approach to SecOps also focuses on integrating TI from security operations into more of the organization's processes to inform architecture, engineering, operations, posture management, and more. TI is also fused with **business intelligence** (**BI**) to form a shared security intelligence context to guide prioritization and other decisions. Security intelligence is described in more detail in the playbooks.

*Without ASCOs, organizations will be much less effective at responding to the continuously increasing severity and complexity of attacks.*

*Each incident that enables attackers to steal, alter, or destroy data and system functionality undermines the organization's revenue, customer trust, and competitive differentiators.*

These key capabilities collectively enable an organization to become agile, resilient, and secure.

## Capability integration

These capabilities do not exist in a vacuum; they are integrated with each other and with business and technical capabilities in the organization.

*Figure 4.9* from *The Open Group Zero Trust Reference Model* illustrates how security capabilities and teams work together to continuously improve security:

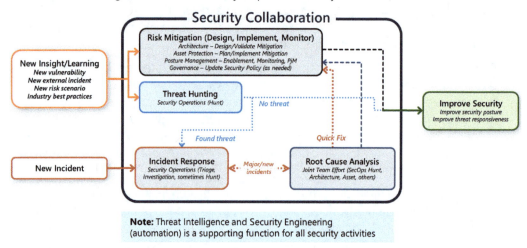

**Figure 4.9 – Security continuous learning reduces risk**

In a Zero Trust approach, the organization learns and grows stronger with each event. Whether the organization directly experiences an attack or learns from the experience of others, the learnings are fed into an improved ability to prevent attacks, detect them, respond to them, or recover from them.

In summary, these Zero Trust security capabilities enable organizations to pursue new opportunities and business models with much lower security friction, more security and risk context, and much higher security assurances than classic security approaches.

# Does Zero Trust include network security?

Yes—network security is part of Zero Trust, but networks no longer define the security paradigm as in classic security approaches. Network security is a key part of security zones and other access control capabilities (alongside identity, application, data, and other technologies).

While network security once dominated security thinking and tooling, its role will be diminished to "one technology among many." This is because the business assets to be protected are increasingly hosted on networks you don't control, requiring the use of other technologies for effective security controls. Additionally, attackers are evading network-only protection strategies with phishing, credential theft, supply chain, and other attack techniques—adding to the requirement for other controls and technologies.

*Figure 4.10* illustrates this dynamic:

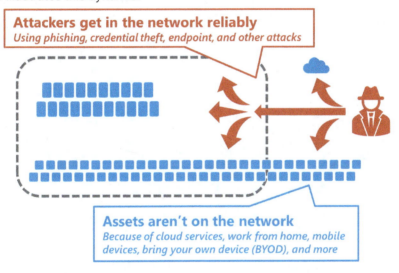

**Figure 4.10 – Limitations of network perimeter security**

### Does Zero Trust require removing firewalls?

*No!* Existing firewalls and related network controls will stay in place to protect existing workloads (which are now "legacy" in the cloud era), but there will be limited value in investing in network security perimeters beyond maintaining existing controls.

We also expect to see more business-aware security technologies emerge and mature (often called microsegmentation) that enable and reinforce security zones with network, identity, and other control types.

This blending of classic security approaches with new approaches allows us to use Zero Trust to protect legacy assets of 30 years ago, all the way to new assets that just went online 30 minutes ago.

## Summary

In this chapter, we reviewed the Zero Trust components using *The OSSpen Group Zero Trust Reference Model*, describing each key Zero Trust capability and the important context for each.

This helped us to get a clear picture of Zero Trust and its key capabilities. When everyone knows what we are building, everyone is on the same page, and we are much more likely to be successful on this critically important journey.

In the next chapter, we will see how Zero Trust allows us to manage big changes from AI, a new technology that is disrupting business, technology, security, and society at large.

# 5
# Artificial Intelligence (AI) and Zero Trust

*Change happens whether or not we are ready for it!*

**Artificial intelligence** (**AI**) is a powerful technology that is introducing disruptive effects across business, technology, security, and society. This technology has been evolving for some time but recently shifted into high gear with the availability of a new generation of generative AI technology.

This chapter provides a summary of AI and its impacts, limitations, and relationship with Zero Trust. Detailed guidance on AI and security for each role is included in each playbook.

This chapter answers these important questions:

- What is AI?
- What will the impact of AI look like?
- What are the limitations of AI?
- How can we manage AI security risks with Zero Trust?
- How will AI impact Zero Trust?

Let's start with the first basic question regarding what AI is.

## What is AI?

AI is the simulation of intelligent human behavior using computers. There are many focus areas within AI, so this book will only provide a brief summary of AI and its implications for security and Zero Trust.

It's important to distinguish between two different types of AI capabilities:

- **Classic AI**: The role of AI in security began by capturing and scaling expert human experience over large datasets with **machine learning** (**ML**). This takes the form of human experts training and tuning *supervised ML* models ahead of time and having *unsupervised ML* models identify clusters or patterns in the data that they surface to human experts for analysis. ML enables humans to identify patterns and anomalies in large amounts of data that can be used to identify security weaknesses, attacks, and other insights in the large complex technical estates of a modern organization.

- **Generative AI**: Recently, **large language models** (**LLM**) have enabled the analysis and generation of human language, pictures, and other media, which has *dramatically changed the way people interact with computers and information*. These models are trained on large amounts of human-generated artifacts (conversations, pictures, poems, songs, news articles, computer code, and more), enabling computers to "understand" (analyze) and generate similar artifacts.

The most impactful use of this technology so far is the use of chat interfaces (such as ChatGPT) where people can have these models (and other connected systems) perform tasks for them. Unlike previous voice interfaces, such as Apple's Siri feature, which was limited to preconfigured commands, these generative AI interfaces can continue to interact with users to further clarify the request and refine the outputs (update and change the pictures, song lyrics, computer code, and more).

This technology was rapidly put into products by Microsoft, Google, and many others. The most common form so far is a co-pilot or guided assistant that enables people to rapidly perform existing tasks and start performing new ones. Additionally, early success stories include providing internal roles (such as customer support roles) with chat assistants that suggest answers to customer questions and the ability to ask questions to perform rapid research.

Because people can rapidly learn how to use this interface (very similar to chatting with humans), it is likely to become a preferred computer interface for many tasks and may even become the default way that vendors build some new features and capabilities.

> **Note**
> Generative AI does not replace classic AI. Generative AI capabilities often use other systems to perform specialized tasks, many of which use the ML models of classic AI.

Now, let's take a look at the kind of impact AI technology will have.

# What will the impact of AI look like?

The impact of AI will be significant and will be difficult to predict in detail, but clear themes are emerging on the kind of impact it will have on organizations.

Generative AI allows anyone with access to the internet to generate impressive content with very little training. People can use generative AI to produce photo-realistic pictures, drawings, articles, song lyrics, poems, computer code, and much more simply by requesting it in a simple chat interface.

*AI will have a large, fast, and ongoing impact across every organization* because of the ease of use and wide availability of this powerful technology. The disruptive impact of AI will likely resemble the PC and internet revolutions that transformed business processes, the consumer economy, and many aspects of society.

### AI adoption will be fast

Unlike the PC revolution, AI does not require distributing new devices to have a broad and deep impact across society. This generation of technology uses (and builds on) the existing devices, internet, and cloud infrastructure to enable rapid access by everyone.

Additionally, *most people can quickly learn how to create value with AI without any specialized skills*. People will require limited or zero training to get started because of how similar the chat interface is to an existing human interaction. Advanced skills and scenarios are emerging in a discipline called **prompt engineering**, but these aren't required to get started.

*AI enables anyone with a computer to quickly use advanced functions* that previously required expert skills and advanced training.While the speed of AI adoption depends on many factors (availability of needed AI skills, speed of organizational adoption, and more), AI adoption faces fewer native limitations than previous disruptive technologies like PCs, Internet, mobile devices, and cloud technology.

### AI will have a broad, ongoing, and deep impact

AI will have a powerful effect across many roles in organizations, disrupting assumptions and norms for years (or even decades) to come.

This disruptive effect will be ongoing and powerful because *generative AI fundamentally changes how people interact with computers*. AI enables people to easily access advanced computing capabilities without requiring technical knowledge and training. As more people discover AI, they will combine their specialized role skills and knowledge with these advanced capabilities (and their imagination). As people create new ways to generate business value using AI, others will discover them and build new ideas on them, and still others will build on those new ideas, and so on.

The resulting growth of the AI economy will likely resemble the growth of applications and programs following the availability of **graphical user interfaces** (**GUIs**) in the 1980s and 1990s. When people could click on what they wanted to do instead of having to memorize and type commands, they were inspired to use computers, write applications, and start software businesses. The natural language interfaces of AI are likely to do the same as more and more people discover how easy it is to use sophisticated capabilities to access, change, and generate documents, pictures, songs, and more.

*Any role that creates or processes information will be affected by AI*, including business executives, managers, artists, scientists, journalists, lawyers, legislators, regulators, business analysts, customer service professionals, administrative professionals, technologists, security professionals, and many more.

This is changing how scammers and criminals work as they are already adopting this technology to fake people's voices and imitate their writing styles.

This large amount of disruption will cause widespread excitement, fear, and confusion – resulting in both opportunity and risk for organizations.

### Some AI impacts on security are predictable

While nobody can precisely predict the future, some changes from AI are extremely likely to impact security. These are based on the nature of the AI technology, early observed AI impacts, and learning from past disruptive technologies such as PCs, the internet, mobile devices, cloud computing, and social media.

The impact of AI on security will likely follow these themes:

- **AI will show up everywhere**: AI is and will continue to be introduced to business, technology, and security workflows across the organization, vendors, partners, customers, attack groups, and more. People are using AI to generate resumes based on job descriptions, business collaboration tools are integrating AI copilots and chat assistants, security vendors are adding generative AI features, attackers are using AI to trick people by imitating real voices and writing styles, and more.

  - **Security implication**: Security, technology, and business teams must quickly learn about the technology and its implications on security risk to develop policies and controls that both reduce organizational risk and enable the business to pursue opportunities with the technology. Everyone must share what they've learned early and frequently to ensure the organization can keep up with the continuous changes from AI.

- **AI will generate a lot of content**: AI can generate a high volume of content, so we will see a flood of AI-generated text, pictures, videos, websites, and more. This content will likely vary widely in quality, utility, and accuracy. This will resemble the explosive growth of email resulting from the low cost of sending emails, including everything from high-value messages to junk (spam) email and everything in between (newsletters, marketing, group email, and more).

  - **Security implication**: This explosion of convincing and personalized content of questionable value will require mitigations such as user education and specialized products to measure the quality, accuracy, and utility of content.

- **AI will generate a lot of confusion**: As AI usage grows, people will get confused by content created by AI such as convincing "deepfake" impersonations of people in video, voice, and email conversations. Additionally, many people will misunderstand what AI technology can and can't do because they don't have a good reference point – the current AI technology is very different than how AI has been portrayed in movies and TV shows for decades. Some people will be overly excited and exuberant about using the technology while others will be overly fearful and cautious with this technology – each extreme can create unnecessary risk.

  - **Security implication**: Organizations should urgently focus on education, managing expectations, security/financial processes and controls, and setting clear policies.

- **AI increases the need for data-centric security**: AI models need good data, dramatically increasing the focus on data security and data quality. Every organization's internal data quickly increased in value because AI models need human-generated data and the internet is already flooded with AI-generated content.

  AI models trained on AI-generated data result in very low-quality results (similar to how a photocopy of a photocopy is of lower quality), a dynamic called **model collapse**. *Figure 5.1* illustrates model collapse by showing the difference between training an AI model on human-generated data versus AI-generated data:

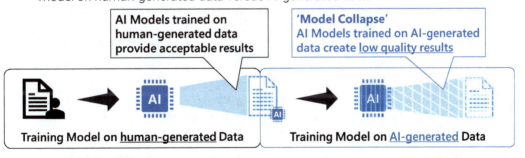

Figure 5.1 – Illustration of model collapse for models trained on AI-generated data

Because of the value of AI models and the need for original human-generated content to train them, human-generated data such as the internal data in most organizations becomes extremely valuable for AI models. This further increases the value of data, and we are already seeing attackers target organizations to steal their data for this reason.

- **Security implication**: Organizations must urgently adopt a data-centric Zero Trust security approach to protect their data and their newly discovered competitive differentiator. Traditional network-centric security approaches will not be able to effectively protect data against attacks.

- **AI success will inspire further disruption**: The successes of generative AI will also encourage investment and funding of additional technological innovations and disruptions. As organizations embrace AI technology, they will apply it to more and more scenarios that push the boundaries of what computers can do, such as measuring and understanding people's emotional states (sometimes called affective computing). Each of these advances will generate more conversations and requirements for guidance, policy, education, and more.

  - **Security implication**: Business, technology, and security teams will need to work together to understand these changes and build policies and controls that allow the organization to responsibly adopt these technologies. Organizations will have to constantly learn how to manage these disruptions so that they enable the business to grow and thrive while reducing risk. The agile security approach of Zero Trust will be a key asset to do this.

As you can see, AI will have widespread impacts that require business, security, and technology teams to work together using a Zero Trust approach. The per-role guidance in each playbook goes into more detail on the implications of AI for each role.

---

**AI transformation will resemble digital transformation**

The AI transformation at your organization will be similar to your digital transformation in many ways. Each transformation will replace existing business processes with new processes based on more advanced technology that is more effective and efficient. Both transformations will also be a source of continuous change and disruption from both external organizations and internal innovation.

---

For additional information on how to think about various types of AI risk, the NIST AI Risk Management Framework is a good resource: `https://www.nist.gov/itl/ai-risk-management-framework`.

While AI will create many new opportunities and risks, there are very real limitations regarding what AI technology can currently do.

# What are the limitations of AI?

AI technology will be powerful and transformative, but AI is not a magic silver bullet solution for security or any other problems. AI has very real and significant limitations, and it is far from the fully independent human-like **artificial general intelligence** (**AGI**) we frequently see portrayed in movies and TV shows.

The main limitation is that AI models don't truly understand content in the complex and rich ways that humans do. AI will also naturally reflect and propagate any biases in its data, whether or not these biases are known and documented.

Let's take a quick look at these key limitations of AI.

## AI models do not "understand" anything

While generative AI appears to "understand" things on the surface, it is only imitating the original content it was trained on. This extremely shallow "understanding" is similar to fake buildings (façades) on a Western movie set – these façades look like buildings to carefully placed cameras but don't function as buildings at all.

*Figure 5.2* illustrates the difference in how a human versus an AI sees and understands something:

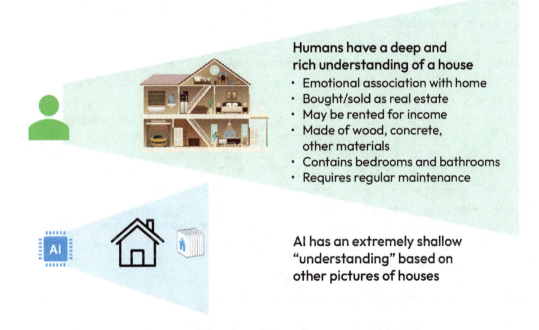

**Figure 5.2 – Artificial intelligence versus human intelligence**

While humans can naturally infer rich meaning and facts from content such as a picture of a house, AI can only recognize and generate new content that's similar to what it was trained on. The contents (documents, pictures, videos, and so on) may appear realistic, but they are just shallow representations of the underlying subject:

- Visual models efficiently analyze and generate visual content, but they don't fully understand the objects in the picture and how they interact with the **three-dimensional (3D)** world around them.

- Language models know how to analyze and generate text, but they don't natively understand the ideas, concepts, or models in the text. They can only predict what words are likely to come next in a particular context (a document, article, poem, movie script, or other format).

During this process, AI models also often make AI-specific errors that humans would never make. For example, the first releases of visual models often get things such as fingers and hands wrong when generating pictures (too many or too few fingers, unnatural proportions, unnatural positions, and more). This is because the visual models don't understand fingers and hands like a human would (hands typically come with four fingers and a thumb, finger length comes in certain proportions, fingers can only move in certain ways, and so on). The visual models only "understand" the visual depiction of patterns in its training data.

Identifying and correcting these errors (or preventing them in the first place) requires a human doing **quality assurance (QA)** or using an automated QA mechanism.

> ### AI capabilities and limitations will change over time
>
> Over time, many of the limitations of AI will evolve as use cases are identified and found to be helpful, profitable, or otherwise beneficial.
>
> Researchers and developers will focus on identifying and resolving AI limitations related to those use cases such as correcting the depiction of fingers and hands, providing technical or medical QA terminology in document generation using existing databases and document repositories, correcting software security issues in code, and more.

**Security implication**: Organizations will need policies and controls to ensure quality, accuracy, security, privacy, ethical use, and other required attributes. The policies and controls should cover the organization's own AI applications as well as the organization's use of external AI applications.

## AI models reflect any biases in their data

Additionally, AI often replicates biases in the data that it processes, including the original training data and other data sources it's connected to, as well as any biases in the chat conversations with the user. This is because AI models are based on mathematical probabilities that don't understand human factors such as moral and cultural values, privacy, security, and more.

For example, the AI model can replicate certain biases in the data, such as having more pink flowers than other colors, more people with a certain color of skin, more cat pictures than people pictures, a high proportion of profanity in the text, and the overuse of certain functions and APIs in source code.

*Any biases in the data used by AI will show up in the AI-generated content* unless quality assurance mechanisms are applied to remove them. Biases can also be introduced (intentionally or unconsciously) in the design or implementation of the AI model itself.

**Security implication**: QA will become an increased priority for content and code generated by AI to ensure outcomes from AI are trustworthy, accurate, ethical, and meet security, privacy, compliance, and other requirements.

QA may take the form of humans or automated QA tools in the process that enforce these qualities. Classic AI typically requires trained professionals to interact with it (data scientists and subject matter experts), which naturally introduces some QA oversight. Generative AI models allow anyone to provide input through ongoing chat conversations, making the explicit inclusion of QA critically important for this technology.

**AI usage often requires an ethical framework**

While ethical frameworks are beyond the scope of this playbook series, it's important to note that AI usage by an organization almost always requires establishing an ethical framework (or updating an existing one). This is because QA processes may identify biases in the use of AI, including those with security, ethical, privacy, or other negative implications.

## How can Zero Trust help manage AI security risk?

A Zero Trust approach is required to effectively manage security risks related to AI. Classic network perimeter-centric approaches are built on more than 20-year-old assumptions of a static technology environment and are not agile enough to keep up with the rapidly evolving security requirements of AI.

The following key elements of Zero Trust security enable you to manage AI risk:

- **Data centricity**: AI has dramatically elevated the importance of data security and AI requires a data-centric approach that can secure data throughout its life cycle in any location.

    Zero Trust provides this data-centric approach and the playbooks in this series guide the roles in your organizations through this implementation.

- **Coordinated management of continuous dynamic risk**: Like modern cybersecurity attacks, AI continuously disrupts core assumptions of business, technical, and security processes. This requires coordinated management of a complex and continuously changing security risk.

  Zero Trust solves this kind of problem using agile security strategies, policies, and architecture to manage the continuous changes to risks, tooling, processes, skills, and more. The playbooks in this series will help you make AI risk mitigation real by providing specific guidance on AI security risks for all impacted roles in the organization.

Let's take a look at which specific elements of Zero Trust are most important to managing AI risk.

## Zero Trust – the top four priorities for managing AI risk

Managing AI risk requires prioritizing a few key areas of Zero Trust to address specific unique aspects of AI. The role of specific guidance in each playbook provides more detail on how each role will incorporate AI considerations into their daily work.

These priorities follow the simple themes of **learn it**, **use it**, **protect against it**, and **work as a team**. This is similar to a rational approach for any major disruptive change to any other type of competition or conflict (a military organization learning about a new weapon, professional sports players learning about a new type of equipment or rule change, and so on).

The top four priorities for managing AI risk are as follows:

1.  **Learn it – educate everyone and set realistic expectations**: The AI capabilities available today are very powerful, affect everyone, and are very different than what people expect them to be. It's critical to *educate every role in the organization*, from board members and CEOs to individual contributors, as they all must understand what AI is, what AI really can and cannot do, as well as the AI usage policy and guidelines. Without this, people's expectations may be wildly inaccurate and lead to highly impactful mistakes that could have easily been avoided.

    Education and expectation management is particularly urgent for AI because of these factors:

    - **Active use in attacks**: Attackers are already using AI to impersonate voices, email writing styles, and more.

    - **Active use in business processes**: AI is freely available for anyone to use. Job seekers are already submitting AI-generated resumes for your jobs that use your posted job descriptions, people are using public AI services to perform job tasks (and potentially disclosing sensitive information), and much more.

    - **Realism**: The results are very realistic and convincing, especially if you don't know how good AI is at creating fake images, videos, and text.

- **Confusion**: Many people don't have a good frame of reference for it because of the way AI has been portrayed in popular culture (which is very different from the current reality of AI).

2. **Use it – integrate AI into security**: Immediately begin evaluating and integrating AI into your security tooling and processes to take advantage of their increased effectiveness and efficiency. This will allow you to quickly take advantage of this powerful technology to better manage security risk. AI will impact nearly every part of security, including the following:

   - Security risk discovery, assessment, and management processes
   - Threat detection and incident response processes
   - Architecture and engineering security defenses
   - Integrating security into the design and operation of systems
   - ...and many more

3. **Protect against it – update the security strategy, policy, and controls**: Organizations must urgently update their strategy, policy, architecture, controls, and processes to account for the use of AI technology (by business units, technology teams, security teams, attackers, and more). This helps enable the organization to take full advantage of AI technology while minimizing security risk.

   The key focus areas should include the following:

   - **Plan for attacker use of AI**: One of the first impacts most organizations will experience is rapid adoption by attackers to trick your people. Attackers are using AI to get an advantage on target organizations like yours, so you must update your security strategy, threat models, architectures, user education, and more to defend against attackers using AI or targeting you for your data. This should change the organization's expectations and assumptions for the following aspects:

     - **Attacker techniques**: Most attackers will experiment with and integrate AI capabilities into their attacks, such as imitating the voices of your colleagues on phone calls, imitating writing styles in phishing emails, creating convincing fake social media pictures and profiles, creating convincing fake company logos and profiles, and more.

     - **Attacker objectives**: Attackers will target your data, AI systems, and other related assets because of their high value (directly to the attacker and/or to sell it to others). Your human-generated data is a prized high-value asset for training and grounding AI models and your innovative use of AI may be potentially valuable intellectual property, and more.

- **Secure the organization's AI usage**: The organization must update its security strategy, plans, architecture, processes, and tooling to do the following:

  - **Secure usage of external AI**: Establish clear policies and supporting processes and technology for using external AI systems safely

  - **Secure the organization's AI and related systems**: Protect the organization's AI and related systems against attackers

In addition to protecting against traditional security attacks, the organization will also need to defend against AI-specific attack techniques that can extract source data, make the model generate unsafe or unintended results, steal the design of the AI model itself, and more. The playbooks include more details for each role to help them manage their part of this risk.

*Take a holistic* **approach**: It's important to secure the full life cycle and dependencies of the AI model, including the model itself, the data sources used by the model, the application that uses the model, the infrastructure it's hosted on, third-party operators such as AI platforms, and other integrated components. This should also take a holistic view of the security life cycle to consider identification, protection, detection, response, recovery, and governance.

- **Update acquisition and approval processes**: This must be done quickly to ensure new AI technology (and other technology) meets the security, privacy, and ethical practices of the organization. This helps avoid extremely damaging avoidable problems such as transferring ownership of the organization's data to vendors and other parties. You don't want other organizations to grow and capture market share from you by using your data. You also want to avoid expensive privacy incidents and security incidents from attackers using your data against you.

  This should include supply chain risk considerations to mitigate both direct suppliers and Nth party risk (components of direct suppliers that have been sourced from other organizations). Finding and fixing problems later in the process is much more difficult and expensive than correcting them before or during acquisition, so it is critical to introduce these risk mitigations early.

4. **Work as a team – establish a coordinated AI approach**: Set up an internal collaboration community or a formal **Center of Excellence (CoE)** team to ensure insights, learning, and best practices are being shared rapidly across teams. AI is a fast-moving space and will drive rapid continuous changes across business, technology, and security teams. You must have mechanisms in place to coordinate and collaborate across these different teams in your organization.

Each playbook describes the specific AI impacts and responsibilities for each affected role.

**AI shared responsibility model**: Most AI technology will be a partnership with AI providers, so managing AI and AI security risk will follow a shared responsibility model between you and your AI providers. Some elements of AI security will be handled by the AI provider and some will be the responsibility of your organization (their customer).

This is very similar to how cloud responsibility is managed today (and many AI providers are also cloud providers). This is also similar to a business that outsources some or all of its manufacturing, logistics, sales (for example, channel sales), or other business functions.

Now, let's take a look at how AI impacts Zero Trust.

## How will AI impact Zero Trust?

AI will accelerate many aspects of Zero Trust because it dramatically improves the security tooling and people's ability to use it. AI promises to reduce the burden and effort for important but tedious security tasks such as the following:

- Helping security analysts quickly query many data sources (without becoming an expert in query languages or tool interfaces)
- Helping writing incident response reports
- Identifying common follow-up actions to prevent repeat incident

Simplifying the interface between people and the complex systems they need to use for security will enable people with a broad range of skills to be more productive. Highly skilled people will be able to do more of what they are best at without repetitive and distracting tasks. People earlier in their careers will be able to quickly become more productive in a role, perform tasks at an expert level more quickly, and help them learn by answering questions and providing explanations.

*AI will NOT replace the need for security experts, nor the need to modernize security.* AI will simplify many security processes and will allow fewer security people to do more, but it won't replace the need for a security mindset or security expertise.

Even with AI technology, people and processes will still be required for the following aspects:

- Ask the right security questions from AI systems
- Interpret the results and evaluate their accuracy
- Take action on the AI results and coordinate across teams

- Perform analysis and tasks that AI systems currently can't cover:

  - Identify, manage, and measure security risk for the organization

  - Build, execute, and monitor a strategy and policy

  - Build and monitor relationships and processes between teams

  - Integrate business, technical, and security capabilities

  - Evaluate compliance requirements and ensure the organization is meeting them in good faith

  - Evaluate the security of business and technical processes

  - Evaluate the security posture and prioritize mitigation investments

  - Evaluate the effectiveness of security processes, tools, and systems

  - Plan and implement security for technical systems

  - Plan and implement security for applications and products

  - Respond to and recover from attacks

In summary, AI will rapidly transform the attacks you face as well as your organization's ability to manage security risk effectively. AI will require a Zero Trust approach and it will also help your teams do their jobs faster and more efficiently.

The guidance in the *Zero Trust Playbook Series* will accelerate your ability to manage AI risk by guiding everyone through their part. It will help you rapidly align security to business risks and priorities and enable the security agility you need to effectively manage the changes from AI.

Some of the questions that naturally come up are where to start and what to do first.

## Summary

In this chapter, we reviewed what AI is, its impact, the limitations of current AI technology, how to manage AI with Zero Trust, and how AI will affect Zero Trust.

In the next chapter – *Chapter 6, How to Scope, Size, and Start Zero Trust* – we'll talk about agile security and answer the most common questions around scoping, sizing, and starting Zero Trust.

# 6

# How to Scope, Size, and Start Zero Trust

*The journey of a thousand miles begins with a single step.*

*– Lao Tzu*

Now that we understand Zero Trust and its role in managing **Artificial Intelligence** (**AI**) security risks, let's address the top questions about planning and getting started with a Zero Trust transformation.

This chapter covers the following topics:

- **Agile security – think big, start small, move fast** – Zero Trust enables agile security that overcomes perfection myths to enable continuous improvement and prioritization.

- **Scoping, sizing, and starting Zero Trust** – common questions on how to plan a Zero Trust transformation and tailor playbooks to your organization.

- **Key terminology changes and clarification** – addresses key wording changes in Zero Trust as well as common points of confusion with terminology that is used differently by different teams in an organization.

Let's start by clearly setting expectations on agile security.

## Agile security – think big, start small, move fast

*Security must be agile!*

As we discussed in *Chapter 3, Zero Trust Is Security for Today's World*, security must continuously adapt to ongoing changes in business conditions, technology platforms, and attackers who are creative, intelligent, and motivated to learn and adapt.

Staying adaptive to these changes requires an agile approach to security that assumes failure (assumes compromise) and *focuses on incremental progress rather than deferred perfection*.

## What is agile security?

Agile security is simply acknowledging that the real world is messy and unpredictable, and adapting to that.

*Zero Trust enables an agile approach to security.* Zero Trust enables security to be agile and keep up with continuously changing requirements (business requirements, technology platforms, security threats, and more).

While this is simple, it isn't easy to adopt this way of thinking if you have been used to classic security for a long time. The playbooks will guide all the roles in your organization through the process of building an agile security approach.

Now let's cover some of the hallmarks of what agility looks like in practice.

## Applying agility in practice

The goal of agility is to get the benefits of a planning process (context, analysis, teamwork, prioritization, focus, motivation, and more) without being constrained by a plan that was made three months or three years ago.

Security agility requires focusing on these two driving principles to get this effect:

- **Focus on progress instead of perfection.**
- **Always ruthlessly prioritize.**

## Focus on progress instead of perfection

*It's more important to get started than it is to choose the perfect place to get started.* The Zero Trust agile security approach embraces the mindset of starting somewhere and rapidly learning and adapting as you go. You won't get everything right all the time, but you can experiment and evaluate in a cycle of learning.

While a guiding North Star is critically important to frame and direct people's thinking and activities over time, *you need to take action to make a change.*

Focus on making progress instead of trying to achieve some perfect state of security to enable you to get started and take the first step.

The playbook series gives you a process and framework to do this in a productive way.

## Always ruthlessly prioritize

Regardless of the size of your Zero Trust efforts, you should always rigorously and intensely prioritize your effort, ensuring you are continually focused on driving quick wins and incremental progress. *Focus on what is important to the organization regardless of the size of the budget and team that are assigned to Zero Trust.* Align Zero Trust efforts to the current pain points and business priorities. We discuss this more in the *What is the best place to start Zero Trust?* section in this chapter.

Now let's look at the other side and get into some of the myths and misconceptions that keep organizations from embracing agile security.

## Myths and misconceptions that block security agility

There are several extremely common myths about security perfection and agility that often get in the way of adopting security agility. We will directly address each of these:

- **Pursuing perfect security is a delusion.**
- **Pursuing perfect solutions is a perfect waste.**
- **Perfect plans are perfectly fragile.**
- **Agility isn't skipping important requirements for speed.**

## Pursuing perfect security is a delusion

The greatest obstacle to security success is assuming and expecting that perfect security is possible (or worthwhile to pursue). Security isn't about creating a perfect ivory tower; it's about reducing risk from actual attacks while enabling the organization we actually work for to grow and thrive.

This shift in mindset is described more in the *Assume Compromise (assume breach)* section of *Chapter 7*, *What Zero Trust Success Looks Like*.

## Pursuing perfect solutions is a perfect waste

There is no such thing as a single "silver bullet" solution that solves everything in security (despite what any security vendors may claim ☺).

Classic security approaches often focus on a perfect end state of compliance, a perfect network configuration, or a "perfect new tool" that fixes everything as their ideal end state. Regulatory standards can't keep up with attackers, network security perimeters aren't enough, and no single tool or technology can stop determined human adversaries.

*Building security resilience is a journey of many steps and learnings, not a single plane flight to a predetermined destination.* While we all wish there was a simple shortcut for security, the businesses and technical estates we defend are complex. No single solution will ever keep business assets safe from every creative attacker and their learnings/evolution.

We need to ask the hard questions that matter (which often don't have clear, simple answers) and focus on the hard work of answering them (which often involves creativity). Wasted effort is often the only thing that results from trying to reshape the questions to match the solutions we already know about.

We already discussed the limitations of network security perimeters in *Chapter 4, Standard Zero Trust Capabilities*, and will discuss how to establish strategic objectives aligned to the business in *Chapter 8, Adoption with the Three-Pillar Model*, and *Chapter 9, The Zero Trust Six-Stage Plan*.

## Perfect plans are perfectly fragile

*No plan survives contact with the enemy.*

*– Attributed to Helmuth von Moltke ("The Elder")*

Building a detailed plan for a big long-term project is a waste of effort in today's world. While planning is a valuable activity, any details you plan today for six months from now will be wrong by the time those six months have passed. The business priorities, technical platforms, and threats will have changed in that time, requiring you to revisit all of those details anyway.

The time and effort wasted on planning future details could be better spent on executing quick wins and incremental progress now or establishing a strategic vision and plan if you don't already have one (as described in the strategic pillar in *Chapter 8, Adoption with the Three-Pillar Model*).

Agile security requires abandoning these ideas of security perfection and focusing on real-world constraints and real risks to assets of value.

### Agility isn't skipping important requirements for speed

Agile approaches aren't about skipping inconvenient requirements to speed up delivery and avoid unpleasant work. While some teams may try to skip important requirements such as security and documentation in the name of agile methodologies, they are missing the point. Agility is about teams working together and understanding each other's requirements so they can continuously learn and adapt to the changing world.

Agile security is about embracing critical thinking and constantly questioning assumptions so you can see the organization and its technical estate and applications, and the way the attackers see them. It's about working closely with other teams, allowing security to change quickly when new requirements are discovered, and blending what you already know with what you have just learned.

Security agility helps build resilience and enables you to be stronger each day and stronger after each failure by learning and adapting (sometimes called antifragility).

The foundational mindsets of an agile security approach are described in more detail in the next chapter, *Chapter 7, What Zero Trust Success Looks Like*.

Now that we understand the agile security approach of Zero Trust, let's answer some of the most common questions about where to start and what to do first.

# Scoping, sizing, and starting Zero Trust

*There is only one way to eat an elephant: a bite at a time.*

*– Desmond Tutu*

You can start Zero Trust in many different ways. In fact, many organizations have already started on parts of Zero Trust without realizing it or without calling it *Zero Trust*. This could include ensuring the integration of security risk into business risk management, adopting modern security operations practices, updating access control and other security approaches for the cloud, and more.

A Zero Trust transformation involves changes across many teams and *connecting teams together to work as a team of teams*. This is a large scope of changes for an organization to understand, plan, and execute. This naturally leads to questions on how best to scope, size, and start the Zero Trust journey.

The top questions that often arise are the following:

- **Will Zero Trust work in my organization?** How will it apply to our size, industry, culture, and processes?

- **Should I plan smaller projects or a big Zero Trust program?** How do I ensure I plan the right Zero Trust size and scope for my organization?

- **How do I ensure Zero Trust stays on track?** How do I ensure Zero Trust continues to deliver value over the long term?

- **What is the best place to start Zero Trust?** How do I get the most value quickly for my organization?

Let's answer those questions.

## Will Zero Trust work in my organization?

Yes! Zero Trust applies to organizations from large, well-established, global organizations using traditional program and project management approaches to smaller, digital-native, "born-in-the-cloud" agile organizations, and everything in between.

The playbooks help you adapt Zero Trust to a wide range of organization types and industries. They include specific guidance to quickly adapt the guidance to your unique organization and Acme examples across different industries to make them realistic.

No two organizations are exactly alike, but most could be classified as larger established organizations, smaller established organizations, or digital-native organizations. These examples illustrate how to use the playbook guidance to adapt Zero Trust to each of these profiles:

- **Larger established organizations** often have complex organizational structures, well-established existing processes, and highly specialized roles. They also often have a large amount of technical debt from legacy applications acquired over decades. Larger organizations often have a history of mergers and acquisitions that may or may not have been fully integrated, which further complicates adoption. Fully executing a major transformation such as Zero Trust requires top-down executive sponsorship and coordination across different teams and roles in the organization.

    The three-pillar model and six-stage plan guide large, established organizations through navigating common obstacles that often stall large transformations such as Zero Trust. The plan guides you through establishing the following:

    - **Strategic integration**: Integrating Zero Trust into the organization's business strategy establishes an organization-wide context required for success and catalyzes the creation of inter-team priorities, goals, and processes.

    - **Executive sponsorship** and **organizational culture**: Senior organizational leaders must establish a clear direction for Zero Trust, signal its importance to all stakeholders, and establish (or reinforce) critical cultural elements. These are required to overcome the natural resistance to changing "the way it's always been done" and natural collaboration gaps between organizational silos common at larger organizations. These top-down signals help overcome resistance to change and increase execution speed and agility by empowering people to challenge assumptions and change existing processes and priorities.

        *Chapter 7, What Zero Trust Success Looks Like*, describes the key success factors in detail.

        *Chapter 9, The Zero Trust Six-Stage Plan*, summarizes how each role establishes, propagates, and monitors these changes, and each playbook for those roles provides detailed guidance.

- **Smaller established organizations** share some challenges with larger organizations but also differ in several significant ways. Strategic integration, executive sponsorship, and cultural change are still required in smaller organizations, but execution often happens much faster because there is less organizational complexity and size to accommodate.

Smaller organizations also have limited budgets and smaller teams for technology and security (and some don't have any dedicated security roles). Technical and security roles are more generalized in a smaller organization where people have a broad range of skills (sometimes called being a "jack of all trades"). These roles often collaborate more closely with each other and with business teams compared to larger organizations. Additionally, many smaller organizations engage in outsourcing services for technology and security functions.

*Ruthless prioritization* is a critical skill for technology and security teams in a smaller organization because they have limited resources (though ruthless prioritization is also a best practice for any size organization). Smaller organizations should focus Zero Trust prioritization on two key areas:

- **Prioritizing projects and outcomes**: Smaller organizations must ruthlessly prioritize what gets done (and what doesn't!) because a smaller staff doesn't have time to learn and execute everything at the same time. These organizations often prioritize projects based on cost-effectiveness and **Return on Investment** (**ROI**).

    Smaller organizations still need to understand the full set of choices to choose what to do first, just as in larger organizations. Think of this like a smaller group of 4-6 people visiting a restaurant. They may order fewer appetizers than a group of 20-25 people, but they still need to see the whole menu.

    The playbook's three-pillar model and six-stage plan guide these smaller established organizations (and all others) through building a tailored and agile roadmap based on their needs and available resources. *Chapter 8, Adoption with the Three-Pillar Model*, describes these pillars in detail (including an example of applying it to Acme Bank), and *Chapter 9, The Zero Trust Six-Stage Plan*, provides the step-by-step plan to execute that model. Many other Acme examples are provided throughout the playbooks to show how to apply these to organizations of various industries and organization sizes.

- **Prioritizing role skills and specialization**: Smaller organizations must carefully plan investments in role specializations and skills because generalists have limited time to learn and perform deeply specialized tasks.

    The *Role Mission and Purpose* and *Role Creation and Evolution* guidance help smaller organizations identify where to invest people's time. These organizations can evaluate the relative value of each role specialization and what typically triggers organizations to invest in these specializations as they grow. They can then choose whether to invest in the specialization, defer investment to a future point, or engage with an outsourced provider to provide the specialization. See *Chapter 10, Zero Trust Playbook Roles*, for morvve on this role-specific guidance.

- **Digitalvv-native** organizations are sometimes referred to as "born in the cloud" and have used agile approaches and cloud technology since their inception. Digital-native organizations need Zero Trust to protect against the threats of today, but their journey has a different starting point and focuses on different priorities. This is comparable to how mobile phone technologies were often adopted faster by countries that didn't already have a copper phone line infrastructure.

  These organizations often operate using agile practices such as the **Scaled Agile Framework (SAFe)**, DevOps, and **Continuous Integration/Continuous Delivery (CI/CD)** models. The technical estate of digital-native organizations is often based more on cloud services and custom applications versus the on-premises data centers and installed software of an established organization.

  These are common priorities for digital native organizations adopting Zero Trust:

  - **Adding rigor to agility**: Digital-native organizations often need to focus on introducing or amplifying security rigor in culture and processes for Zero Trust because they already often have the required agile cultural elements.

    This helps them achieve the required balance between agility and rigor that all organizations need for Zero Trust. They just approach this balance from a different direction than established organizations. Rigor is required to ensure security practices are consistently applied as adversaries are effective at finding and exploiting gaps in security hygiene. Agility is required to adapt to changes in the threat landscape, technology, and business priorities.

    *Stage 2 – Set up an Operating Model* of the six-stage plan enables digital-native (and all other) organizations to embed security into the organization's culture, processes and practices, and technical and development team skillsets. The playbooks describe how to apply the technical elements in daily processes and CI/CD tooling and automation.

  - **Different platforms and different technical debt**: Digital-native organizations often rely heavily on cloud services that are maintained and secured by cloud vendors and custom applications and systems:

    - **Cloud services** help limit operational overhead versus on-premises data centers because the cloud vendor performs most security and operations work (though not all of it). This avoids limits on how much technical debt is accrued from keeping aging infrastructure up to date (which is required for on-premises data centers).

    - **Custom applications and open source components** require managing the life cycle of open source and custom application components (where most established organizations focus more on managing the life cycle of installed applications). This causes digital-native organizations to prioritize application and product aspects of Zero Trust early, including managing the security of *software supply chain components*.

These differences in platform composition cause digital-native organizations to shift the priority and order of initiatives, but they are still on the same Zero Trust journey.

The playbooks guide digital-native organizations through building an agile strategic roadmap with short-, medium-, and long-term elements tailored to their unique needs. This process is described in more detail in the *The strategic pillar* section in *Chapter 8, Adoption with the Three-Pillar Model*.

As you can see, organizations of all sizes and types can use this playbook series to adopt Zero Trust, from well-established global organizations to brand-new start-ups that are born in this digital world.

A common question is whether you need to do a big Zero Trust program or whether you can start small.

## Is it better to go big or plan smaller projects?

People often ask whether a large project is required to get value from Zero Trust or whether smaller project(s) are effective.

From a sponsorship and strategic planning perspective, *you should go as big as you can*. What does this mean? Make it strategic, align it with the company's technology, business and operating models, and roadmaps, and ideally get executive sponsorship. Strategic Zero Trust initiatives sponsored by organizational leadership and aligned with business goals and risks are much more effective at delivering value than small, disconnected technical projects.

Smaller Zero Trust initiatives can deliver meaningful value quickly, but smaller projects are limited in how much value they can deliver compared to a full transformation across teams. To get the full value and benefits of a Zero Trust transformation, you will need a full transformation program with executive sponsorship from organizational leadership.

It's important to keep in mind that *large transformations are a coordinated and intentional series of smaller changes* (often guided by a roadmap, as in the case of Zero Trust). Like every large transformation, Zero Trust is ultimately a series of bite-sized decisions and actions aligned to a larger strategic goal. The playbooks break this transformation down into actionable elements that can be executed by each role, often independently of others.

Regardless of the size of the Zero Trust program or initiative, you should *focus on planning and executing it in small increments and adjusting as you* go so you can stay agile to changing requirements.

Key considerations for planning the size and scope of a Zero Trust initiative(s) are the following:

- **Large Zero Trust transformations are the most effective** and require executive sponsorship.
- **Good communication can catalyze the executive sponsorship** that is required for a large transformation.
- **Starting small is sometimes required**, but is slower and delivers smaller value.

Let's take a look at each in more depth.

## Large Zero Trust transformations are the most effective

The most effective approach to Zero Trust is a commitment to larger transformation sponsored by the organization's CEO (or equivalent) and guided by an agile strategic roadmap like the one embedded into the *Zero Trust Playbook Series*. This full transformation with executive sponsorship and business integration enables Zero Trust to fully deliver on all promised benefits.

A full Zero transformation requires coordination across the organization, an intentional plan, and supporting cultural elements. Smaller initiatives operated within technical and security teams will have limited impact compared to a full transformation. The playbook series is designed to take you through this full process.

*Chapter 9, The Zero Trust Six-Stage Plan*, provides a description of the six-stage plan that incorporates all of these elements.

## Good communication can catalyze executive sponsorship

A lack of executive sponsorship for Zero Trust (or for security in general) is often driven by gaps in awareness, understanding, and communication, *not a lack of interest by organizational leaders*.

The communication gaps are often driven by a lack of awareness and understanding:

- **Business leaders**: Most organizational leaders are concerned about risks to business operations and intellectual property but aren't clear on how to evaluate, judge, and manage security risks. Some even mistakenly believe that security is simply a "technical problem" that technical teams should be able to handle without business leadership involvement (versus a dynamic risk driven by intelligent human criminals and other actors).

  These gaps in understanding arise simply because most business leaders don't have direct experience with security and haven't had formal training on how to manage security risk effectively in their role.

- **Security leaders**: Many security leaders may be unfamiliar with business terminology and processes, leading them to communicate security risks using the technical terminology and framing they know. This approach is unfamiliar to business leaders and confuses them, often reinforcing the incorrect belief that security is simply a technical problem.

This dynamic makes it difficult for business leaders to accurately judge security risks and participate in productive security risk discussions with security leaders, leading to a lack of sponsorship for Zero Trust or security at large.

The playbooks help overcome these gaps by providing clear guidance for each stakeholder's role and perspective. This establishes a foundational understanding that helps catalyze productive conversations and collaboration on security risk. There is always more learning to be done in today's continuously changing world, but the playbooks will help get the positive cycle started.

## Starting small is sometimes required

Smaller Zero Trust initiatives have limits in terms of value, but sometimes you have no choice but to start small to prove Zero Trust before getting executive sponsorship. In this situation, you will have to build credibility and momentum for Zero Trust by starting with smaller targeted projects within teams that understand the value of Zero Trust. This organic "bottom-up" approach is slower but is still more valuable than not adopting Zero Trust at all.

This approach requires increased focus on communicating the value of Zero Trust as you execute it. Teams driving a Zero Trust project(s) must regularly communicate to organizational leadership how Zero Trust enables business goals and delivers value. This helps build the case for additional investment, business integration, and sponsorship for a full Zero Trust program.

In these situations, the teams championing Zero Trust must focus on driving quick wins that immediately deliver and show tangible value compared to traditional security approaches (increased ease of use, reduced organizational risk, and so on). The teams often must build a sense of momentum by continuing to build on these quick wins with incremental progress.

You will need to establish enough of a Zero Trust vision to guide the teams as they get moving for the first few agile projects. This vision should be informed by the organization's strategy and direction as best as it can be known.

## How do I ensure Zero Trust stays on track and continuously delivers value?

Organizations on a long-term Zero Trust journey need to guide and monitor it to ensure value is delivered quickly upfront and the program continues to sustain and grow its value over time.

Keeping a large program such as Zero Trust on track requires a **clear vision** of where it's going, translating that vision into **actionable guidance** for all the affected roles, **continuous visibility**, **governance** to monitor progress and mitigate any components that are going off-track, and **agility** to adapt all components to the continuous changes of the world.

The three-pillar model and six-stage execution plan in this playbook include those elements and the *Zero Trust Governance* capability sustains these over time. This updated version of a security governance capability is adapted to the modern digital world based on Zero Trust core principles such as assuming compromise, reducing the threat space, and asset and data centricity.

This is a quick summary of key elements in the six-stage plan (described more in *Chapter 9, The Zero Trust Six-Stage Plan*) that will keep your Zero Trust transformation on track:

- **Establish a clear vision**: This clearly articulates the ideal end state everyone is working toward, which helps guide countless daily decisions by people across the organization to ensure they align in the same direction.

  This vision is established in *Stage 1 – Set vision and capabilities*, which builds this vision, aligns it with the organization's business capabilities, identifies the prioritized Zero Trust capabilities, and creates a strategic plan to get there – the **Zero Trust roadmap**. This creates a unique tailored vision and plan for your organization that addresses your most important security, business, technology, and compliance drivers. Another critical step is in *Stage 2 – Set up an operating model*, which ensures this vision is aligned with the organization's operating model and processes.

- **Actionable guidance** makes the vision and capabilities real for each role so they know *what* their part is, *why* it's important to their role, and *how* to execute it.

  Actionable guidance is established in *Stage 3 – Create architecture and model* to guide the technical and business teams. This includes the development of the solution **architecture** that describes the details of the end state vision and components, the **policies and procedures** that establish the rules of the road, and the plan for establishing Zero Trust operations that will bring it to life and keep it running day to day.

  This is further tailored to the organization as it's implemented in *Stage 4 – Tailor to business*, which aligns Zero Trust and the roadmap to the operating model, product model, daily processes of the organization, and other business constraints.

- **Continuous visibility and governance** ensure that Zero Trust stays on track by monitoring for and addressing issues in project progress, operational effectiveness, and other aspects of the initiative. The playbook series leverages standards such as those from The Open Group's *Zero Trust Reference Model* to provide a robust foundation for governance and monitoring.

  *Stage 2 – Set up an operating model* establishes key governance and visibility elements including decision rights and accountabilities, guardrails and monitoring, as well as training and cultural change. This is implemented as Zero Trust capabilities are implemented in *Stage 5 – Implement and improve* and are continuously operated and refined in *Stage 6 – Continuously Monitor and Evolve*. The *posture management* capability plays a key role in monitoring and reporting information from across the technical estate.

- **Agility** ensures that the organization's plan (formed in the past) doesn't prevent it from meeting the continuously changing security demands of today and tomorrow.

  The design of the playbook is focused on providing agility without sacrificing consistency of execution. This is accomplished by adopting the three-pillar model that is executed through all six playbook stages.

The *Agile Strategic Roadmap* is the central element to guide actions across teams, stages, and pillars that maintains consistency (this is the plan) while maintaining agility (the plan can change). The agile roadmap approach prioritizes tasks into short-, medium-, and long-term priorities that each change at a different rate, enabling you to drive ongoing transformation while continuously adjusting to changes in the world as needed.

The roadmap and related activities are informed by the initial plan as well as other information sources, such as security intelligence, which fuse business intelligence and threat intelligence into actionable insights in the most effective ways to reduce risk. The roadmap is described more in *Chapter 8, Adoption with the Three-Pillar Model*.

This combination of **clear vision**, **actionable guidance**, **continuous visibility**, and **flexibility** will enable you to rapidly get the benefits of Zero Trust while keeping you on the right long-term path for transformation. This combined approach is necessary to be able to sustain long-term, consistent focus while staying agile to adapt to the rapidly changing requirements of today's business, technology, and threat environments.

### The natural tension between governance and agility is healthy

Security is a complex space, so some decisions will require balancing various conflicting requirements and making judgment calls. *The speed of change in the threat environment often outpaces the ability of standards to keep up.*

There is and always will be a natural tension between compliance-focused governance functions and the real-time attacker evolution that changes which risks are most important (and sometimes introduces new risks).

This tension between staying consistent to meet (mostly static) regulatory standards while staying agile to keep up with attacker evolution must be constantly managed. These situations require you to consider multiple perspectives and make the best prioritization decision you can (and expect that you may have to change that later as well).

> **Note**
> In many ways, this tension mirrors the classic tension between "by the book" characters and "follow their gut" characters in many TV shows and movies.

*Both compliance and security are necessary and the tension between them is valuable to drive informed and intelligent decisions.*

Both the compliance and real-time attacker risk perspectives are valid and valuable, but neither has a monopoly on the truth. Either one taken to an extreme can increase risk for the organization if not balanced by the other.

Here are some examples to illustrate why both priorities have to be addressed in your roadmap:

- **What's old is new again**: Sometimes attackers find ways to exploit older techniques to get access to an organization's resources. Mitigating these requires applying well-known recommendations covered by compliance regulations such as installing security updates (sometimes called security patches) or applying well-known security configuration recommendations.

  One example of this is the highly damaging WannaCry/WannaCrypt worm in 2017, which exploited organizations that didn't apply an update to fix a software vulnerability released by the vendor two months prior (and was advertised as urgent by many organizations and the press). Organizations that invested in this basic hygiene maintenance task would have mitigated a significant amount of this damage.

  Zero Trust's asset-centric approach addresses this naturally by focusing on assets throughout their life cycle. These basic hygiene maintenance tasks are addressed as part of the **Asset Centricity** capability described in *Chapter 4, Standard Zero Trust Capabilities*.

- **Compliance can't keep up**: On the other side of the equation, we find that compliance standards often can't keep up with today's threats. Additionally, obsolete compliance standards can be harmful for a long period before they are updated.

  For example, *password complexity* requirements were once thought to be the strongest account protection, and this requirement was included in many compliance standards.

  Unfortunately, we have learned in today's world that *password complexity requirements actually weaken security* because they cause people to create repetitive, guessable passwords and do very little to protect against the most prevalent password attacks. Because of this, the industry has moved on to focus on other newer solutions such as solutions such as **Multifactor Authentication** (**MFA**), behavior analysis, and passwordless (which is actually easier to use as well). *Many regulations today still have explicit requirements for password complexity that waste resources, create user frustration, and increase risk.*

While compliance and security will be aligned most of the time, it's critical to recognize there are times when they aren't. You should expect these situations and make the best judgment call you can with the best information you have (including *security intelligence* that fuses business intelligence and threat intelligence insights).

In summary, the *Zero Trust playbook series* provides you with the guidance and mechanisms you need to successfully keep your Zero Trust initiative on track and aligned with the realities of business risk and security threats.

Now let's get to a common question people often ask after seeing the full scope of Zero Trust and the value it can offer.

## What is the best place to start Zero Trust?

Organizations may not be able to fully commit to all Zero Trust initiatives at once, so it's important to ask what to prioritize first.

Organizations should always focus on quick wins that can show progress in a short amount of time and prioritize areas with the highest impact on the organization's business initiatives and security risk.

What is most important will vary for each organization, but many organizations often start by prioritizing these Zero Trust capabilities:

- **Adaptive access**: Establishing strong modern access control that enforces MFA and Conditional Access to resources is often a top priority. This is critical because traditional network security perimeters can no longer provide this basic protection against current threats and for current assets.

- **Asset-centric security operations**: Establishing strong detection, response, and recovery capabilities for common modern attacks is often another top priority. This is critical because traditional approaches based on static query **Intrusion Detection Systems/ Intrusion Protection Systems (IDSs/IPSs)** and firewall logs are not effective against modern attack techniques on identity, endpoint, cloud, and other assets.

- **Asset-centric protection for cloud assets**: Organizations that have migrated or established new business-critical assets in the cloud must adopt modern data-centric and system asset-centric approaches to protect business-critical data and systems. Organizations often find that legacy network security perimeter approaches block core cloud functionality, which restricts business agility. Zero Trust enables organizations to protect cloud data and systems such as business websites and **Application Programming Interfaces (APIs)** without losing agility or security assurances.

> **There is no wrong place to start!**
> Don't let perfection get in the way of making progress. The playbook series provides a complete set of guidance to plan a full-scale transformation, but *it enables anyone to start anywhere on any scale*, including a manager or an individual employee.

Now let's take a moment to provide clarity on some words that often cause confusion because they mean different things to different people.

## Key terminology changes and clarification

One of the side effects of connecting business, technology, and security teams together is terminology confusion. As these teams start working more closely together, they often face points of confusion around language, terminology, and its meaning.

Some terminology and concepts are new to teams that haven't worked together before, some of the same (or similar) terminology has different meanings to different teams, some terminology is new to everyone, and some common terminology is just outdated and misleading.

The most common points of confusion typically center around the use of the words *assets* (and related words), *operations* (and related words), and *the network* (or *the enterprise*).

## Newer terminology – technical estate

The series uses "technical estate" or "technology estate" to refer to all technology used by an organization to get work done, including all data and all **IT**, **Operational Technology (OT)**, and **Internet of Things (IoT)** systems.

This newer term replaces the use of outdated and misleading terms including *the network* or *the enterprise* to refer to all organizational technical resources.

The books avoid using *the network* because this term is both of the following:

- **Wrong**: The organization's assets are no longer hosted exclusively on their private network(s).
- **Distracting**: Protecting a network takes focus away from the assets of different values that may (or may not) be on it.

The book series also avoids using *the enterprise* because it implies that Zero Trust only applies to larger "enterprise" organizations when Zero Trust is equally important to smaller organizations.

These older terms also imply that all work is done on the organization's own equipment and networks, which is no longer true. The technology estate that can impact business risk now includes data and systems owned and operated by the organization, partners, cloud providers, software suppliers, government regulators, employees and contractors (personal devices), and others.

## Disambiguation – operations, operational, operating model, and so on

This model and the playbook series contain multiple variations of the word operations. These words are used extensively throughout business, financial, technology, and security teams. These variations all share a common theme to reference something about the operational phase of business, technology, or security, but each has evolved to a specific meaning or aspect of operations.

This is a quick summary of the main variations seen in practice and in the playbooks:

- **Operational**: This business term refers to the daily business operations and activity of the entire organization producing products and services. This is also the name of one pillar in the three-pillar model used in the playbooks, which is described more in *Chapter 8, Adoption with the Three-Pillar Model*.

- **Operating model**: This business term refers to *the way that the organization operates*, the abstract model under which all operations and processes are organized. This big-picture view enables you to see the organization as a whole and provide good oversight and governance over all of it. This is also the name of a pillar in the three-pillar model, which is described more in *Chapter 8, Adoption with the Three-Pillar Model*.

- **Operating Expenses (OpEx)** (and **Capital Expenditures (CapEx)**): OpEx is a financial term referring to day-to-day expenses that occur as the business operates. This contrasts with CapEx, which refers to major purchases that often involve extensive planning ahead of time. Many IT and security costs are shifting to an OpEx mode from a CapEx mode because cloud services have a "pay for what you use" dynamic instead of larger one-time purchases of hardware and software licenses for on-premises technology. Additionally, this fundamentally changes the nature of how technology is financed and reported because OpEx is accounted for as a short-term budget expense while CapEx results in financial "assets" that must be amortized or depreciated over time. Because of how fast things change in the digital era, an OpEx model is often preferable because it is more flexible and because it avoids financial reporting issues where large capital investments (CapEx) become obsolete before their planned amortization and depreciation dates.

- **IT operations**: This primarily refers to the organizational function (and team) that implements, operates, and maintains IT. Sometimes this may refer to all operational functions of IT, and sometimes to a specific part such as service desk and user support functions (separate from an infrastructure operations team) or traditional on-premises teams (separate from the cloud service operations team).

- **OT**: This is a category of computing technology at the level of **IT** and **IoT** classifications. OT refers to computer systems that control or monitor physical processes, such as computer control of manufacturing, windmills, fluid valves, power generation and distribution, and others. This is sometimes also referred to as **Industrial Control Systems (ICSs)** or **Supervisory Control and Data Acquisition (SCADA)**.

- **Security Operations (SecOps)**: This is sometimes referred to as a SOC (short for security operations center). This security term refers to how your organization manages attacks by detecting, responding to, and recovering from incidents (caused by attackers). This refers to both the name of the security discipline (and associated processes) and is often also the name of the team performing that function.

> **Note**
>
> SecOps is not the only operational security function; security posture management is a complementary function that focuses on preventing attacks. These two functions are described more in *Chapter 8, Adoption with the Three-Pillar Model*.

## Summary

In this chapter, we answered some common questions around scoping, sizing, and starting Zero Trust, which helped us think about structuring the approach to meet the unique needs of an organization. We saw how these playbooks are compatible with any size organization and any style, from well-established organizations to digital-native organizations.

Next up, in *Chapter 7, What Zero Trust Success Looks Like*, we will take a look at common causes of technology project failures and how to avoid them on this Zero Trust journey.

# 7
# What Zero Trust Success Looks Like

*"Begin with the end in mind."*

> – Stephen Covey

Now that we understand why Zero Trust is so important and what it involves, let's take a look at what success looks like for this (continuous) journey.

To be blunt, the world is littered with failed technology-related projects. You can confirm this with a quick internet search for *"IT project failure rate"* or ask any experienced colleague in your organization for a story about a failed technology project. *Zero Trust is simply too important to get wrong.* We can't risk failing because of something we could have easily avoided.

This playbook series is designed to help you avoid failure in implementing Zero Trust by using proven models and applying best practices from real-world deployments of Zero Trust and other technology projects. This helps you avoid common causes of project failure, which are sometimes called *antipatterns*.

This chapter discusses three **Zero Trust success factors** that separate successful projects from failed ones, as follows:

- **Clear strategy and plan**
- **Security mindset and culture shifts**
- **Human empathy**

Focusing on these success factors as you move forward with Zero Trust will help you avoid the most common sources of project failures and slowdowns.

> **On antipatterns**
>
> An antipattern is a common response to a recurring problem that is usually ineffective and risks being highly counterproductive. For example, many organizations deprioritize security in favor of cost or scheduled priorities, which incrementally increases organizational risk over time and frequently results in major breaches later.
>
> The best practices described in *factor 2* will displace one or more common antipatterns that frequently increase organizational risk for Zero Trust progress.

## Zero Trust success factors

*"Good judgment comes from experience, and experience comes from bad judgment."*

*– Fred Brooks*

Let's dive into how to avoid common pitfalls on the Zero Trust journey. These three success factors are based on direct Zero Trust experience and other large technology initiatives we have observed over the years. These three factors represent the hallmarks of successful initiatives and programs, factors that are typically weak or missing on failed projects.

These success factors are embedded into the fabric of the Zero Trust playbooks to make it easier for you to avoid common sources of friction and failure. We will directly or indirectly refer to many of these success factors and how they apply to business leaders, technical leaders, technical managers, architects, and technology practitioners.

> **The job is never done**
>
> It's important to recognize that Zero Trust is a transformation to a dynamic state of continuous improvement, rather than a simple static end state where you cross a finish line and are done.

Three key success factors for Zero Trust transformation include the following:

- **Clear strategy and plan**: The organization needs a clear vision and playbook to guide different roles through this journey so that each set of stakeholders knows their part to play.

- **Security mindset and culture shifts**: You must introduce or reinforce specific mindsets, expectations, and cultural elements for teams to successfully navigate fundamental shifts in assumptions with the transformation to a digital business, cloud technology, and Zero Trust security.

- **Human empathy**: It's critical to recognize that these transformations affect the lives and careers of many people across organizations. You must deliberately address these and actively manage the human aspects of change (expectations, emotions, relationships, and more)—for yourself individually and for your teams.

Now, let's look at these factors in more detail.

# Factor one – clear strategy and plan

To ensure everyone is on the same page and moving in the same direction, it's critical to have a clear strategy and plan to coordinate these efforts. This must be agile, must account for any unique aspects of your organization, and must be integrated into the organization's operating model to sustain it and keep it on track.

*Good news!* You found this book series, which is designed to help you with building a clear strategy and plan!

This book series is structured into reference playbooks designed to guide each role on their part to play in Zero Trust. It includes the reference models, architectures, models, and strategies you need to pull this off. The playbooks include examples of how to integrate Zero Trust into different industries and organizational operating models and how to structure your Zero Trust operating model.

*Tailoring the playbook to your organization and defining clear progress metrics will create clarity and actionability for your organization.*

Now, let's discuss the next success factor.

# Factor two – security mindset and culture shifts

It's critical to establish or reinforce key mindsets and cultural elements to shift security expectations and habits for stakeholders and roles across the organization. These go beyond the literal plan and create an invisible human fabric that helps everyone make similar decisions. This also helps people feel like they are on a common mission and work better together as they figure out this new world.

You can make partial progress on Zero Trust without the organization completely adopting these mindsets, but you will face greater organizational friction each step of the way. The effort will be slower, costlier, and less effective.

This section defines patterns of repeatable behaviors that lead to Zero Trust success and security agility. These patterns help guide organizations through cultural change and adapting to a Zero Trust culture by driving the right mindsets and cultural elements. Each of the following patterns listed is included directly or indirectly in the structure and/or content of the playbooks.

The following patterns map directly or indirectly to defined principles found across industry guidance on Zero Trust, including the *Zero Trust Commandments*. We chose not to define these patterns and elements as another "list of principles" to be mapped to others but as a summary of the collective wisdom from across them.

These are the key security mindset and culture shifts that will help you drive an effective security approach:

- **Security risk is business risk**: Security risk must be understood in the context of (and aligned with) the organization's mission, goals, and risk management framework. Any security issue on any system can lead to business disruption of the entire organization because the technical systems are interconnected with each other.

- **Security is a business enabler**: Overcome the myth that security is only a risk, and treat security as both an enabler of the business and mission and a risk management function.

- **Security is everyone's responsibility**: Security risk is an organization-wide responsibility that nearly any role in the organization can impact, much as with financial responsibility, legal liability, or physical safety. Ensure that everyone considers security risk part of their job and has a basic security literacy and clarity in their role in it.

- **Security risk accountability starts at the top**: The organizational leader (CEO or equivalent) is ultimately accountable for all aspects of an organization's management and operation, including risk from security incidents. As with most disciplines, the day-to-day management of this risk is often delegated within the organization. Anyone who accepts the risk of exceptions must be in an *organizational leadership* role with the following responsibilities:

  - **Accountable for organizational-wide business impact**, not just a local system or a temporary project team (security risk is not just project risk). *If you are not empowered to make organization-wide business decisions, you shouldn't be accepting security risks.*

  - **Keeping fully informed** of all potential business impacts of the decisions, including organization-wide security impact(s) and direct business impacts of exceptions. *If you aren't clear on all the potential impacts, you should learn about them from business, security, and other experts.*

- **Assume compromise (assume breach)** so that all stakeholders and teams have a practical view of security, rather than clinging to a false sense of perfect safety and security. Accepting this assumption leads to more thoughtful and effective risk planning and mitigations.

- **Explicit validation of trust**: In a world where attackers are constantly trying to find ways to trick anyone in the organization, everyone must have a healthy sense of caution. You can't operate a system without any trust (imagine if someone paid you money and you weren't sure you could use that money to buy something else), so you must build reliable and scalable assurances into your systems. We may start from "Zero" Trust, but we must then build trust back up explicitly (rather than assuming it) so that we can work effectively.

- **Asset-centric and data-centric security**: Everyone must frame their security thinking in terms of assets that have value to the organization (data and systems), rather than on networks and network locations. In fact, the **National Institute of Standards and Technology** (**NIST**) and *The Open Group* built that into the definition of Zero Trust itself!

Now, let's take a look at these key mindsets and culture shifts in more detail.

## Security risk is business risk

This risk must be managed by business leaders, as with any other organizational risk (natural disasters, economic and monetary risks, geopolitical risks, and so on). Security is often one of the top five risks every organization faces, requiring the awareness and attention of the CEO and the **board of directors** (**BoDs**) or equivalents.

Security must be understood in the context of (and aligned with) the organization's mission, goals, and risk management framework. This first fundamental shift in mindset ensures that Zero Trust *just makes sense* to all roles and serves as a foundational understanding for many roles across the organization.

A common antipattern we see across organizations is that security problems and challenges are framed only within the scope of a technical lens. This logically leads to the unhealthy assumption that security is a technical problem to be solved (by technical people with a technical solution), *which it is not*. This unhealthy mindset blocks the critically important collaboration that occurs between technology and business teams. (Why bother spending time on security? It's the security team's problem.) We discuss how this "powerless scapegoat" dynamic leads to a no-win situation for the organization in the *Avoiding a dangerous misperception* section a little later in this chapter.

It's critical for everyone to understand the following:

- **Security risk is driven by human attackers** with financial incentives to succeed (or other powerful motivations). These intelligent and creative humans continuously adapt—*so, we need to continuously adapt too!*

- **Security risk affects the whole organization**: Everyone must understand that any security incident can lead to business disruption of the entire organization, similar to how a fire anywhere in a building can quickly spread to burn the whole building down.

  This happens because attackers often abuse the legitimate mechanisms provided to employees, vendors, customers, and suppliers to access your organization's assets. This is similar to criminals using the same phone systems and roadways as citizens to communicate and travel. This also means that a security issue at a supplier or partner organization can cause a security incident at your organization through accounts, devices, systems, or other mechanisms that enable the integration of daily operations.

Now, let's look at how the business risk from security has changed in the last decade or so.

## Security risk has evolved rapidly

The risk organizations face from cyberattacks has changed significantly over the past decade or so, further complicating the management of this risk. These are recent notable major shifts in this risk:

- **Digital business models and cloud computing**: The advent of digital business models empowers business departments and users to select (and sometimes design) the best technology for their needs. This often takes the form of adopting cloud-based applications and platforms, **Internet of Things (IoT)** devices, **artificial intelligence (AI)**, and more.

  These technology changes typically disrupt how organizations manage the risk of security, requiring organizations to *revisit all their security risk assumptions, controls, responsible parties, and user education*. This is because most organizations have based all prior assumptions on a security perimeter model (sometimes called the "castle model") and never considered shared responsibility for security or protecting assets outside this perimeter.

- **Ransomware/extortion**: The introduction of extortion to criminal business models (such as ransomware and threatening to release sensitive data) has significantly increased cybersecurity risk in the past decade. This has increased both the impact and likelihood of damage during a cybersecurity attack, as outlined here:

  - **Increased business impact** of attacks as attackers now *disrupt most or all business operations* of an organization in exchange for an extortion payment.

  - **Increased likelihood** of an attack as these high-profit extortion models are attracting more and more criminal actors, who conduct more attacks and make it *more likely your organization will be targeted.*

- **Criminal business models (affiliate models)**: Additionally, the sophistication of criminal business models has increased over the past decade, enabling more attackers with lower skills to conduct advanced attacks using affiliate models. Many criminals now specialize in offering sophisticated attack toolkits as a service to other (lower-skilled) attackers, often in exchange for a percentage of the criminal profits. This greatly increases the volume of nation-states, hacktivists, and criminals who can use sophisticated attack tools, *increasing the likelihood that your organization will be targeted by these attacks.*

- **Increasing nation-state activity**: Governments are increasingly targeting many types of organizations around the world with cyberattacks to advance their goals. They don't just target other governments, but may also target private sector support and suppliers, academic research programs, and any other for-profit and non-profit organization that can advance their goals. Nation-state objectives may include stealing military and government secrets, stealing **intellectual property (IP)** to accelerate the development of local industry, disrupting competing industries, disrupting infrastructure, supporting active military invasions, preparing for potential future wars, establishing military deterrence, testing new attack techniques on smaller targets, and more.

Nearly every organization faces potential IP theft from nation-states seeking to accelerate their local industry (your competitors) or for national espionage. Some organizations will also be targeted by nation-states with geopolitical disruption goals.

- **Increases in supply chain risk**: Recent years have also seen an increase in the volume and sophistication of supply chain attacks where adversaries compromise **open source software** (**OSS**), business partners, suppliers, customers, and others to get access to a target organization. This supply chain risk requires organizations to change risk assessment scope and assumptions, as well as to develop a program component to manage these external risk sources.

  You must identify which suppliers your organization depends on for security and which customers and partners rely on your security practices. This often requires changes to vendor and partner management processes, purchasing processes, security controls and architectures, and more.

As you can see, security risk has undergone several major changes in recent years that increase its likelihood, impact, and complexity.

Elevating this risk to a business level often requires a shift in mindset. These are some examples that help illustrate this change:

- As **business leaders** hear about security news, they should always ask what the business implications are. It's critical to develop a deeper understanding of security implications beyond just the "Are we protected from it?" question. Business leaders should consider which revenue streams would be impacted, how fast we could recover, how can we make business processes more resilient, and so on.

- **Technical leaders** should always prioritize security projects and work based on their impact on the business. These roles should always translate technical security risks and events into business risks for their business colleagues and translate business risks into technical language for their teams.

- **Security practitioners** should always consider the business and mission implications as they do their specialized work. For example, an analyst in security operations should consider which alerts and incidents are more likely to have a large business impact and prioritize work on those. Also, technical architects and engineers should always prioritize the technical controls that are most likely to mitigate high business impact events (such as ransomware).

Now, let's take a look at security's other key role as a business enabler, an often-overlooked security benefit.

## Security is a business enabler

As people start becoming more familiar with security risks, you may see a hidden myth emerge that *"security is only a risk."* We all know that security is one source (*among many*) of risk, but we often miss that it becomes a business enabler when you use a Zero Trust approach.

As security shifts to an advisory role and learns about business goals and risks, technical expertise and unique perspectives can help to innovate and solve business problems.

> **We're not kidding – security can enable business opportunities**
>
> This may seem unimaginable or impossible if you are still in the "department of no" stage in your organization, but this does happen!
>
> One real-world example is from an organization that was struggling to figure out how to provide new services to consumers without violating customer privacy assurances demanded by the European market. As the security team learned about this, it offered the suggestion of decentralized identity technology, which created a business breakthrough for the business to create a new market and revenue stream.

### *How can security be a business enabler?*

When security is aligned with the business, it is freed of the burden of blame and motivated to help the business.

The most common patterns we see for security enabling the business are set out here:

- **Safety brings speed**: Security is a silent enabler for organizations, just as seat belts and brakes are speed enablers for a car. Without brakes or seat belts to make you feel safe, you aren't likely to drive very fast at all.

  Good security can give teams the confidence to take more business risks and try new approaches. If teams are constantly worried about security incidents that they don't understand, they are less likely and able to take business risks to rapidly meet customer needs before competitors do.

- **A lack of safety is costly**: *Pay now or pay more later*. While some teams skip security and get a short-term speed boost from that, those teams often find themselves with a security mess on their hands once attackers discover weak security in that area. This cancels out much of that initial speed and cost advantage because it takes extra time to clean up and risks customer trust, and the team has a harder job retrofitting the security it skipped (which would have been much easier to do during the original design/implementation process).

- **Rigor brings visibility and efficiency**: The rigor required to do security well often also brings clarity and attention to how underlying systems actually operate (which often goes unnoticed). Security frequently surfaces broken business processes and bizarre organizational acrobatics that often cause massive inefficiencies and hamper business agility. These are often accepted as *"the way it's always been done"* until you shine a light on them. Bringing a critical security eye to these processes helps find and fix these invisible operational inefficiencies and unlock significant organizational potential (in addition to reducing risk from cyberattacks).

Now, let's look in more detail at these common patterns for business enablement by security.

## Security is everyone's responsibility

*Security is part of everyone's job.* It's critical that everyone in the organization believes that "security is part of my job" and knows what to do. Just as safety is everyone's responsibility as they navigate the physical world, security is everyone's responsibility while using the internet, not "someone else's job" you can ignore.

Decisions that affect the security of the organization are not just made by organizational leaders and security teams. Everyone in the organization makes decisions that affect security, even if it's as simple as *"Should I click on that link in my email?"* This is similar to how responsibility for physical safety, financial costs, and legal liability all require everyone in the organization to play some part.

> **Human conflict is timeless and ever-present**
>
> Information security is just an extension of conflict and conflict resolution, which has been a standard part of human history and of our daily life experience forever. Different types of conflict show up in war and politics; in economics, where people vie for control of scarce resources; in games such as chess, poker, and football; in family environments such as brothers and sisters bickering; in businesses competing for market share; in criminal activity; in civil disputes handled by courts; in bullying; and many more places.
>
> We will explore and apply lessons from these other disciplines throughout the series and show how to apply concepts from them in a practical way to business and security.

Making your organization safe from attacks requires making computer security a normal part of the organization's culture and a normal job responsibility for anyone who uses computers for work.

These examples show how the mindset of *security is part of my job* changes decisions made by roles throughout an organization:

- **All users** think carefully about how to keep the organization's data and systems safe as they handle documents and perform daily communications (email, chat, social media, and others). This is similar to how office employees would be careful about what they say in public and which sensitive internal documents are lying around where people can read them. This is also similar to how everyone working in a physical production facility feels responsible for the safety of themselves and others around the heavy equipment operating there.

- **Application and product owners** proactively ensure there is a security review on their releases and carefully evaluate any findings to ensure that their component doesn't become a key enabler for a major security incident. This is similar to how managers, engineers, and others would carefully review the safety aspects of any new equipment to ensure nobody gets hurt during daily operations (potential risks, safety features and their configurations, location and configuration of fire and other safety measures, and so on).

- **System owners and technical operations** prioritize quickly remediating security vulnerabilities to reduce the likelihood that attackers would exploit them and damage the organization. This is comparable to how operations managers would respond quickly to address reported manufacturer recalls, defects, and potential safety issues for their equipment to keep customers and employees safe (and reduce organizational liability).

- **Architects and engineers** ensure that security best practices are applied early during the design phase of their projects to reduce the volume and impact of incidents, as well as to reduce the cost of fixing issues by addressing them early. This is similar to how building architects include fire and other safety systems in the core architecture and building design when it is easy, cheap, and more effective.

- **Software developers** embrace security as a critical part of the quality of their code, focusing on reducing the volume and severity of security issues that could cause disruption of business processes, financial transactions, physical safety, and more. This is similar to construction workers who carefully focus on the quality of their installation of fire alarms, sprinklers, and other building safety measures to protect the building and the people in it.

As you can see, **everyone has a critical part to play in managing security risks**. Everyone working with the organization's systems and data is responsible for some aspect of reducing such risks.

Now, let's take a look at what it takes to enable effective and pragmatic decisions throughout the organization.

### Enabling good security decisions by everyone in the organization

*Everyone doesn't automatically understand computer security risks.* People need sufficient context, guidance, and rules (policies) to help them make good security decisions in the situations they face. This guidance should enable good security decisions that both enable business processes and reduce business risk (or make careful trade-offs when required). The organization's guidance must cover a full range of situations, from well-known scenarios with clear right/wrong answers to new and ambiguous situations where they will need to apply general principles in new ways:

- This guidance often takes the form of written policies and education (training, videos, documentation, and more) as depicted in *Figure 7.1*:

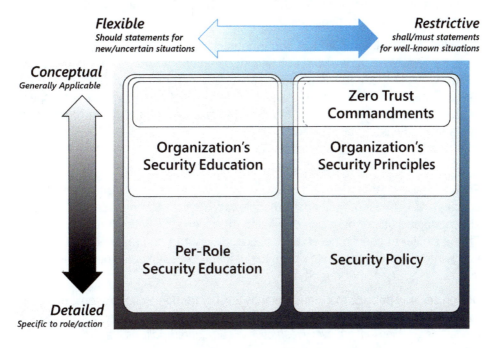

**Figure 7.1 – Organizations need multiple types of security guardrails**

Organizations should start enabling good security decisions with a core foundation from accepted standards such as the *Zero Trust Commandments* and then adapt them into guiding principles, security policy general security education, and per-role security education that are tailored to the unique needs of your organization. This will ensure that you have clear prescriptive guidance where required and general principles to follow to enable effective decisions in agile circumstances.

Cybersecurity is new to many people, and they are often unfamiliar with how to frame their thinking about it and what their role is in it. The design of your security guidance should establish basic security literacy and guardrails throughout the organization.

These are key success factors that enable everyone in the organization to make good security decisions:

- **Establish why security is important**: Security education should help everyone understand the importance of security to the organization and their part to play in it. This should make it clear how security incidents could damage the organization and how they can impact this in a positive way (ideally using guidance that is specific to their role).

- **Ensure education is engaging and interesting**: Security education must relate security to what people already know, and it must be engaging by using gamification and other interactive approaches. Nobody learns much from boring training that they can't relate to their job, lives, or experiences.

- **Establish a security mindset of continuous change**: Security policy and education must help everyone understand that security is an ongoing interactive conflict similar to business competition, international diplomacy, criminal justice, sports, and video games. People must be able to look at their daily work from an attacker's perspective so that they can think about how to defend their unique part of the organization's operations against those attackers. People must also expect that attackers will likely adjust tactics in response to defenses so that they can choose practical measures that will stand up over time and adjust to attacker changes.

- **Enable rapid identification and resolution of common security situations**: Security policies and education must enable people to recognize common security-impacting situations and guide them on addressing them correctly without requiring experts. This is similar to enabling everyone to recognize common fire hazards (a pile of oily rags) and take the appropriate action to get it addressed (clean it up themselves, call in specialists, or another remedy).

- **Design security policies to create a healthy level of friction**: Policies should be designed to set a productive and helpful level of "security friction" in business and technology processes. *Policies that are overly restrictive will be ignored; policies that are too permissive will increase organizational risk from security.*

  The number and type of interruptions in the process must create enough friction to trigger critical thinking so that serious risks aren't missed or ignored, but this friction should not block or slow business processes needlessly. You will need to tailor this level of friction to be healthy for your organization based on the organization's risk appetite and business needs.

- **Ensure security policies and standards are practical and actionable**: Security standards and policies are often very difficult to apply because they are too abstract (high- level), too specific (tied to technologies that later change), or for other reasons. *This usually happens because the people drafting the policies aren't the people using them.* Just as global restaurant brands would never release a new product without user testing, the compliance and security teams drafting the policies and standards should never release them without collaborating with people who will implement and follow them in daily operations.

- **Provide easy access to experts when required**: People should be able to get expert help rapidly and easily for new and unusual security situations that aren't covered by policy and standard procedures. *If people don't have the resources to get help with their security questions, they will assume it isn't important and are likely to ignore it.* This rapid access to expert advice minimizes slowdowns in business processes and avoids the risk of skipping security because they can't wait.

> **Technology disciplines drive more new and unusual situations**
>
> Technology disciplines such as cybersecurity, the cloud, and AI often generate a large volume of opportunities, innovations, new challenges, and new questions than other well-established business disciplines. The questions raised by these dynamic disciplines often require multiple experts to combine their expertise to create new solutions and new rules (that will then be documented in longer-term guidance such as policy and regulatory compliance).

The playbooks include more detailed guidance on how to effectively design and implement security education and policy.

Now, let's see how security leaders can set the organization up for success by establishing a clear and effective security accountability and responsibility structure.

## Security risk accountability starts at the top

*The general rule for risk accountability is "The person who owns and accepts the risk is the person that explains to the world what went wrong (often in front of TV cameras)."*

The organizational leader (CEO or equivalent) is ultimately accountable for all aspects of an organization's management and operation, including security risk. As with most disciplines, the day-to-day management of this risk is often delegated within the organization. This section will discuss how to effectively approach structuring accountability and responsibility for managing security risk.

We have found that *incorrectly assigning accountability is often the biggest obstacle to making progress on security risk* (and Zero Trust) in an organization.

Cybersecurity is a newer risk, and leaders are often unfamiliar with best practices for framing their thinking, measuring, and managing it (for example, who is accountable for accepting risk, implications to consider when deciding to accept risk, and more).

As we discussed earlier in this chapter, security risk is fundamentally different from technical risks that are primarily managed by technology teams. Managing this risk is similar to managing legal, financial, or safety risks because a *single policy violation or policy gap anywhere in the organization can create a major incident and organizational risk*.

This section covers these three topics:

- **Avoiding a dangerous misperception**: Describing how the common mistake of viewing cybersecurity risk as a "technical problem to be solved" creates an obstacle to effectively managing this risk

- **Managing security risk effectively**: Describing success criteria and examples of how to manage business risk from security effectively

- **Acme Energy case study**: Describing how one organization established roles and processes to proactively and effectively manage security risk

The role-specific playbooks for business, security, and technical leadership roles in this series include more details on how to set up effective security risk management.

Now, let's take a look at how a common misperception can prevent organizations from managing business risk from security effectively.

## Avoiding a dangerous misperception

Most common security risk management challenges are driven by a misperception that security risk is simply a "technical problem" that should be "solved" by technical security teams (whether this is an implicit belief or an explicitly stated or written opinion). This misperception creates a "powerless scapegoat" dynamic that leads to poor risk management by the organization. This is an easy mistake to make because of these factors:

- Technical and security experts have limited knowledge and experience framing risks using business terminology.

- Security risk shows up on technical systems managed by technical teams.

- This business risk has been managed as a technical problem in the past.

When operating under the misperception that security problems are solvable, *security teams are held accountable for decisions they don't make* (implicitly or explicitly). This often creates a continuous conflict situation where business decision-makers ignore security requirements ("it's not my problem") and the security teams waste resources protecting themselves from these decisions (as best they can). This often creates a never-ending cycle of blame and conflict that increases risk, slows down business processes, or both.

This unhealthy internal conflict usually takes one of these two forms:

- **If security approval is not required for projects**, security teams (and requirements) will often be ignored, causing decisions to be made exclusively on criteria of speed, profitability, and other requirements. Skipping security increases organizational risk because attackers can exploit nearly any common security vulnerability, even simple ones that can quickly and easily be mitigated. This frequently leads to many more avoidable security incidents, each of which can have a significant or material impact on the organization.

- **If security approval is required for projects**, they will often apply restrictive controls and configurations that are designed to reduce the security risk to as close to zero as possible. This is often referred to as the "department of no" dynamic and often impedes business productivity because decisions are focused only on avoiding the security "failure" they are accountable for (without considering any other business requirements).

  The painful irony in this scenario is that risk actually increases in addition to blocking or slowing business progress and agility. The risk of damage from security incidents increases because business teams get frustrated and often find a way to go around security to deploy "shadow IT" systems. These shadow IT systems and the data on them can have nearly zero security protection or monitoring, leading to more security incidents that have a significant or material impact on the organization.

As you can see, *treating security risk as a technical problem creates a "no-win" situation* that impacts both business productivity and organizational risk. We strongly encourage organizations to reframe how they manage this risk using techniques described in the next part of this section.

---

**An up-close perspective – how bad risk decisions are made**

**Would you want to be held accountable for someone else's decision? Would you make a good risk decision if you didn't understand it or if the consequences of that decision didn't affect you?**

While any reasonable professional would never answer yes to these questions, this is exactly what happens when security is held accountable (for example, the CISO gets fired or pushed out) for the negative outcome of decisions made by others in the organization.

Too many times, we see project managers or executive sponsors treat organizational security risk as a transactional project risk by saying something such as "*I accept this risk; let's keep moving.*" This frequently happens because they aren't aware that these risks will endure for years after the project itself is done (or don't feel accountable for that outcome).

This creates a trap for security teams who expect to be blamed for incidents resulting from these decisions. Security teams often have few (or zero) good choices to avoid being blamed for others' mistakes, often falling back on strictly applying regulatory compliance requirements to get any security requirements considered. This last-ditch technique can block or slow projects, further undermining trust and relationships between teams.

---

Let's talk about how to avoid this trap and drive productive and healthy management of security risk.

### Managing security risk effectively

*Normalize security risk.* Managing this risk effectively requires normalizing security accountability and responsibility throughout the organization, similar to legal, financial, safety, and other risks.

These are the key success factors for effective security risk management that are integrated into the playbook series:

- **Register security formally as organizational risk**: Security risk(s) must be formally recorded and tracked along with other organizational risks in a risk register or similar process. This ensures that this risk is actively managed using standard processes for assessment, monitoring, reporting to oversight (boards) and regulatory authorities, investment into mitigations, and other risk management activities.

  This allows the organization to manage security risks such as those that could disrupt revenue, operations, or mission accomplishment such as natural disasters, geopolitical factors, fire/employee safety, legal liability, and others.

- **Assign security risk with other accountabilities**: Risk accountability must be assigned to roles with broad business ownership and accountabilities across revenue, safety, liability, and more. Larger organizations that delegate risk management must be careful to ensure they don't assign security accountability to separate leaders and create the "powerless scapegoat" dynamic described earlier in the *Avoiding a dangerous misperception* section.

  Security experts should be positioned as expert advisors who have a **duty to inform** and support business leaders who have the **duty to decide** on security risks along with other organizational goals and risks. This expert advisor model is similar to how many organizations structure legal and human resource experts who work with stakeholders throughout the organization.

  *Figure 7.2* illustrates the classic (scapegoat) model and the (recommended) business enabler model:

  In the **Security as Scapegoat** model, which isn't recommended, security (red block on the right) is held accountable for the security outcomes of other's decisions. In the **Security as Business Enabler** model, security teams are positioned as experts who are accountable for providing expert support and advice to the **business units** (**BUs**) that they support.

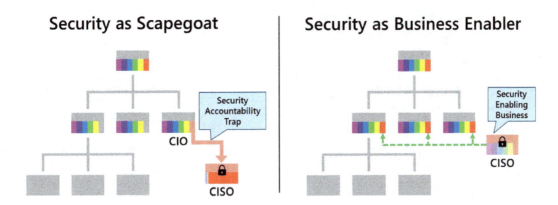

Figure 7.2 – Comparison of security accountability models

A general rule of thumb is that anyone who accepts the risk of exceptions must be in an *organizational leadership* role that has the following responsibilities:

- **Accountable for organizational-wide business impact**, not just a local system or a temporary project team (security risk is not just project risk). *If you are not empowered to make organization-wide business decisions, you shouldn't be accepting security risks.*

- **Aware fully informed** of all potential business impacts of decisions, including organization-wide security impact(s) and direct business impacts of exceptions. *If you aren't clear on all potential impacts, you should learn about them from business, security, and other experts.*

- **Provide business leaders with security context and expertise**: Ensure that business leaders are supported with access to expert security advice in their language and context. This provides business leaders with the critical context they need to make good business risk decisions regarding security. This is particularly important for business leaders who are new to judging security risk and comparing it to other risks and business opportunities (which is most business leaders as of the writing of this book).

  Having security leaders such as CISOs provide this advice helps position them as trusted advisors to business leaders, creating more productive relationships focused on securely enabling the business. See the Acme Energy case study section later in this chapter for an example of how to structure this well.

- **Provide a framework for strategic security risk decisions**: Decision makers need a framework to make security risk decisions at a strategic level. This framework should prioritize outcomes in this order:

  I.   *Seek or create win-win options* that both maximize enablement of business productivity and decrease risk from security incidents.

II.   *Guide thoughtful trade-offs* when win-win options aren't available by considering how to best balance productivity and security risk.

Ensure the use of the same structure and terminology to compare the decision outcomes. For example, compare potential revenue/mission gains (and their probability) from a new proposed system design versus likely revenue/mission losses (and their probability) if that resource is compromised. This calculus should consider positive and negative impacts on other capabilities throughout the organization.

As with any other strategic decisions with a long-term impact, consider both long-term and short-term impacts of security-related decisions. You should also measure and monitor the outcomes of decisions to ensure you are learning how to improve these decisions over time.

- **Provide current context (intelligence) to inform risk decisions**: In today's rapidly changing world, significant security risk decisions should always be informed by current business, technical, and security contexts. Rapid changes in security threats, business priorities, and technical platforms constantly change the options for managing security risk—the best option yesterday may not be the best option today or tomorrow.

Use security intelligence to inform decisions and actions with the current context of real attacks and what they mean to your organization, including risk decisions, policy design, security control prioritization, security architecture, and more.

*Figure 7.3* depicts how security decisions should be informed by a combination of business and security contexts called security intelligence:

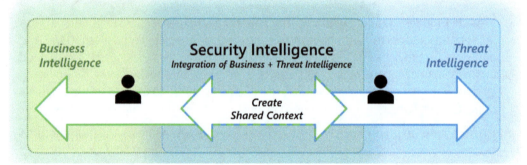

**Figure 7.3 – Security intelligence combines business intelligence and threat intelligence (TI)**

Business and security experts must work together to combine *business intelligence* and *TI* into a shared *security intelligence* context that informs decisions across all teams. Creating this shared security intelligence context requires experts on different teams to work together in a collaborative manner. Security intelligence is discussed more in the security operations and leadership playbooks.

The playbooks include detailed role-by-role guidance to effectively design, implement, and manage security risk across all these success factors.

Now, let's look at a case study of how one organization structured roles and processes in its security program to meet these goals.

### Acme Energy case study – proactive security risk management

Acme Energy's leadership shifted to a proactive strategic approach to security risk management by changing its processes and structures. This helped Acme get out of the repeating cycle of reacting to security incidents and crises and enabled the organization to be strategic in how it managed security risk.

The main components of Acme's change are set out here:

- **Security risk council**: Acme established a new process that enables organizational leaders to strategically plan security risk management and manage urgent security events. This forum includes leaders for each of Acme's business lines, the head of the enterprise risk team, the CIO, the CISO, and the head of the regulatory compliance team.

- **Enterprise security integration role**: Acme established a new role on the CISO's team dedicated to integrating security into business and technical strategy and driving security strategy and risk within the security team. Acme established a dedicated role in the security team called *enterprise security integration* that is modeled after the business strategy roles that support business leaders.

  Using the same structure as business teams helped ease integration challenges with business teams and enabled security to take advantage of best practices and learnings from business teams.

These two components helped Acme drive a massive transformation in cybersecurity risk management. Acme was able to proactively address many existing internal challenges simultaneously because of the following:

- **Human connection and diplomacy**: These two components strengthened the human relationship and collaboration between security, business, and technology teams at all levels from leadership down.

  The *human connection* created by these processes helped Acme smoothly handle many gaps, overlaps, and mismatches between team processes. This helped avoid mishandling big risks and resolve inter-team challenges quickly and effectively by working both sides at once.

- **Strategic integration**: This component enabled Acme to take a genuinely strategic approach to security. The quality of Acme's strategic decisions improved in many ways. Some key highlights include the following:

- **Integrate security in business and technical decisions**: Security was proactively integrated into business strategy and processes, making it an integrated component of business decisions, just as with legal, financial, and other factors. This helped Acme avoid costly oversights by ensuring security issues were addressed early when they were cheaper and easier to solve. This also enabled Acme to respond rapidly and effectively to the regular stream of new security risk events that were constantly coming up.

- **Integrate business priorities in security decisions**: Security teams at Acme began making decisions with the full context of business and technology risks and priorities. This ensured that Acme's security resources were focused on the most important risks to the organization's mission and revenue (in contrast to the previous approach, which resulted in a lot of resources wasted on lower-priority tasks). This also helped the security team be more agile and adjust priorities more quickly to changing business and technology environments.

As you can see, Acme Energy was able to achieve a proactive strategic approach to security risk management. The guidance in the leadership playbook describes how to design and implement these functions in your organization.

Now, let's talk about a key underlying assumption that should frame everyone's thinking about security risk.

## Assume compromise (assume breach)

*There is freedom, gold, and beauty in the new frontier, but also bandits, badgers, and bears.*

Imagine yourself walking in a gorgeous landscape in a wild frontier, with trees, deer, and open green fields laid out before you. There is gold in the rivers, streams, and mountain caves—opportunities waiting for you. This is how the internet looked when we first saw it—full of promise, beauty, and opportunity.

But some dangerous animals and humans live in this landscape too. We have learned from our experience (and from others' experience) that we must keep ourselves safe in this beautiful place. The beauty and opportunity are still there, but the threats are as well. We must learn how to avoid attacks, survive them when they happen, and continue to thrive despite these setbacks.

This mix of opportunity and risk accurately describes the real internet we actually depend on for much of our modern lives.

### Perfection is unattainable in the real world

Information security teams have historically tried to provide a perfectly safe and secure internal network environment for the entire organization and tried to stop all attackers from getting into it. While this vision of a perfectly secure walled garden would be ideal, it has proven impractical in the real world over and over again, despite the best vvefforts of very smart people. You simply can't expect perfection in anything, let alone a large, complex interconnected network with thousands of devices, each connecting to hundreds of arbitrary websites and services every day.

Trying to live in a fantasy of a perfectly secure computer network blinds people to better problem definitions and readily available solutions. When we only focus on a (failing) strategy that attempts perfection, we are neglecting or starving efforts to take a more practical and agile path. We must abandon attempts to perfectly secure networks, salvage the working parts of that strategy, and focus on a better path of Zero (assumed) Trust. We must fully internalize the very reasonable assumptions that attackers are out there, many will target you, and some will succeed sometimes. We must use that recognition to see the world through the lens of the attackers and learn, prepare, and act accordingly.

### How do you get your job done safely in the open countryside?

Zero Trust focuses on enabling business goals and productivity in an internet environment with an assumption of compromise. Zero Trust accepts reality as it is, adapts to what's there, makes the best of it, and improves security as it goes.

Imagine you were told you were going to lead a group of employees (including the CEO) about 10 blocks to a business meeting in a new, unfamiliar city. You would probably not panic, but you would adopt a cautious mindset, think about how people were dressed, what people were carrying, and what route you would take, and make sure everyone knew the plan and communicated. You would also probably remain vigilant and pay close attention to your surroundings, looking for signs that people around you may not have your best interests in mind.

Zero Trust is applying that same kind of thinking to protect your data and systems. Business technology systems operate on the same open internet where every day, people socialize, businesses conduct commerce, and criminals and spies operate. It's not a completely bad place, but it's not completely safe either.

A Zero Trust security strategy simultaneously honors proven and well-established security best practices while boldly challenging flawed assumptions that did not work in practice. While this is a relatively easy thing to accept as a business leader, this can be a worldview-altering event for security folks who have spent their professional careers living under those assumptions. We will cover more of those human changes later in this chapter.

Shifting from assuming you operate in a safe, stable internal space to operating in an open environment is critical to acknowledge as it simply reflects reality. While it's simple to say *"Assume compromise,"* this shift to an agile security approach is a fundamental strategic shift that causes many downstream effects across an organization.

Changing this core security assumption requires people throughout the organization to adopt a new/unfamiliar mindset and think through many details of daily processes, operations, and strategic planning. Security vigilance and security thinking must become a normal, seamless, and low-friction part of daily operations for everyone.

Security must become agile and align with the organization, not a static quality mechanism in an ivory tower that tries to apply the same solution from last month, last year, or a decade ago.

> **Important note**
> *Assume compromise is a recognition of the essential truth that attackers are always trying to attack you and will sometimes succeed.*
>
> *Countless breaches have proven this true.*

This shift in mindset sometimes happens naturally after people experience their first major security incident and realize how fragile their environment can be against a determined attacker. Some teams double down on the old ways of security, but many move forward and start to shift their mindset about security.

You will see references throughout the book series to "assume compromise" as we show how this principle applies to the daily work of operating and securing an organization and its assets.

### Assuming compromise is a pivotal mindset for all roles

This assumption is applied at all levels of the organization and is particularly important for business leaders, technical leaders, and security teams. Here are some examples to illustrate how different roles apply this principle:

- **Business leaders** should assume successful attacks will happen and factor this into risk planning, budgets, productivity forecasts (for example, consider "ensure schedules accommodate security maintenance requirements"), and more.

- **Financial teams** should assume an email account is potentially compromised and never approve large money transfers without additional process controls (especially in today's age of deep fakes using AI).

- **Technical and security leaders** should assume attackers will get access to some business assets and work with business leaders to understand which assets to protect most, which to recover first in an attack, and so on.

- **Technical architects** and engineers should assume any resource could be compromised and ensure system designs include appropriate security controls, monitoring, and response processes to protect against intelligent and creative human attackers.

- **Security operations** should assume an attacker may have gained control of internal resources and proactively hunt for their presence.

Assuming compromise leads you to the conclusion that you cannot assume anything is trustworthy, hence the name *Zero Trust*. Good security begins by assuming Zero Trust.

## Explicit validation of trust

But you can't actually operate a system without trust. Trust is what makes a piece of paper worth money; it enables personal and business relationships to work, it enables people in a complex organization to work with others they haven't met, it enables you to buy products online, and it's required to make security decisions such as "Who accesses which resources?"

Zero Trust shouldn't be interpreted to be "never trust," but as *zero assumed trust*. This forces you to figure out how to make an informed decision using data and telemetry, not assumptions.

The explicit validation of trust requires more work than simply trusting anything on an internal network, but it enables you to build flexible, reliable, and scalable security assurances in a highly dynamic world.

At the end of the day, we will never have perfect security, but we can make it as difficult and expensive as possible for attackers to hide in our systems and impersonate our legitimate employees, devices, identities, and more.

Trust and security decisions improve with more data, better fidelity on that data, and more diversity within the data to triangulate assumptions. It's easier for adversaries to hide when the only data is simplistic and one-dimensional; it is difficult to hide anomalous activities in a high-detail, high-fidelity, and diverse dataset. Hiding your identity from a grainy black-and-white security camera is easier than hiding it from a high-definition color video with sound.

## Asset-centric and data-centric security

Another key mindset shift (particularly for technical teams) is the need to become business asset-centric and data-centric.

*This is needed to counteract a common antipattern where technology teams have a technology-centric or network-centric view of the organization.*

Security teams are mission-oriented and committed to keeping the organization's assets safe but often aren't aware of what is important to business leaders. This forces them to try to protect all assets equally (without regard to what is most valuable to the organization).

Trying to protect everything equally in the complex and fast-moving world of today is a recipe for failure. They won't be able to succeed no matter how much they want to.

Security teams need to be comfortable asking "How much does this matter?", and business teams need to answer those questions (both reactively and proactively) to get to a better place.

As we discussed earlier, data is becoming the key enabler for a business to rapidly innovate and stay competitive (or stay relevant and meet the needs of citizens, in the case of a government).

*Figure 7.4* is a diagram from The Open Group that captures the essence of how the world's organizations have become interconnected through technology systems, affecting each other in real time:

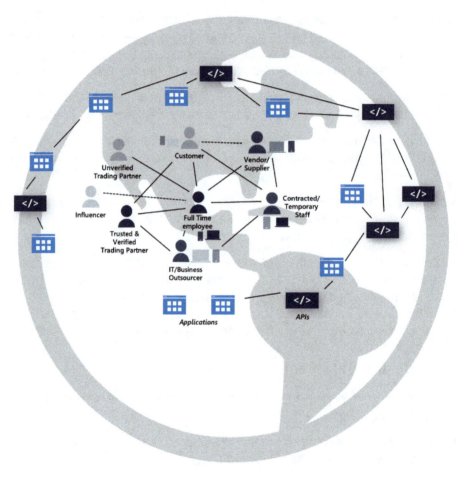

**Figure 7.4 – The Open Group diagram on the interconnection of businesses**

Let's take an example from retail to illustrate this. Buying an item in a large or medium-sized retailer in most countries today initiates a series of events that are completely automated by computers. The money you pay will be automatically added to databases used for reporting revenue and forecasting future sales. This data will also frequently be used to automatically order more items from the manufacturer and notify shippers and distributors that more products will need to be moved from those factories to this specific store.

There may still be some humans involved in reviewing or approving some orders and payments, but most repetitive tasks are automated these days, and this trend will only continue. More and more automation will be used because computers handle these repetitive tasks better and more accurately, it's cheaper this way, and most people don't like doing these kinds of jobs anyway.

In practice, for a modern business, *data is a key business asset*. Where and how it's produced, how it's modified and shared, how easily it can be shared, and how it's monetized impact businesses significantly. For example, ransomware works by locking your ability to use your data. In another example, how fast you can enter a new market is often dependent on how fast you can share your data—securely. If you can't, you may not be able to add that new trading partner or use that new vendor. But as mentioned earlier, not all data is created equal.

A picture in an online catalog available to the public may be of lower value than a credit card number. Also, remember that data can have many forms. So even a utility company cares about data in its operational systems—for example, if you can't route the electricity, you can't deliver it. Those operations involve data too, only in another form than a credit card.

Shifting the mindset of technical teams to be asset-centric and data-centric is critical to success. Security must be focused on the value of the business assets—the data and applications most valuable to the organization. Just as when you move to a new house or apartment, you don't put your most treasured and valued items in any random box; you put them all into a few boxes, pack them carefully, and pay extra close attention to those boxes to ensure they don't get lost.

This is often a significant shift in mindset, particularly for technology practitioners who have been operating under a network-centric model for many years. The execution of Zero Trust will leverage a lot of existing skills, knowledge, and technologies, but they will be applied in new ways that focus on data and applications of importance. *Figure 7.5* captures this transformation visually:

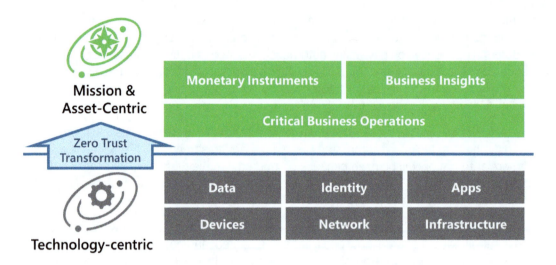

**Figure 7.5 – Diagram showing a shift in mindset**

This diagram illustrates how organizations need to transform from focusing on the technical environment to focusing on the mission and assets of the organization.

### Making data- and asset-centric security real

Business leadership will need to lean in to help technology teams get the context they need to protect what matters. Business and technology leaders work together to *ask and answer hard questions that may never have been discussed before*.

The overall process requires figuring out the following:

- Which data and applications are most important to the organization? Which would cause the most impact if they were lost, stolen, or altered (losing assurances of confidentiality, integrity, availability, or physical safety)?

- Which systems do they depend on (both internal and external to the organization)?

- How well are those secured and monitored?

Getting answers to these questions requires people across the organization to work together, including business leaders, technology leaders, employees within BUs, technology practitioners, and more.

As with all longer-term journeys, *incremental progress is better than deferred perfection*. Focus on quick wins and incremental progress that get you the most risk reduction for the least amount of effort, ensuring that you are always working toward the ideal end state. These quick wins will then be built into a continuous life cycle that leads to improvements in both security and productivity as you gain insights into your business processes.

This asset discovery process will be addressed in more depth later in the playbooks.

## Cybersecurity is a team sport

*"Alone we can do so little; together we can do so much."*

*– Helen Keller*

*Collaborate across organizations.* While it can sometimes feel like you are alone against the world in cybersecurity, nearly every organization on the planet faces the same challenges as you do. Every business, government, and organization on the internet faces nearly the same threats, attack groups, and attack techniques as you do. Each of these organizations has learned something from its journey and is a potential ally and source of wisdom. Regardless of your role, you should make it a priority to reach out to your peers at other organizations to talk about cybersecurity and share learnings with each other. Join existing communities or attend conferences if available, and if they are not, create a community for you and your peers to share and help each other.

*Collaborate across teams and departments.* Additionally, organizations where teams work together effectively are far more likely to be successful at enabling business goals and reducing security risk. This is true for both teams within a discipline working together (security teams working with each other, IT teams working with each other) as well as teams working across disciplines (business, security, and IT teams working together) that we described in *Chapter 3, Zero Trust Is Security for Today's World*

When people work together on a common goal, the formal silos of where people report fade away a little bit and people focus more on what they have in common than how they are different. This allows them to share opportunities, tips, and perspectives that would otherwise be lost or never be created. This also helps integrate security earlier into the process and solve security problems early when it's easier, faster, and cheaper. This reduces risk and cost by reducing the likelihood and severity of security incidents and their resulting organizational damage.

*Chapter 10, Zero Trust Playbook Roles,* covers how the playbooks describe the key relationships for each role that represent the minimum interactions for cross-team processes.

---

**Teamwork doesn't have to be formal**

Sometimes, simple informal connections and interactions can be surprisingly impactful.

Something as simple as a CEO or business leader taking the time to visit the security teams to thank them for protecting the organization can be a huge morale boost and motivation source for people who are used to working hard without recognition of their efforts.

Security people with have friends in IT and business groups often have a lot of context and insight that helps them do their job better.

---

# Factor three – human empathy

*I cannot solve problems that I don't see or understand.*

The third critical success factor that enables digital, cloud, and Zero Trust transformations to go smoothly is the use of human empathy—focusing on the human experience of the transformation.

We can't overstate the importance of the human side of this simultaneous transformation. Managing the human experience of change within ourselves and within our teams is a critically important success factor for the following reasons:

- **These transformations are made by people on your teams**, and we all feel the impact of these transformations on our lives, jobs, careers, and more. Additionally, we are moving from static business processes (designed to be carried out by any qualified person in a role) to dynamic business processes where judgment calls and empathy are required to understand customers and their needs and ensure the organization is meeting them.

- **Change is hard**. These transformations upend many of the assumptions people have taken for granted for all of their careers, creating additional stress and distractions as they figure out new processes (and, sometimes, new jobs).

- **These transformations are about people**. The purpose and value of technology changes are to better serve people's needs. These changes ensure products and services are safe for customers, business investments are safe for shareholders, and critical services and missions are provided safely by governments and non-governmental organizations. *This requires empathy with customers, citizens, partners, and other stakeholders.*

---

**Transformations will hit some harder than others**

While these transformations will touch everyone differently, some of the strongest effects will be felt by security and technology professionals. This is similar to how the shift to working from home during the COVID-19 pandemic affected junior employees living in apartments with multiple roommates much more than senior management who had larger homes with extra rooms.

While senior managers have visibility of the workings of business and the confidence of having already changed their careers multiple times, practitioners have often heavily invested their careers in specific technologies and knowledge. Security and technology professionals have often built a significant professional identity around a technology they mastered—for example, I am the "firewall person" at the company. It's critical to understand which roles are impacted by which changes and provide them the support they need.

---

As with any transformation, people across the organization will experience large and small changes in what they do for their jobs and how they are paid for success. In this case, we are shifting to a world of continuous, rapid changes that don't conveniently show up on a preset schedule. People need to adapt in real time as the organization shifts the business model, the technology platform to support it, and the way it secures all of it. This amplifies the need to focus on cultural acceptance of this new normal of constant uncertainty.

## Zero Trust provides a competitive advantage

*When we feel our voice is heard, we want to share our best ideas and insights.*

Organizations that manage the human aspect of these transformations well will differentiate themselves from their competitors in the marketplace. While a job change is stressful for anyone, having awareness of the change and influence over the definition of their new job is empowering and motivating and can increase productivity.

## Key cultural themes

These are the key themes of the human changes everyone should expect to experience and manage through the transformation. These key themes show up throughout the playbooks as we explore how Zero Trust transforms organizations and their approach to security. Your individual experience of these may differ depending on your role in the organization, background, experience, and other factors.

### Normalization of continuous change

Technology, businesses, and security are changing and will keep changing continuously. This is the new normal, and we must all accept that as a basic assumption. What we have been experiencing is not a simple one-time change but *the start of an era of continuous changes*. We must assume that business drivers, technology platforms, business models, and security threats will continuously evolve, and build that into our models and perspectives.

Just taking a quick glance at the horizon, we see our world will continuously change with advances in and the proliferation of AI, IoT, and affective computing. We will also see geopolitical affairs and regulatory changes to privacy and security evolve in response to these, further affecting organizations. More on these changes in the *Zero Trust Futures* play book.

*Change is normal.* The guidance for each role in the playbooks describes how each role adapts to this world of continuous changes.

### A growth mindset and continuous learning

**Win, learn, or both!** Continuous change means continuous learning. Learning means taking chances, trying something new, and making mistakes. We must focus on learning from mistakes and encouraging others to learn as well. People cannot learn quickly and effectively unless they feel safe making mistakes as they learn.

## A calm and rational view of attackers

While much of the security industry seems determined to scare everyone about security (often to encourage buying a product), this leads to a warped view of security risk that doesn't enable good decision-making. Worrying about a shadowy figure hunched over a keyboard with potentially infinite resources and skills doesn't help you make good, clear decisions about real-world security risks. It's a lot easier to make good decisions if you have a rational and calm understanding of the relevant risk context.

The threat of criminals and nation-state espionage is now simply another part of daily life for business leaders, technical leaders, and technical teams. *Everyone should be informed about the actual motivations, methods, and capabilities of attackers* appropriate to their role.

We covered a summary of the dynamics briefly in *Chapter 1, This Is the Way*, to get you started. The security operations and leadership playbooks detail how to set up security intelligence and TI capabilities and integrate them into your processes.

There are also good free TI reports such as the Verizon **Data Breach Investigations Report (DBIR)** or the **Microsoft Digital Defense Report (MDDR)** that you can use to get informed. There are many other good external reports and services, but there are also plenty that try to stir up fear to sell products. Pay close attention to the language, framing, and profit models of the reports you read.

## Inclusion and diversity

What got us here won't get us there. We see organizations succeed more often when they are willing to disrupt established thought patterns within the organization and try new things. Security needs to take advantage of existing hard-earned experience and wisdom but must apply it in new ways to grow into the new world.

Diversity of ideas and perspectives is a critical element to help break people out of existing thought patterns. Considering new perspectives and integrating wisdom from other sources helps nudge us out of our normal habits and see things we know about in a new light (or see completely new things). This is especially true in information security, where problems have been defined in a very literal technical way that often ignores the business and human sides of security.

Security teams should be constantly seeking out different perspectives from people of different personal and professional backgrounds that can help approach these highly complex and challenging problems in different ways. There are many sources of different thinking patterns in other parts of our organization, from new hires outside the organization, from outside consultancies, from existing team members studying other human disciplines, and more.

Here are some examples to illustrate this:

- The economic question of *"How do attackers decide who to attack?"* can help you better prioritize which technical defenses to invest in (rather than simply analyzing technical data).

- A parent who has dealt with stubborn kids probably has many creative ideas on how to help inspire people to change their work habits and processes.

- A finance expert can better identify human process controls to prevent executives from being tricked into approving money transfers than a technical professional who only understands the technology.

- Someone who has seen a childhood classmate get caught up in crime will have a clearer picture of how criminals think and what kinds of things they may try.

Engage the full set of expertise you have in your organization and try to include as many diverse perspectives and people as you can find. They will make your security approach much richer and more effective.

### Everyone needs to work together

Organizations that work well together across departments and teams are much more likely to have a smooth and productive Zero Trust transformation than organizations with teams that are constantly arguing. Building a common identity and strategic partnership between teams enables organizations to transform faster, adopt new technology successfully, and better keep up with a seemingly endless river of threats.

The growing sophistication, volume, and scale of attacks now make it critical to include security in business strategy, requiring security and business to get to know each other better and develop common language and priorities. In short, everyone needs to work together as a team to keep up with the rapid pace of change and support each other's success.

## Summary

In this chapter, we examined three key success factors to help avoid common causes of failures—having a clear strategy, security mindsets and cultural shifts, and human empathy. These help you avoid common antipatterns (common mistakes) seen in Zero Trust and other technology initiatives. Each playbook includes specific antipatterns to avoid—for business leaders, technical leaders, architects, and technical managers, and for IT and security practitioners.

Next up, in *Chapter 8, Adoption with the Three-Pillar Model*, we will describe how the three-pillar model helps you meet these success factors.

# 8
# Adoption with the Three-Pillar Model

*"No one can whistle a symphony. It takes a whole orchestra to play it."*

*– H.E. Luccock*

Now that we have a clear overview of Zero Trust and what success looks like, *it's time to shift into planning mode*. The remaining chapters will focus on the playbook approach that enables you to achieve and benefit from the promised benefits of Zero Trust.

This chapter discusses the three-pillar model used as the foundation of the playbooks that helps you orchestrate Zero Trust and integrate it with your whole organization. The next chapter will cover the six-stage plan based on these pillars that guides the overall journey. The final chapter describes the role-based guidance in the playbooks that make Zero Trust personal, actionable, and crystal clear to every role.

The key topics covered in this chapter are as follows:

- **Introduction to the three pillars** that enable you to transform an organization and integrate security, technology, and business into one interconnected system

  - The **strategic** pillar sets the direction

  - The **operational** pillar guides integration and execution

  - The **operating model** pillar monitors, adjusts, and sustains over time

- **Playbook structure**, including a deeper analysis of each pillar and showing how they are made real using an *Acme Bank* example

- **Stitching it all together with the Zero Trust Playbook**, which introduces the detailed elements that are executed in the six-stage plan described in *Chapter 9, The Zero Trust Six-Stage Plan*

We use a detailed example of how *Acme Bank* planned Zero Trust by working through each pillar of the playbook. Zero Trust enabled *Acme*'s digital transformation and market expansion with an integrated approach to security.

Now, let's take a look at the three pillars.

## Introduction to the three pillars

What matters to an organization? The ability to conduct business, achieve its mission, and grow its business.

Doing this in today's dynamically changing world is like navigating a constantly changing obstacle course. You must have a clear plan to get to your objectives and you must keep moving forward, but you also have to be flexible and adjust based on what you learn on that journey.

To enable this, we recommend using a simple three-pillar model based on *The Open Group's SOA for Business Technology* guide (`http://www.opengroup.org/soa/source-book/wp_soa4bt/p2.htm`).

At its very simplest, this is a *plan → do → run* framework, but it has been tailored to Zero Trust and the complex and continuously changing business, technology, and threat environments of today.

This model provides much-needed clarity on how to integrate security and Zero Trust into an organization's strategy, processes, and daily operations. It provides a high-level structure that enables the agile security approach of Zero Trust by connecting and guiding organic local activity across teams.

*Figure 8.1* illustrates these three pillars:

**Figure 8.1 – The three pillars of the Zero Trust Playbook**

The first pillar (*strategic*) establishes a strategy and creates a roadmap to deliver on a long-term vision, creating a clear direction for all. The second pillar (*operational*) is where you execute that plan and integrate it into the daily running of the business, which is producing products and services. The third pillar (*operating model*) addresses governance and culture to enable and sustain Zero Trust—the people part of it.

This model is designed to be as follows:

- **Consistent but flexible**: This common three-pillar model sets a foundation to balance rigid structure with flexibility, providing clear direction without suffocating the creativity and agility needed for success. The consistent strategy keeps Zero Trust from floundering because people move in different directions (which happens frequently in large or complex organizations). At the same time, the model enables flexibility to apply that strategy differently to existing organizations in different industries, with different cultures and structures.

- **Actionable**: Enabling you to rapidly deliver on clear short-term goals while also constantly moving you toward long-term objectives. In this hyper-competitive agile world, you need to deliver with precision when *performing* against current responsibilities while *transforming* to meet continuously evolving needs. This model weaves strategy into your existing assets, structure, and personnel in a journey that has clear governance guardrails to monitor and keep it on track.

The playbooks use this three-pillar model to drive progress forward in an integrated way while maintaining the visibility and flexibility you need to be agile and adjust your course as you go.

Now, let's take a look at the playbook structure.

# Playbook structure

Now that we understand the model, let's dive into the playbook structure and how it is woven throughout the playbooks. This chapter will take a deeper dive into each of the three pillars (strategic, operational, and operating model) and then summarize how they tie together into a single, coherent, detailed model that is implemented in phases. We will use *Acme* examples for different industries throughout this chapter and the rest of the playbook to show how to apply these in real life in different industries.

## Playbook layout

The playbook series provides a single overarching approach that is then detailed in role-specific guidance. This naturally provides immediate actionable guidance while keeping everyone in the organization focused on working in the same direction. This approach also provides clarity and structure while maintaining flexibility to adapt the playbook to your organization and changing requirements. You can start anywhere and continuously improve on it, but we encourage business leadership to sponsor a larger initiative to improve coordination across teams. While a musical instrument can be used by a musician to play a song solo, music sounds better when played by a full orchestra.

For each element of the playbook, we will cover what it is, why the element is important to include, who will do it, and how to do it.

*Figure 8.2* illustrates how this book contains a high-level summary of the whole journey, in which each playbook adds greater detail for each role:

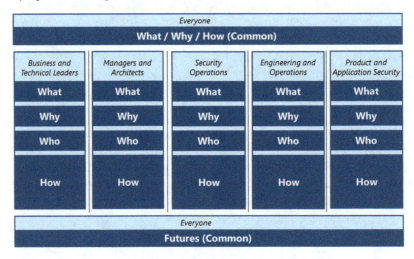

**Figure 8.2 – The playbook structure**

In the playbook, the strategic pillar sets Zero Trust up for success, the operational pillar executes it in your organization, and the operating model pillar provides governance (guardrails), cultural changes, and training to smooth the path.

It's worth noting that the Zero Trust strategy and operating model pillars tend to be very similar across organizations and industries. The operational pillar is where you will tailor it to your organization's current structure, culture, and industry requirements.

### Introducing the Acme Bank example

*"Tell me and I forget. Teach me and I remember. Involve me and I learn."*

*– Benjamin Franklin*

Concepts become more meaningful when they are applied to a real example. We will use the *Acme Bank* example in this chapter to explain how the three-pillar model works in the real world.

*Acme Bank* is undertaking a large, complex digital transformation initiative. *Acme* is migrating new developments and many existing workloads to the cloud, and it is opening three new financial service businesses. This includes the introduction of **peer-to-peer** (**P2P**) payments that will operate in Europe, the US, Japan, and India. The bank prides itself in providing cost-effective, secure capabilities for its customers to borrow money, with a focus on the retail banking sector. The organization faces significant security and compliance challenges in supporting these initiatives across multiple jurisdictions. The CISO and the board have decided to follow a Zero Trust approach to provide a unified security strategy to manage risk.

## The strategic pillar

*"By failing to prepare, you are preparing to fail."*

*– Benjamin Franklin*

*Figure 8.3* illustrates the strategic pillar in the three-pillar model:

**Figure 8.3 – The strategic pillar**

A strategy sets the direction for the organization by defining the end state (mission and vision), what it takes to achieve that end state (goals, capabilities, and strategic models), and how to get there (agile roadmaps).

To be clear, organizations don't make money (or accomplish their mission) by doing Zero Trust. Zero Trust is an *enabler* for an organization, enabling a business to accomplish its mission and make money by *preventing loss and enabling business opportunities*. Zero Trust provides critical safety and security assurances that make the organization resilient to (intense and growing) security risks.

Because Zero Trust isn't the organization's actual mission, it's critical to focus and prioritize your Zero Trust efforts on enabling that mission and reducing risk to it. To do this, you need to understand your organization's vision, mission, capabilities, and direction so that you can identify how Zero Trust prevents loss *and* enables opportunity.

---

### What if we don't have a written business strategy?

Note that your organization may not have a current strategy clearly documented in an easy-to-consume format (many don't). The question *What are the organization's capabilities and direction?* may not have been asked, fully answered, written down, or communicated broadly at your organization (or the written answers may be out of date).

*This is okay, and you can still do Zero Trust.* We will explain as we go and provide examples of what we see at most organizations to help you get started with Zero Trust. In particular, you should focus on *starting with the digital transformation strategy* as this is likely the most relevant aspect of the business strategy (and is more likely to have current documentation).

We do recommend that you work on getting clearer insights on your organization's business strategy in parallel as this adds clarity to your digital transformation and Zero Trust work.

### *An agile roadmap*

*"Plans are of little importance, but planning is essential."*

*– Winston Churchill*

One of the most critical elements of a strategy is a roadmap that lays out how to achieve that business vision. In today's world of constant change, that *roadmap must be agile* so that it can be adapted and changed as you learn.

*Figure 8.4* illustrates how this agile roadmap helps guide your organization in the short-, medium-, and long-term phases of a project:

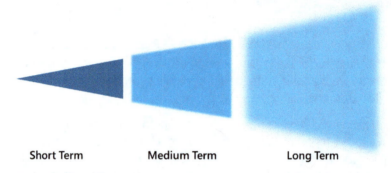

Short Term          Medium Term          Long Term

**Figure 8.4 – Short-, medium-, and long-term planning in an agile roadmap**

**What is an agile roadmap?** An agile roadmap is very clear in the short term and is more vague or fuzzy over time. An agile roadmap is designed to evolve with the continuously changing external environment (triggered by regular processes and significant external events). Let's take a closer look at this:

- **Short term**: Elements are defined very clearly with a high level of confidence that they will be achieved as planned.

- **Medium term**: Elements are still concrete but are defined in a more abstract manner. These are all attainable with work and prerequisites but have less confidence in the specifics of how and when they will be achieved.

- **Long term**: Elements are defined more aspirationally and with a much lower level of detail and confidence.

The exact requirements for how you define short, medium, and long term can vary with your organization's culture, industry, and other factors (such as urgency to act quickly after a recent security incident). To help frame your thinking, short-term objectives are typically measured in months (no more than 6 months), and long-term objectives are typically no more than 3 years out (and no shorter than 1 year).

The strategy (and the roadmap) should be expected to adjust to changing conditions. When goals and priorities change, we need to be able to adapt to that change. Often, this is simply reprioritizing what gets done earlier or later, but sometimes it involves new additions to the roadmap or taking something off entirely (for example, the organization shelved a project, so we don't need to protect *"xyz" technical capability* anymore). To deal with this kind of regular change, you need to set an expectation and build a process to handle both expected and unexpected roadmap updates.

*Most importantly, an agile roadmap is still a roadmap, with a vision and goal. It just adapts to changing conditions on a more frequent basis.*

---

**Microsoft – an example of agile roadmap planning in a cloudy world**

One example of agile roadmap planning you can take inspiration from is Microsoft's "semester" planning system. Microsoft uses this approach to structure agile development planning using 6-month intervals.

Development teams across Microsoft use this process to coordinate planning. Each team conducts its own individual semester planning exercise every 6 months to prioritize requirements and identify which work can be completed in the next semester versus what will be deferred to a later semester. Additionally, leaders from across all teams conduct joint planning exercises to coordinate work on joint projects and inter-team dependencies to ensure that everyone is delivering consistently as expected. These plans are regularly revisited by development teams throughout that 6-month period to make adjustments based on changes (typically reprioritizing existing tasks based on customer feedback or shifts in the competitive landscape).

The semester-planning process itself is also optimized and adjusted regularly based on what has been learned from previous semesters. 6 months may be too fast or too slow for some industries, but this real-world example helps get you thinking about how to make agile planning real.

---

## What does an agile roadmap mean in the context of Zero Trust?

A Zero Trust approach to the security of assets in a technical environment is fundamentally about protecting the assets you actually have against the actual threats to them (to the best of your ability). Security must constantly keep tabs on critical business assets as they are being created and changed, as well as tracking current and likely threats as they evolve. The roadmap with the planning and implementation of the appropriate security capabilities and controls simply evolves to reflect this new information as it comes in.

Two main themes you should keep in mind as you develop an agile roadmap for Zero Trust are as follows:

- **Build flexible core capabilities**: The Zero Trust capabilities you build should be flexible so that they can be used across many asset types, including inventory and access control, security operations (incident detection, response, and recovery), and governance.

- **Integrate security early**: Keep security teams plugged closely into application teams that are developing new assets in a DevOps/DevSecOps manner. This ensures new business capabilities meet current security standards when they release (and steadily improve with each iteration of those processes). This is sometimes called *shift left*—a reference to integrating security earlier into timelines.

Now that we understand what an agile roadmap looks like in the context of Zero Trust, let's see how the strategic process enables building this roadmap.

### Building a Zero Trust strategy

This process in *Figure 8.5* shows how to build a *Zero Trust strategy that is informed by and aligned with the business strategy*:

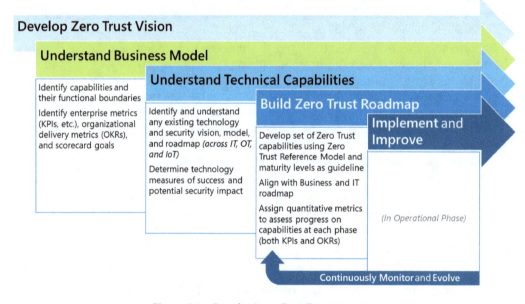

**Figure 8.5 – Developing a Zero Trust strategy**

The process of building out the strategic pillar is as follows:

1. **Develop a Zero Trust vision**: Aligned to the organization's vision, mission, and quantifiable goals. This helps you create a focused and measurable Zero Trust strategy.

2. **Understand business capabilities**: Identify your business capabilities and their functional boundaries (if they are not already defined) and map them to your Zero Trust capabilities. As described in *Figure 8.6*, Zero Trust capabilities are informed by and connected to business capabilities. Stakeholders in *both security and business teams* will need to understand these capabilities and their relationships with each other.

3. **Understand technical capabilities**: Identify your technical capabilities and their functional boundaries, then map them to your Zero Trust capabilities. As described in *Figure 8.6*, Zero Trust capabilities are informed by and connected to technology capabilities. You will need to ensure that stakeholders in *both security and technology teams* understand these capabilities and their relationships with each other.

   If you have an existing high-level enterprise technology capability map, it's critical to map these capabilities to it.

4. **Build a Zero Trust roadmap**: This phased roadmap lays out the journey to be followed in priority order. This is described in more detail in *Chapter 9, The Zero Trust Six-Stage Plan*.

5. **Implement and improve**: As the roadmap is implemented (*in the operational phase that follows*), you will inevitably learn about changes in the technical, business, and threat environments that require you to reprioritize projects or add, change, or remove projects on the roadmap.

---

**A quick reminder on capabilities**

This is a quick reminder of a critical concept and term that we introduced earlier. To provide goods or services, organizations must have *capabilities*—things such as being able to price a product, deliver a product or service, assess cybersecurity risk, detect a cybersecurity attack, or recover from a cybersecurity attack.

Defining capabilities allows us to abstract *what* the organization does away from *how* it does it (which can change over time and vary between organizations). This allows us to manage and improve an outcome consistently over time.

---

To summarize, the strategic phase brings together all the business and technical contexts to inform the Zero Trust capabilities (which also connect and unify those capabilities). The strategic process sets the direction and sets the organization up for success, as shown in *Figure 8.6*:

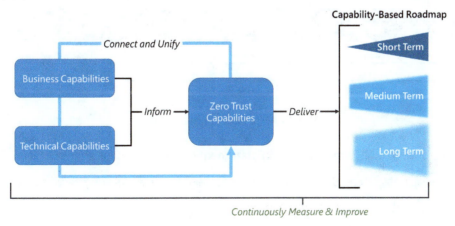

**Figure 8.6 – Strategic model**

**Business capabilities** and **technical capabilities** *inform* the Zero Trust capabilities of the organization. These **Zero Trust capabilities** are *delivered* over the **short, medium, and long term** with a **capability-based roadmap**.

*To be clear, Zero Trust very much starts with what you already have and builds on it to meet today's needs.*

As we deliver these capabilities, they are continuously measured, monitored, and improved in an agile manner. This ensures that we incorporate current top priorities and context, as opposed to sticking exactly to yesterday's plan that was made when we knew less and was based on priorities that often have evolved. This approach allows Zero Trust security to be agile and adaptable and stay aligned with evolving business, technical, security, and Zero Trust capabilities.

---

**Measuring how well you transform while you perform**

You should measure the ability of the organization to *rapidly adapt to the new environment* and how well you are *executing the transformation while continuing to operate* the current business.

We cover how to measure success with scorecards and other metrics later in multiple parts of the playbook.

---

## Acme example – strategic pillar

We are going to use an *Acme Bank* example to show how the strategic pillar comes together. *Acme Bank*'s workflow is described in *Figure 8.7*:

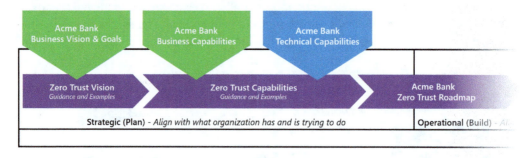

Figure 8.7 – Acme Bank's strategic pillar

First, *Acme* developed a **Zero Trust vision statement** based on its business vision:

*Zero Trust will enable Acme Bank to become a secure global retail banking services provider.*

Then, *Acme* developed a **Zero Trust mission statement** to apply that vision to *Acme's* mission:

*Zero Trust at Acme Bank will enable a "customer for life" model where customers can securely bank anywhere, while also allowing employees to securely work anywhere to support those customer needs.*

*Acme* then set aspirational business goals with clear **objectives and key results (OKRs)** to form its *Roadmap to the Digital Enterprise* initiative.

The business goals were as follows:

- **Goal**: Enable modern end-to-end experiences from anywhere:

  - **Objective**: Enable a *Securely Work Anywhere* initiative, with a long-term goal of supporting fluid hybrid work in perpetuity:

    - **Key result**: 80% of all employees will be able to work from anywhere in the US and European jurisdictions in 3 months, and globally in 6 months.

    - **Key result**: 99% of authentications will use strong authentication across employees, partners, vendors, and transitions between relationships.

  - **Objective**: Enabling a *Bank Anywhere* initiative to support a strong, agile global branding capability:

    - **Key result**: 70% of all customers can bank using any channel within 12-18 months.

- **Goal**: Enable sustainable growth given the volatility, increased risk, and cost:

  - **Objective**: Enable the ability to deliver *P2P* financial services globally:

    - **Key result**: 80% of all US and European systems will be able to support adaptive authentication to support global markets.

    - **Key result**: 90% of key **protected health information (PHI)**, **personally identifiable information (PII)**, or **personally identifiable financial information (PIFI)** data will support data tokenization in 1 year.

- **Goal**: Invest in infrastructure and support systems to enable and sustain this change:

  - **Objective**: Provide a global hybrid multi-cloud environment:

    - **Key result**: Migrate all core operations to a global hybrid multi-cloud model within 2 years, with 80% of applications hosted on cloud platforms.

- **Goal**: Develop a **continuous learning (CL)** culture to deal with continuous change:

  - **Objective**: Develop the skill sets required to support continuous change in a sustainable manner, establishing knowledge retention and frictionless operation:

    - **Key result**: Launch a skill set-enhancement program that supports incremental learning for all roles based on continuing professional education credits within 6 months.

  - **Objective**: Develop an agile enterprise value system that emphasizes security and rapid change:

    - **Key result**: Develop processes, education, governance, and communication to educate, promote, and communicate the organizational value system in 6 months.

    - **Key result**: Establish a culture of *assume compromise*, *verify explicitly*, and *least privilege* for security across all business functions within 6 months.

*Acme* identified key **business capabilities** required to support these goals, including deposits, risk management, fraud, payments and remittances, cards, and unsecured loans.

*Acme* also identified key **technical capabilities** required to support these goals, including building a microservice-enabled architecture that works across a hybrid multi-cloud platform.

Based on that business and technical context, *Acme* then designed key **Zero Trust capabilities** required to support these business goals based on the Zero Trust Reference Model. These included the following:

- **Adaptive access control** to provide centralized, consistent, and policy-based authentication and authorization across multiple jurisdictions (and their evolving compliance needs)

- **Data-centric protection** to ensure that **customer data** and **intellectual property (IP)** are consistently protected across technical environments

- **Security zones** to provide simplicity and consistency of protections to meet security goals and compliance requirements

*Acme* developed a phased **Zero Trust roadmap** to establish these capabilities over a 2-year period. This *Roadmap to the Secure Digital Enterprise* initiative is based on this playbook and tailored to *Acme*'s business goals, OKRs, and capabilities.

The roadmap helps *Acme* decide when and how each capability will be enabled, links it to business and technical capabilities, and helps the company understand how people and processes will be tied into operations and the operating model. The roadmap contains tangible actions associated with key business, technical, and Zero Trust objectives, metrics, and specific initiatives.

*Acme* plans to revisit the priorities in this roadmap every 3-6 months to ensure that they are still in alignment with its needs (competitive, technical, threat landscape, and so on).

## The operational pillar

The operational pillar focuses on the execution of the strategy to make it real in your current environment. This pillar focuses on how to integrate Zero Trust into your daily operations, organizational structure, business functions, and business processes:

**Figure 8.8 – The operational pillar**

Most organizations are not start-ups defining everything from scratch; they are running a successful business with everyday accountabilities (often including reporting earnings quarterly for public companies).

*Organizations can't stop production to do Zero Trust; they must operate daily and perform while they transform.* Organizations must continue producing products and services while simultaneously transitioning to the new approach in the Zero Trust (and digital transformation) strategy. For example, a shipping organization must operate a fleet of vehicles every day even while it is updating them.

This dual requirement means that you must understand how the organization provides goods and services so that you can keep it up and running while updating processes and technology. What is the organizational structure like? What are the business processes used to run the business? What are the teams, departments, divisions, and functional units that provide these services (business functions) every day?

### Security operations integration

Zero Trust influences several aspects of the operational environment. Operational disciplines also benefit from the Zero Trust approach in different ways.

> **The sprawling technical estate**
>
> The digital technical estate is constantly at risk of sprawling out of control, and technical teams are constantly managing this dynamic. The digital world makes it easy to copy and change any digital asset at incredible scale and speed (files, pictures, and so on), creating the potential for both rapid business growth and rapid growth of problems.
>
> While digital resources themselves are easy to copy, people and financial resources don't scale up as fast or as easily. Shifting to Zero Trust from classic models helps the organization get visibility and control of this sprawling estate so that assets aren't stolen or abused by hostile parties.

Two operation disciplines typically found in the security team are **security operations (SecOps)** and posture management. Let's look at them in more detail:

- **SecOps**: This security team performs rapid attack detection, response, and recovery (effectively the security equivalent of a firefighting organization). This reduces risk to the organization by reducing the time that attackers have access to your business assets, limiting their ability to inflict damage.

  A critical assumption of Zero Trust is that attackers can and will reliably penetrate a network perimeter. This assumption creates several specific requirements for a mature sec operations approach to manage this new reality. That's not to say that some of these may have already been adopted at your organization in response to evolving threats, technology platforms, and organizational processes.

  *Zero Trust implications for security operations include:*

  - **Origin and composition**: Security operations teams (aka SecOps or the SOC) are often one of the first security specialties to be created in an organization to handle alerts and active incidents. Depending on the size and maturity of the team, SecOps may also include proactive threat hunting (to find attacks that slipped past detections), **incident management** (**IM**, to manage non-technical aspects of major attacks), and **threat intelligence** (**TI**).

  - **Evolution of security technologies**: Assuming compromise in a Zero Trust approach requires SecOps to expand beyond traditional networking skill sets and tooling into other technologies (identity, endpoint, applications, data, and so on). This broadening of visibility is required to manage attacks on assets inside the corporate network and attacks outside the network perimeter (on cloud services mobile devices, and more).

    Some organizations have already begun the process of diversifying data sources and skills, which gives them a head start on Zero Trust. Rapidly and reliably containing attacks on any business assets before damage spreads requires fully adopting Zero Trust capabilities described in *Chapter 4*, *Standard Zero Trust Capabilities*, and in the playbook for security operations roles.

- **Integration with other operations teams**: Assuming compromise in a Zero Trust approach also requires SecOps to integrate with other operational teams to provide effective coverage across key business stakeholders (legal, communications, human resources, and so on) and the technical estate (IT operations, DevOps, and **operational technology (OT)** operations teams). Some organizations have already begun this process in response to changes in the technology estate, technology release cadence, and threat landscape—Zero Trust embraces and builds on cross-team integrations you already have in place.

- **Metrics maturity**: Zero Trust also requires security operations success metrics to be aligned with the business outcome of limiting the time attackers have access to the technical estate (for example, dwell time), often measured by **Mean Time to Remediate (MTTR)** after an incident.

  Organizations with a mature risk management approach may have already adopted similar success metrics, which gives them a head start on Zero Trust. Additional success metrics are discussed in the playbook for security operations roles.

- **TI**: Zero Trust requires SecOps to build or mature a TI capability to inform stakeholders around the company of current security threats and insights. This function is required to ensure that business leaders, technical leaders, architects, and practitioners are aware of current top threats so that they can make informed decisions appropriate to their role.

  Some organizations may have started building a TI capability to capture and share what they've learned, and some may have matured this capability to provide strategic insights (versus only tactical technical information). These will give organizations a head start on Zero Trust for security operations, which is discussed more in the playbook for security operations roles.

- **Security posture management**: This (new) security team is an active operational function of governance that actively monitors potential risk. This function reduces risk by finding virtual "holes" in the environment that attackers can use to gain access to business assets and inflict damage. They work closely with asset protection teams to plug these holes.

*Zero Trust implications for posture management include the following:*

- **Origin and composition**: Posture management teams are new and often created as part of a Zero Trust strategy. This function fuses together previously separate security functions, including vulnerability management and compliance auditing. This function is often created as a reaction to the availability of new tools that allow the **continuous monitoring (CM)** of potential risks (which can be exploited by an attacker). This long-desired capability only became practical recently with the advent of cloud tooling that provides on-demand insights across large portions of the technical estate.

---

**A close partnership**

SecOps and posture management teams are closely related functions that are distinct but must closely collaborate and communicate. These functions manage two different aspects of the same risk—posture management handles potential risk and preventive aspects of operations, while SecOps (or SOC) teams focus on rapid response to a realized risk.

This is similar to the relationship between firefighters (SecOps/SOC) and fire inspectors (posture management).

---

Security responsibilities also become integral to normal technology operations responsibilities and include the following:

- **Security asset protection**: This is the responsibility of teams in IT and **business units (BUs)** that manage technology assets (IT, OT, IoT, and DevOps) throughout their life cycle (deployment, uptime, maintenance, support, and so on). *The asset-centric nature of the Zero Trust strategy requires protecting assets wherever they are across their life cycle, which often requires changes.*

  *Zero Trust implications for asset protection include the following:*

  - **Integrating security with daily operations**: These teams in IT and BUs need to integrate security practices and teams into their processes. This helps prevent security incidents, quickly contain the risk of an active attack, and rapidly resume normal business operations. This involves updating metrics, processes, and tooling to ensure these teams can successfully integrate security into their mission.

  - **Prioritizing security maintenance**: The Zero Trust strategy assumes that attackers can and will get access to an organization's network, requiring each asset to be protected (rather than relying on the broken assumption that "attackers won't get onto the network"). This creates a requirement to prioritize the reliable execution of basic security hygiene elements to all assets throughout their life cycle. Basic security hygiene includes measures such as rapidly installing security updates/patches and applying recommended security configurations for both new and existing assets. If these security tasks are a low priority, the organization will experience more security incidents and more damage from each incident.

  - **Integrating security into infrastructure automation**: Security tasks should be integrated into automation processes, such as **Infrastructure as Code (IaC)**. Organizations are increasingly adopting these approaches to manage the cost and complexity of a technical estate that is continuously adding more assets and asset types. Integration of security and compliance tooling early helps prevent security issues and additional cost/complexity from retrofitting it later.

- **DevOps becomes DevSecOps**: Adding security to the DevOps process of creating and updating applications makes it DevSecOps. DevSecOps lowers cost and security friction because more security issues are found and fixed early in the process when it's cheap and easy to fix them (often called *shift left*). This requires teams that create and own assets to integrate security practices early in the development process. DevSecOps helps mitigate supply chain security risks such as those that affected SolarWinds in 2020.

---

**What are DevOps and DevSecOps?**

The classic IT model has separate teams for software **Dev**elopment and IT operations (**Ops**). Many organizations are on the journey to adopting a modern DevOps approach that fuses these into a single organizational function. Adding **Sec**urity makes it into **DevSecOps**.

---

*Integration is key to operations success*—a siloed approach to operations will not work. In future chapters, we take a deeper dive into operational dependencies, which roles are involved, and what each role does to enable the integration.

---

**Where is "security management"?**

The term *security management* (or information security management) is sometimes used to describe multiple operational and operating model disciplines that have a close relationship with **IT service management** (**ITSM**). We chose to break security management down into its core capabilities to increase clarity and actionability.

Security management is addressed by Zero Trust with the following:

- **Security governance** sets the security policy and standards in partnership with operational teams. This discipline also supports compliance-reporting activities for external requirements and internal policies and standards, includes security architecture, and has an emerging responsibility to collate and distribute strategic TI (high-level summaries of security threats) to stakeholders.

- **System asset protection** applies security policy and standards to system assets. This is typically performed by the IT, DevOps, and business-line teams that operate and manage the assets.

- **Posture management** ensures the policy is being followed and enables asset protection teams to be successful. These teams monitor dashboards and engage with various teams to help them execute the policy, identify challenges to meet the policy, and provide feedback to governance teams. The feedback could include context on noncompliance trends, suggestions on improving policies, identification of gaps in tooling or education, and so on.

Now that we understand the operational pillar of Zero Trust, let's see how to make this pillar real for your organization and industry.

### Tailoring is key to the operational pillar

While a Zero Trust strategy can be similar across different organizations, the operational pillar must be adapted to your organization. We need to understand the organization and how it operates to integrate Zero Trust successfully. We need to understand the unique products, business processes, business functions, and organizational structure.

We need to understand who is involved and the business functions they support. The following are some examples of different operational models:

- A **healthcare payer** (insurance company) works with patients, providers (doctors and nurses), and so on, providing business functions such as claims processing and provider credentialing.

- A **manufacturer** works with distributors, part suppliers, and raw material suppliers and then provides the design and assembly of parts, finished goods, or equipment. Manufacturers rely on OT such as **industrial control systems** (**ICSs**) to control physical processes.

- A **financial institution** works with individual consumers, corporate clients, and government regulators in the context of offering loans, investment services, advisory services, and so on.

We have included many *Acme* examples throughout the series to help you tailor Zero Trust to your organization.

### On business functions and business processes

For reference, **business functions** are the big elements of the business, such as *production*, *claims processing (in the case of insurance companies)*, or *sales*. These functions can also be further broken down as needed, such as breaking sales into *corporate sales* and *small business sales*. Each business function is typically associated with one or more **organizational units** (**OUs**) and a set of **business processes**.

For example, *sales* might have business processes such as *lead generation* and *deal closing*. Business processes can also cross business functions and organizational boundaries to deliver business services (providing customer feedback, updating pricing, and so on). *Figure 8.9* illustrates how business processes span across multiple business functions:

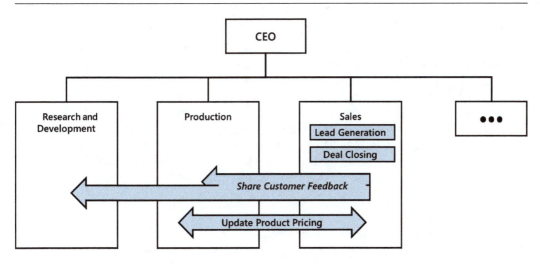

Figure 8.9 – Business functions and business processes

Now let's take a look at how to build the operational pillar.

## A process for building our operational pillar

*"Without strategy, execution is aimless. Without execution, strategy is useless."*

*– Morris Chang*

This process shows how to integrate your Zero Trust strategy into your existing operational environment:

1. **Determine your product model** to align the Zero Trust roadmap to products (goods and/or services) that your organization produces and the way you produce them.

2. **Determine business functions**, including the organizational structure, **standard operating procedures** (**SOPs**), and business processes in general. Business functions may sometimes be referred to as departments, divisions, units, or teams. While Zero Trust doesn't change what these are, it may impact the organizational structure and will probably modify business processes.

3. **Determine business processes** that run across the organizational structure and business functions to enable the production of goods and services. Zero Trust requires a high-level understanding of business processes as they are likely to be changed, modified, created, or automated during a digital transformation (sometimes multiple times).

> **Note**
>
> This is where **data and asset centricity** *significantly improve organizational agility and productivity*. Think about a business asset as a file with sensitive data that is protected wherever it goes (rather than relying on the security of every system that accesses it). Instead of having to revisit the security of every system that touches this file every time there is a process change, the data file simply stays secure the whole time. Zero Trust limits the effort required to be secure and the friction to adapt processes to new requirements, enabling teams to go faster and be more secure with less effort (and cost). This results in increased business agility and improved productivity of the business, enabling teams to work together toward a common goal instead of working against each other.

4. **Develop Zero Trust services and components**: Zero Trust introduces new services and components that will interact with existing technical services and components in the environment. As we develop the Zero Trust solution architecture, we define a set of core Zero Trust services and the components needed to enable them, which are then used across the technology estate to enable business processes.

   Some examples are provided as follows:

   - **Asset-centric architecture** ensures that all business assets have an identity to enable simple and flexible security decisions. This provides simplicity and clarity that both accelerates business agility and reduces organizational risk. Asset-centric architecture establishes identities, classifications, and/or labels for *all* business assets, including applications, data, users, devices, and so on that persist through their life cycle. This allows easy authoring and maintenance of policies that can keep up with the speed of business (changes in roles, asset sensitivity, business partnerships, vendor relationships, and so on).

   - **Adaptive access control** enables organizations to deal with the continuous evolution of relationships with partners and other entities in the digital ecosystem, and the volume of entities involved. It does this by using a policy-based model and supporting it with modern technologies such as AI to dynamically manage changes in an automated manner (including the business model, technology, and security threat/regulatory changes). Finally, it allows the automated self-service and self-registration of people and devices.

   - **Data centricity through rights management**: Enables organizations to protect existing sensitive documentation through their full life cycle. This reduces the risk of a data breach (because sensitive documents are always protected) and reduces the cost and effort of doing so (because you don't have to protect them in dozens of different ways across different systems).

- **Data-centricity support through tokenization services**: These reduce the number of copies of sensitive systems that the organization has to protect. Setting up a tokenization service allows data to be shared with reduced risk by replacing multiple copies of sensitive data with a reference to a single well-protected main copy of the sensitive data. This also empowers business, technology, and security teams dealing with agile delivery through dependency reduction (teams don't have to wait on other teams to update their encryption component or firewall, and so on) and becomes a huge enabler in frictionless evolution. As teams deal with different scenarios— **software as a service (SaaS)** providers, new partners and clients, entry into new business domains, or scenarios such as remote work and evolving organizational structures—this becomes a source of competitive advantage, reducing cost and risk and increasing agility.

- **Endpoint and application threat detection**: Organizations often develop components and services that enable security analysts to detect and clean up infections on computer operating systems (aka endpoints) and applications. As more and more teams develop websites and mobile applications to enable digital experiences, these development teams should use common Zero Trust components so that they don't have to build their own component (or operate without this basic security protection).

- **Privacy-by-design programs**: Organizations frequently develop a program to manage privacy in response to the constant flow of privacy regulations, such as the European Union's **General Data Protection Regulation (GDPR)**, the **California Consumer Privacy Act (CCPA)**, or Brazil's **Lei Geral de Proteção de Dados (LGPD)**.

Each of these operational pillar elements is described in much more detail later in the playbook.

### Acme example – operational pillar

*Acme* now transitions to operationalizing its roadmap and focusing on making it *actionable* to capture quick wins and make continuous incremental progress. This requires understanding the operational model of the business and mapping Zero Trust to it. *Figure 8.10* illustrates the operational pillar at *Acme Bank*:

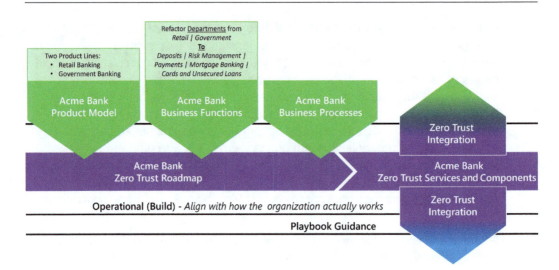

**Figure 8.10 – Acme Bank's operational pillar**

**For its product model**, *Acme*'s products (goods and services) are retail and government banking.

Currently, *Acme*'s **business functions** to support this product model are organized under retail banking and government banking, but *Acme* found this duplication of each capability slows down agility. As a part of its roadmap, *Acme* is reorganizing all departments against its business capabilities—deposits, risk management, payments, mortgage banking, cards, and unsecured loans—with each supporting both retail and government markets as appropriate via sub-capabilities.

*Acme*'s Zero Trust initiative is the security part of this roadmap and focuses on the early prioritization of the following:

- **Asset-centric architecture** to simplify *Acme*'s ability to apply policy across many individual assets, setting up a foundation for adaptive access control

- **Adaptive access control** capability to ensure strong access control for assets during regular and expected process changes

- **Data centricity** to simplify sharing data securely and reduce friction during the frequent evolution of business processes

- A centralized **privacy-by-design** capability to allow easy entry and access to new jurisdictions

**Zero Trust integration** changes *Acme*'s business processes:

- **Asset-centric architecture** creates a responsibility for *Acme* business leaders to identify business owners for its most valuable assets to determine risk and access policy. This ensures that the risk to these assets is understood and managed well by those who understand the impact of these business assets, rather than relying on security teams to protect all assets equally without context.

  *Acme* expects this will reduce the "blast radius" of damage and business impact for common attacks such as ransomware or **denial of service** (**DoS**). This is because *Acme*'s policy-based access will reduce the potential number of assets that can unnecessarily communicate with each other and be affected (similar to how reducing the amount of human contact limits the spread of a disease). Coupled with adaptive access control, this will also allow *Acme* flexibility to deal with an evolving digital ecosystem.

- **Data centricity** speeds up *Acme*'s partner onboarding for credit/debit card authentication because *Acme* no longer needs to share full copies of sensitive data to onboard a partner. It also significantly reduces the risk profile of the organization and makes compliance simple to implement, as the number of processes with sensitive data is reduced.

- **Adaptive access control**: *Acme* will build on the asset-centric architecture by implementing modern policy-based access control to provide flexibility and strong security that doesn't interrupt users and disrupt business processes.

  The policy-based enforcement provides the agility to keep up with the fluid evolution of business relationships—today's partner in a digital world might be tomorrow's subsidiary and then a competitor or client shortly after that.

  Adaptive access control also integrates silent security mechanisms, such as TI and **behavior analytics** (**BA**) to catch anomalies such as known bad locations, deviations from normal user behavior patterns, and connections using noncompliant or infected devices. Additionally, *Acme* is adopting strong authentication that provides strong (often **passwordless**) logins, which are both easier to use and more secure.

*Acme* focuses on *reusable* **Zero Trust services and components** that enable these capabilities for multiple business processes and functions. *Acme* is prioritizing the creation of an adaptive access control architecture, a data classification scheme, a token architecture and token service, a privacy-by-design service, and an asset-centric architecture.

When procuring and building these components and capabilities, *Acme Bank* will align these with different business functions so that changes in business processes and organizational structural impact are seamless. *Acme* will also map its current technology estate and security policies against industry standards such as the **SOA Reference Architecture** (**SOA RA**) standard and the Zero Trust Reference Model. This allows *Acme* to use existing infrastructure and industry standards to inform them on what to procure (or build), how it fits into current technology estates, and how it impacts the business.

This approach ensures that *Acme*'s Zero Trust initiatives are actionable and produce the desired and promised outcomes, ensuring the roadmap enables and secures *Acme Bank* in a world of continuous change.

---

**A mindset shift at Acme Bank**

*Acme* recognizes that this is a significant shift in mindset.

*Acme*'s current model is analogous to protecting a country's leader and their data by protecting their house (for example, the network) and restricting them to never leaving it.

*Acme* is focusing on shifting its mindset to the Zero Trust approach of *attaching security to the person and their data wherever they are and go*. This gives *Acme* the freedom to do business anywhere, *securely*.

---

## The operating model pillar

*"Bad companies are destroyed by crisis, good companies survive them, great companies are improved by them."*

*– Andy Grove*

You always have to steer the car as you go, no matter how well you have planned your journey. The operating model elements monitor and adjust the strategy and the execution as you go, keeping them aligned and on track, as shown in *Figure 8.11*:

Figure 8.11 – The operating model pillar

The operating model pillar *reflects and governs the way that the organization operates*. Zero Trust is an enterprise-level initiative that needs to be integrated into and harmonized with the organization's business operating model to be successful.

This starts with awareness—is the organization operating as a single monolithic organization? Or multiple independent subsidiaries? Or something in between?

A major change such as this also requires recognizing that it impacts more than just the literal business and technology capabilities; people change too. People make decisions and do the work, the processes they follow will keep the business going, and the organizational culture will guide decisions when people face a new or difficult situation.

The operating model elements of Zero Trust effectively provide the glue that holds Zero Trust together. These include the following:

- **Business operating models** control organizational focus and rhythms. These models determine funding, metrics, and support from senior leaders and mid-level management. Zero Trust initiatives don't often change the operating model but must discover it, understand it, and align it with how the organization actually works.

  You don't want to allow autonomy if the organization is one single entity (as that will fracture the strategy and execution). You also don't want to waste effort trying to impose control across autonomous BUs (which can and will choose to ignore you when they want, regardless of how hard you try).

- **Governance** lays out the guardrails to keep people on track, enabling them to work together seamlessly. Governance determines decision rights (who makes which decisions) and lays out process frameworks to connect teams and guide how they work and interact with each other. The governance process frameworks operate at strategic, team, and practitioner levels in the organization.

  *Figure 8.12* shows how these governance process frameworks tie together:

Figure 8.12 – Different parts of a Zero Trust governance process framework

- **Cultural norms** create a CL organization by establishing learning processes and instilling values into the organizational culture. You must ensure that your organization's cultural framework establishes and reinforces a shared value of CL. A CL culture is critical to agility as it enables people to acquire the right skill sets as they go while executing efficiently.

  *Without a culture that reinforces the importance of a value, policies and rules will always fall by the wayside and fail.*

Because of the disruptive nature of Zero Trust and digital transformation, we must ensure people have clarity on this new (and potentially unfamiliar) cultural norm. Reinforce the message and signal its importance by delivering and modeling it consistently on all channels—in processes, metrics, the wording you choose in team meetings, and so on.

The following diagram describes the points in the business operating model where you integrate measures such as governance to sustain Zero Trust:

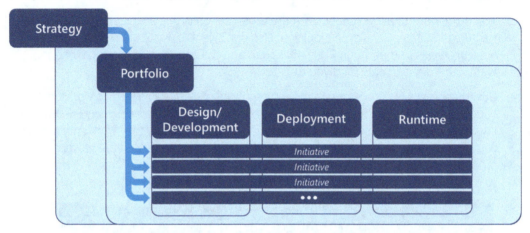

Figure 8.13 – Zero Trust operating model process

Strategy influences the whole organization, the portfolio applies to all initiatives, and then each initiative includes a design/development, deployment, and runtime (ongoing operations) phase.

Let's look at an *Acme* example to illustrate how to apply these Zero Trust operating model elements in the real world.

### Acme example – operating model pillar

How does *Acme Bank* weave in Zero Trust and become a CL organization across the whole enterprise? *Figure 8.14* illustrates the operating model pillar at *Acme Bank*:

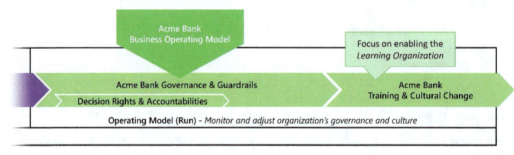

Figure 8.14 – Acme Bank's operating model pillar

First, the leadership assessed the current **business operating model** and determined that they currently have a *unified model* enterprise with a single unified enterprise approach across all business lines in the organization.

The unified model means that all stakeholders (including the IT and business organizations) must undertake a common journey and work together as a single organization. This also influences all technology decisions (such as component reuse, infrastructure purchases, and so on).

A key enabler and success criterion for an enterprise Zero Trust initiative is the development of a framework for **governance and guardrails**. (Note that some organizational cultures favor the use of the term *guardrails* instead of *governance* to signal a proactive empowerment approach to oversight.) Governance and guardrails permeate people, processes, and technology—laying the foundation for people to work together, for risk to be managed, and for changes to be well understood.

*Acme* started its Zero Trust governance framework by capturing **decision rights and accountabilities**—which is effectively a modern agile approach to what was once handled by a **Responsible/Accountable/Consulted/Informed** (**RACI**) framework. *Acme* started with existing business decision makers in control of business assets, functions, and business processes, then added Zero Trust-specific decision owners.

The governance framework also includes the organizational structure for Zero Trust and guardrails for the following:

- *Strategic process model* covering strategic processes (such as developing and maintaining the roadmap)
- *Operational processes* for things that are in use (including IT operations and security operations)
- *Development processes* to ensure the reuse of Zero Trust components

Concurrently, *Acme* is moving toward establishing a CL organization through **training and cultural change**. *Acme* decided to build on its existing training infrastructure but pivoted to preferring **Massive Open Online Courses** (**MOOCs**) and favoring **just-in-time** (**JIT**) training over prescheduled courses when possible. *Acme* also focused on gamification and rewarding continuing professional education rather than static qualification and certification approaches. *Acme* also defined, funded, and staffed an internal **communication plan** that detailed communication vehicles (webinars, podcasts, and so on) and ensured Zero Trust communications are done on a recurrent, consistent basis.

*Acme*'s leaders also hold themselves accountable for CL using those same courses, and *Acme Bank* executives are encouraged to publicly discuss their own mistakes and learnings during this transformation to give "social permission" for everyone in the organization to do the same.

Finally, *Acme* is extending the organizational core values to include a **Zero Trust value system** that integrates concepts such as *least privilege*, *assume compromise*, and *verify explicitly* into the organizational thinking, language, and metrics, such as performance reviews.

In summary, the operating model keeps *Acme*'s Zero Trust strategy and execution (operations) on track. This is done by integrating Zero Trust into the business operating model and governance mechanisms and by reinforcing a culture of CL.

## Stitching it all together with the Zero Trust Playbook

Now that we have all three pillars of the model, we can put them together and move forward on making it real at scale. We now implement *sustainable and effective* Zero Trust capabilities that all fit together in an actionable, living, breathing strategy—the *Zero Trust Playbook*.

We will next look at the overall system of three interconnected pillars and their individual components. We will introduce the six-stage plan in *Chapter 9*, *The Zero Trust Six-Stage Plan*, and then proceed to build it throughout the rest of the playbook.

*Figure 8.15* describes each playbook component and how they all flow together, much like a blueprint describes all aspects of a building's architecture:

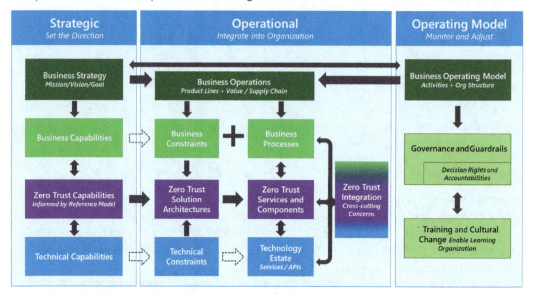

Figure 8.15 – Zero Trust Playbook overall components and relationships

This diagram explains the relationships in the overall system:

- Each of the dark green boxes at the top of the pillars represents an existing business element of the organization, the *business strategy*, *business operations*, and *business operating model*.

- In the **strategic** pillar, *business capabilities* and *technical capabilities* align with and support the business strategy. The *Zero Trust capabilities* you define (starting with The Open Group Zero Trust Reference Model) provide modern digital era security to *business capabilities* and *technical capabilities*, linking them together. Note that existing technical security capabilities are included in *technical capabilities*.

- In the **operational** pillar, *business operations* are informed by the *business strategy* and *business operating model* from the other pillars:

  - In the left column of this pillar, the *business constraints* you operate under are informed by *business capabilities* (in the strategic pillar) and are aligned to *business operations*.

    *Technical constraints* are informed by *technical capabilities* (in the strategic pillar).

    The *Zero Trust solution architecture* is built based on *Zero Trust capabilities*, *business constraints*, and *technical constraints*.

  - In the right column of this pillar, business operations come to life as *business processes* (*and business functions*), while the *technology estate* reflects *technology constraints*. *Zero Trust services and components* are hosted in the *technology estate* and interact with *business processes*.

  - The *Zero Trust integration* drives cross-cutting changes in *business processes*, the *technical estate*, and *Zero Trust services and components*.

- In the **operating model** pillar, *governance* and *guardrails* keep Zero Trust on track, critical components of which are *decision rights and responsibilities*, which ensure clear ownership of decisions. *Training and culture change* helps support *governance* and *guardrails* and drives the transformation to a learning organization.

## Zero Trust integration drives changes

*Zero Trust integrations* are how *Zero Trust services and components* realize value from Zero Trust investments. This integration drives cross-cutting efforts that ensure Zero Trust services and components become a normal part of business processes, business functions, and the technology estate of the organization. "Cross-cutting" concerns are those that span several of these elements (processes, functions, and technical services) within the organization:

- **Adaptive access example**: Take an example such as modern policy-based adaptive access control that explicitly validates the trust of the user account and the device before allowing access to assets. This *Zero Trust service* has potential value, but that value isn't realized until it is integrated into the technical estate and business processes. *Once it has been integrated*, this service increases security and enables *ease of doing business*—the organization can easily add new partners and customers, employees can easily and securely work from home, and policies can be easily modified and updated as risks and threats change.

- **Data tokenization example**: Another example is a data tokenization service that allows you to reduce the number of copies of sensitive data (such as PII) that you have to track, secure, and report on. This is comparable to using a token for playing video games at an arcade instead of actual cash—you are less worried about the token getting stolen because using that token requires coming back to your systems to use it. Once this is used widely as a *Zero Trust integration*, you will have fewer copies of data to secure, so there will be a lower impact of breaches (reducing blast radius), and your application development and partner onboarding will be much faster and more agile because of the drastic reduction in security and compliance work.

You should target Zero Trust integrations consistently across most or all application and system architectures in the technology estate and business operational model. This creates concrete and measurable value as organizations fully realize value from Zero Trust capabilities such as asset and data centricity, adaptive asset management, and security zones.

We will expand on this further in later chapters of the playbook.

## Summary

In this chapter, we learned about the three pillars of the playbook and how they enable security agility and security integration with the organization's business and technical priorities and processes. We learned about how the strategic roadmap is formed and the context that goes into it, how the operational pillar implements this roadmap, and how the operating model allows you to monitor and adjust Zero Trust to keep it on track.

Next up is *Chapter 9, The Zero Trust Six-Stage Plan*, which describes the six-stage approach that resolves the three pillars into specific implementation stages and prescriptive actionable steps to coordinate the overall journey across roles. The role-by-role guidance in the playbook translates these into the language and culture of each role, outlining changes with Zero Trust and what the resulting daily tasks and routine look like for each role.

# The Zero Trust Six-Stage Plan

*Vision without execution is just dreaming.*
*Execution without vision is just chaos.*

Now that we have a clear picture of Zero Trust and the three-pillar model that integrates it into your organization, let's map out the journey in more detail.

In this chapter, you will learn about the six-stage plan the playbooks use to guide the planning and rollout of Zero Trust to the whole organization. These stages enable you to build, sustain, and continuously improve Zero Trust.

These stages help you avoid common causes of project failure by ensuring all the right stakeholders in the organization are involved at the right time and have the right context to make decisions. This helps avoid waste and confusion that result from not having critical context (or from being overwhelmed with too much irrelevant detail). The six-stage plan provides a central reference point that enables people to clearly understand what will be done, why it needs to be done, when it will be done, who will do it, and how it is supposed to work.

This chapter includes the following topics:

- **Overview of the six-stage plan**, introducing the overall approach and a summary of each stage
- **The playbook stages in detail**, including steps for each stage, key stakeholders, and a description of each step:
  - **Stage 1 – Establish a strategy**
  - **Stage 2 – Set up an operating model**
  - **Stage 3 – Create the architecture and model**
  - **Stage 4 – Tailor to the business**
  - **Stage 5 – Implement and improve**
  - **Stage 6 – Continuously monitor and evolve**

> **Getting closer to launch!**
>
> We are nearing the end of the first book, which acts like a big kickoff meeting to get all the stakeholders on the same page. Once we all understand the six stages in this chapter, we will learn about the roles-based approach in the next (and final) chapter and move on to the playbooks that guide our execution!

The six-stage approach blends the best of agile approaches with the best of traditional strategic planning. This enables flexibility and speed without losing focus on the end-to-end transformation by combining short-term immediate action with long-term strategic direction.

This will help security teams transform into full partners of business teams throughout the six stages, naturally integrating security into business processes. This process enables security to become agile and support an agile business that is continuously evolving to meet changing business needs.

Now, let's learn about the six-stage plan that will be used throughout the Zero Trust playbook series.

## Overview of the six-stage plan

Now, it's time to lay out the stages that are used throughout the playbooks. These stages guide the end-to-end implementation of Zero Trust, much like a building project plan helps plan the order of executing tasks (for example, pouring concrete foundations first, then framing the building, then the electrical wiring and plumbing, and so on).

The six-stage process establishes a solid foundation of Zero Trust based on proven architectures that are also tailored to your organization's unique needs and business operating model. The process also enables you to involve the right stakeholders across the organization, ensuring you have diverse internal perspectives involved to sidestep avoidable challenges and common miscommunications. This inclusive approach carefully balances standard approaches and your unique organizational needs to set you up for success with Zero Trust.

*Figure 9.1* shows the six stages overlaid over the playbook components described in the previous chapter:

These six stages will be used throughout the playbooks to guide the Zero Trust initiative:

- **Stage 1 – Establish a strategy**: This first stage gets the Zero Trust initiative pointing in the right direction. It starts with orienting **Zero Trust** to the context of where we are by discovering the *business strategy* and developing a Zero Trust strategy with a *mission*, *vision*, and *goals* that complement it. Next, we learn about the existing *business capabilities* and *technical capabilities* so that we can define our *Zero Trust capabilities* that build on and connect them. This process is also informed by the current *business operating model* (how the business works day to day) so that Zero Trust will be successful when it lands.

*Stage 1* also defines the goals, objectives, and key results that will be used to measure the progress and impact of the Zero Trust strategy overall.

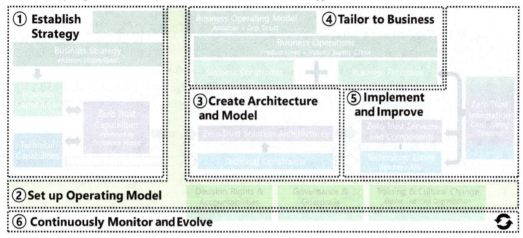

Figure 9.1 – Overview of Zero Trust playbook implementation stages

- **Stage 2 – Set up an operating model**: The next stage is to define an operating model to manage Zero Trust that aligns with your *business operating model*. This operating model includes the definition of *decision rights and accountabilities* so that it's clear who makes what decisions. This stage also sets up the *governance and guardrails*, which set the rules and policies for Zero Trust across the organization.

  The final part of the operating model enables focusing on the *human empathy* critical success factor, which we discussed in *Chapter 7, What Zero Trust Success Looks Like*. This introduces a *learning and experimentation* element to your culture and a sense of a unified organization. This empowers everyone to navigate the continuous flow of challenges and unfamiliar situations that they will face with continuous transformation. This also allows people in your organization to work together across teams in an agile way, which is critical to success for continuous transformation.

  The training and cultural element also enables people in the organization to answer *what* changes Zero Trust brings, *why* these are important, and *how* they are expected to support it. When the answers to these are clear, Zero Trust becomes real and teams are inspired to share ideas and plan improvements to their daily work experience and productivity.

- **Stage 3 – Create the architecture and model**: Next, we plan the foundational Zero Trust capabilities for the organization. This stage establishes the core *Zero Trust solution architectures* based on the *Zero Trust Reference Model* from The Open Group (cited throughout the playbook series). Because this will be implemented in the current technical environment, we align it to the *technical constraints* of the platforms and technologies in use (based on the technical capabilities discovered in *Stage 1*). This stage also establishes key required operational disciplines for security (or updates them for Zero Trust).

- **Stage 4 – Tailor to the business**: After planning the foundational components of Zero Trust, we integrate and align them in finer detail. This ensures Zero Trust is normalized into day-to-day operations and adjusted to your organization's unique needs. In this stage, the models and architectures are tailored to the unique *business constraints* and *business processes* in your organization's *business operating model* and *business operations*.

- **Stage 5 – Implement and improve**: Now that we have the full context of the business and technical environments, we can plan and build the specific *Zero Trust services and components* without fear of being tripped up by something big we should have expected. This stage is when Zero Trust goes live and is available in the organization's *technology estate*. This may require small adjustments to the plan as we implement and learn new things.

  The most significant aspect is the *Zero Trust integration* of the services and components with business processes that drive cross-cutting changes in business processes and the technical estate. *This integration is what enables Zero Trust to create value for the organization by changing it for the better.*

- **Stage 6 – Continuously monitor and evolve**: Zero Trust must continuously evolve like any other part of your dynamic organization, even if the initial project team has moved on to something else. Monitoring for changing requirements and making adjustments is primarily done through governance and guardrails. The *training and cultural change* enables an overall learning organization and provides critical cultural foundations to support this ongoing change, giving everyone permission to see the changing needs and propose changes to meet them. The well-defined *decision rights and accountabilities* provide clarity to help you quickly identify owners and approvers for any needed changes.

*Figure 9.2* shows which elements are addressed by each stage:

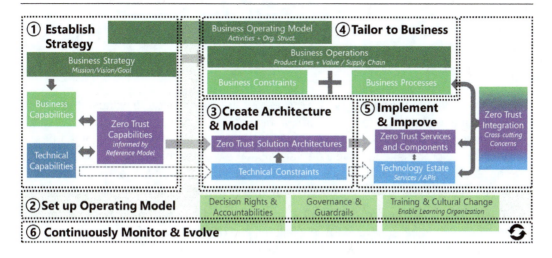

Figure 9.2 – Detailed view of Zero Trust playbook implementation stages

Now, let's talk about using the playbook approach.

## Using the playbook stages effectively

To help you use the six-stage approach, we will provide tables later in this chapter to break down each stage into more granular steps. Each step includes a description and a list of the stakeholders involved. This creates a concise summary of the playbook approach that you can reference quickly as needed.

**The order matters**. When executing, we strongly recommend the order presented for building the various elements. This ideal ordering for Zero Trust work will guide organizations of all sizes, up to and including large global organizations. We have carefully balanced rapid execution and value realization while ensuring the key dependencies are in place before they are required.

Your organization can still get value if teams skip ahead or build individual projects without cross-organizational support, but you won't be able to realize the full benefits of Zero Trust without the larger framework in place. This recommended ordering is based on decades of experience of what consistently works well (and what doesn't) in large initiatives such as Zero Trust.

## Key concepts

Before we get into the details, let's explicitly define a couple of critical concepts that are used in the playbooks:

- **Minimum viable product** (**MVP**): Throughout the playbooks, we will use the MVP technique to start with the minimum viable version of any playbook element. This approach enables your team to both learn fast (maximize the amount of learning early in the process) and rapidly deliver value. We will use this approach throughout the playbooks for both strategy and implementation, applying it to the overall strategy roadmap and individual capabilities and initiatives as well.

- **The learning organization**: This describes an approach where everyone in the organization shares a cultural assumption to view failures and obstacles as opportunities to learn and improve. Digital transformation, cloud transformation, and Zero Trust all require adopting this mindset of continuous learning and improving the people and processes in an organization.

This mindset becomes real through the following aspects:

- **Human empathy**: As described in *Chapter 7, What Zero Trust Success Looks Like*, this is where leaders evangelize new behaviors and publicly practice them for all to see.

- **Organizational processes**: These ensure learning is actively captured in documentation, institutional knowledge, and process changes instead of being lost or forgotten.

- **Learning systems and processes**: These aspects enable and encourage on-demand continuous learning. They are typically structured in small, bite-sized learning experiences that use modern techniques such as gamification to increase engagement, enjoyment, and retention.

We will use *the learning organization* throughout the playbooks to describe an organization that has integrated this mindset into its culture.

## Agile delivery and the playbooks

Agile delivery and processes are being extensively adopted across industries today, and they are often associated with the *modern digital enterprise*. These processes can vary widely by organization as the playbooks are not tied to any specific process methodology. Additionally, some organizations still follow *waterfall* approaches (or quasi-waterfall) due to culture, compliance, or business drivers. How does this playbook series blend the best of agile and waterfall processes to drive a Zero Trust outcome?

Let's take a look:

- **A roadmap, but an agile roadmap**: The roadmap created by the six-stage approach is built on a capability-metric-culture approach that allows for both clear direction and flexibility. It has a process model (which should be tailored to fit an organization's delivery model) and lays out an approach that provides high levels of confidence in the short term, a reasonable level of confidence in the mid-term, and a general high-level direction for the long term. This gives clear, actionable direction for multiple teams while simultaneously enabling the organization to adapt and change using periodic roadmap reviews.

- **The playbook stages have a logical relationship between stages**: This structure helps create agility by ensuring that efforts to address immediate priorities will constantly move the organization forward to the North Star ideal end state. Some of these stages don't change as frequently as others – for example, governance frameworks, business operating models, and capabilities evolve at a slower rate.

- **Roadmap time frames can be adapted**: Some organizations may have very mature agile processes and delivery teams that run through all roadmap phases every 6 to 12 months. Others may have 1- to 2-year roadmaps. The length of your roadmap will depend on the organization's operating model and drivers (business, technical, security, Zero Trust, regulatory, and other unknown disruptive drivers). You can and should tailor the time frames to your organization or ecosystem.

- **The playbooks integrate agility into the implementation**: Stages 3, 4, and 5 may often be rapidly iterated through as we implement what was developed in stages 1 and 2. Stage 6 will be a continuous process of iterations, again based on the organization and the environment it is in. Digital organizations are continuous learning organizations that are continuously evolving, and Zero Trust supports just that – the ability to keep updating to meet that evolving digital environment.

- **The playbooks provide tailoring guidance with examples**: Each playbook will take a deeper look at how the stages are implemented and provide a how-to guide for tailoring them to your organization.

**Avoid analysis paralysis and overengineering**

One antipattern to avoid is teams falling into an *analysis paralysis* trap, which happens when they're trying to engineer the *perfect* solution for each stage (often because teams fear they can never change it once launched). The playbooks avoid this by integrating an iterative approach into the dynamic roadmap, operating model, and other processes to ensure that agility, continuous adaptation, and continuous learning are normalized. This reduces wasted time and resources on overengineering and avoids approaches that will run against the organization's operating model (and are more likely to fail). The iterative process frees teams up to use agile approaches to validate decisions and the roadmap as they go, without looking for the *perfect* solution that may not exist or be visible with the information available during planning.

*Always ensure that teams understand the operating model, the operating environment, and drivers so that they can best determine what is "good enough" for each iteration.*

# The playbook stages in detail

The following tables explain the steps in each stage and who owns and drives them. These tables provide a detailed view of the end-to-end journey. The playbooks resolve these into role-specific details and guidance to provide full clarity for each role. *Chapter 10, Zero Trust Playbook Roles*, provides an illustrative reference for these roles and the guidance that is provided for each role.

## Stage 1 – Establish a strategy

The first stage sets you up for overall success – defining a clear vision and direction, laying out the plan and prioritized roadmap to achieve it, and getting buy-in from senior stakeholders across the organization. This ensures everyone is moving in the same direction so that different teams aren't working against each other.

Here are the steps in this stage:

1. Develop a Zero Trust vision.
2. Understand the business capabilities.
3. Understand the technical capabilities.
4. Finalize the Zero Trust capabilities.
5. Build the Zero Trust roadmap.

*Table 9.1* takes a look at these steps in more detail:

| Playbook Step | Who | Description |
|---|---|---|
| **Stage 1 – Establish a strategy** | | |
| **Develop a Zero Trust vision** | • Organizational senior leaders (especially Business, Risk, and Compliance leaders)<br><br>• Technology senior leaders (especially Security, Risk, and Technology /IT leaders) | *This step establishes the vision that will guide all other Zero Trust work.*<br><br>**Security leaders** own the Zero Trust vision and author this with input from their teams. The leadership playbook includes guidance and examples.<br><br>**Business leaders** provide ownership, engagement, input, and alignment on the changes and impact on the business. They lay out the guardrails from a business perspective and define the business impact in terms of opportunity and returns.<br><br>**Technical leaders** provide input on the impact on technology domains, vision, and roadmap.<br><br>To ensure broad awareness and buy-in, the vision, mission, and goals should be reviewed by leaders across the technology and business leadership of the organization. |
| **Understand the business capabilities** | • Organizational senior leaders<br><br>• Technology senior leaders<br><br>• Architects (especially enterprise architects if present) | *This step captures the business capabilities that the Zero Trust capabilities align with.*<br><br>Security leadership performs a business capability assessment to capture insights into the business capabilities of business leaders. This often requires gathering input from business leaders and collating the capabilities into a single capability-based view of the organization. The final product should be reviewed, validated, and approved by the business leaders of the organization.<br><br>This assessment will typically include a capability map – for Zero Trust, this is usually limited to a high-level document. An organization's enterprise architecture and business leadership team may take this deeper and define a full business landscape, but that is not normally necessary for Zero Trust. |

| Playbook Step | Who | Description |
|---|---|---|
| **Stage 1 – Establish a strategy** | | |
| **Understand the technical capabilities** | • Security leaders<br>• Technology leaders<br>• Enterprise architects (if present) | *This step captures the technical capabilities that Zero Trust capabilities will build on and integrate with.*<br><br>Security leaders should collaborate with technical leaders to jointly assess the technical capabilities. Because IT and security teams often don't collaborate closely, this activity should be used to start catalyzing collaborative relationships. The discovery process must explicitly include both IT capabilities and security capabilities, and the output should be shared across *both IT and security teams*.<br><br>The technical capability assessment will typically include a capability map and a high-level technology landscape. For Zero Trust, this is usually limited to a high-level document.<br><br>The capability assessment should use a standard document. Standards such as **The Open Group Reference Architecture Standard** should be used to leverage a common, shared definition of capabilities (Acme examples are included throughout the playbooks) to both accelerate the process and start from an accepted industry understanding. An organization's enterprise architecture and business leadership may take this deeper and define a detailed landscape, but that is not normally necessary for Zero Trust. |

| Playbook Step | Who | Description |
|---|---|---|
| Stage 1 – Establish a strategy | | |
| **Finalize the Zero Trust capabilities** | • Organizational senior leaders (especially risk and compliance)<br><br>• Technology senior leaders (especially security and technology leaders)<br><br>• Architects (especially security and enterprise architects if present) | *This step defines the Zero Trust capabilities that will be integrated into business processes and the technology estate.*<br><br>Security leaders and their teams identify and finalize the organization's Zero Trust capabilities with risk leaders, compliance leaders, and enterprise architects (if present). This should start with The Open Group Zero Trust Reference Model, which defines high-level industry-standard Zero Trust capabilities.<br><br>Note: The Zero Trust capabilities are composed of Zero Trust components and services defined later in the architecture. |

| Playbook Step | Who | Description |
|---|---|---|
| Stage 1 – Establish a strategy | | |
| **Build the Zero Trust roadmap** | • Organizational senior leaders<br>• Technology senior leaders<br>• Architects (especially security and enterprise architects if present)<br>• Managers | *This step defines the Zero Trust roadmap, which identifies which Zero Trust capabilities are in scope, which will be delivered first, and how each will be integrated into business and technical capabilities.*<br><br>This roadmap is executed in phases aligned with the organization's business operating model and release cycles and focuses on identifying the MVP for each capability and initiative. Each phase establishes a Zero Trust capability, enhances an existing one until a target level of maturity is reached, or integrates one with business or technology processes. The impact of these goals should be quantifiable and measurable as **key performance indicators** (**KPIs**) or **objectives and key results** (**OKRs**) and captured in the roadmap.<br><br>The roadmap phases are in a high-level, prioritized order for capabilities and initiatives, balancing quick wins and incremental progress while establishing foundational dependencies first.<br><br>Each initiative in the roadmap includes estimates for associated resources, risks, dependencies, and metrics. It also identifies targeted key results for each Zero Trust capability and KPIs for each phase.<br><br>The implementation of the roadmap extends through the *implement and improve* stage.<br><br>This is ideally built by security architects and managers in close partnership with business and technical managers (and enterprise architects if present). This is sponsored and approved by security, business, and technology leadership.<br><br>In a smaller organization without those formal roles, you can get IT architects, technical managers, or technology leaders to coordinate and author these in partnership with technical teams. |

**Table 9.1 – Stage 1 – Establish a strategy**

## Stage 2 – Set up an operating model

This stage ensures that Zero Trust is aligned with how your organization works. This sets you up for success and proactively clears potential obstacles for Zero Trust in your organization's culture, governance, and operating model.

Here are the steps in this stage:

1. Determine your business operating model.
2. Develop your governance framework.
3. Develop your cultural change and skillset development.

*Table 9.2* covers these steps in detail:

| Playbook Step | Who | Description |
|---|---|---|
| Stage 2 – Set up an operating model | | |
| **Determine your business operating model** | • Organizational senior leaders<br><br>• Technology senior leaders<br><br>• Architects (especially security, enterprise, and business architects)<br><br>• Enterprise security integration (deputy CISOs and staff, security [business] analysts) | *This step captures the business operating model that you will use to focus and prioritize your strategy, governance framework, and policies.*<br><br>This is owned by security leaders and involves security analysts, business architects, and business leaders.<br><br>This should include discovering how your business operates as well as the risk management framework your organization uses to govern it.<br><br>Note: Remember that the roadmap will need to be updated so that it aligns with the business operating model. |

| Playbook Step | Who | Description |
|---|---|---|
| **Stage 2 – Set up an operating model** | | |
| **Develop your governance framework** | • Organizational senior leaders<br><br>• Technology senior leaders<br><br>• Architects (especially security, enterprise, and business architects)<br><br>• Enterprise security integration (security [business] analysts) | *This step builds a governance framework to guide your Zero Trust operating model that is aligned with your business operating model.*<br><br>This framework provides the organizational glue that holds everything together, including these key components:<br><br>• Organization structure<br><br>• Process model<br><br>• Goals<br><br>• Principles<br><br>• Policies<br><br>This is usually owned by the security leaders and built by business architects with the support of security architects and analysts. Enterprise architects are involved in embedding and weaving elements of the governance framework into the organization's technology delivery governance framework. |

| Playbook Step | Who | Description |
|---|---|---|
| Stage 2 – Set up an operating model | | |
| **Develop your cultural change and skillset development** | • Organizational senior leaders (including **human resources (HR)** and business)<br><br>• Technology senior leaders<br><br>• Enterprise security integration (deputy CISOs and staff, security [business] analysts)<br><br>• Architects (especially security architects)<br><br>• Adjacent roles (business analyst, trainers, and internal readiness and communications teams if present) | *This step identifies the required organizational culture changes and plans how to implement them.*<br><br>This step builds on your understanding of the business operating model.<br><br>This includes the following:<br><br>• Assessing your business culture and value system<br><br>• Assessing who needs training for technology, business processes, and more<br><br>• Developing a plan to implement this change<br><br>The resulting plan usually includes elements such as the following:<br><br>• Setting OKRs for teams<br><br>• Setting goals in the employee performance review process (including senior executives to model the behavior)<br><br>• Establishing a training plan (including a continuous process for sustainment)<br><br>• Establishing a communications plan (including a continuous process for reinforcement)<br><br>This is owned by security leaders and supported by other roles. The entire organization is impacted, and hence business leaders and technology leaders must support this. |

**Table 9.2 – Stage 2 – Set up an operating model**

Next, we are ready to plan the architecture and processes.

## Stage 3 – Create the architecture and model

This stage creates the specific plan that will guide the technical and business teams, ensuring that architecture, processes, and daily operations establish all the needed components for Zero Trust.

The following are the steps in this stage:

1. Develop your Zero Trust solution architecture.
2. Develop your policies and procedures for Zero Trust.
3. Establish Zero Trust operations.

*Table 9.3* covers these steps in detail:

| Playbook Step | Who | Description |
|---|---|---|
| Stage 3 – Create the architecture and model | | |
| **Develop your Zero Trust solution architecture** | • Technology senior leaders (especially security, risk, and compliance)<br>• Architects (security, technology, and enterprise architects if present) | *This step builds the tailored Zero Trust model and architecture for the enterprise.*<br><br>This step translates the reference model and architecture into concrete and actionable documents for your organization. You will tailor the reference documents to the organization's technical estate and map the capabilities to formulate a Zero Trust solution architecture. This is a fundamental part of what is done through the operational pillar, and we will lay out a detailed process in the playbooks.<br><br>This task is done by security architects and will involve technology architecture. |

| Playbook Step | Who | Description |
|---|---|---|
| **Stage 3 – Create the architecture and model** | | |
| **Develop your policies and procedures for Zero Trust** | • Risk and compliance roles (risk team, compliance team) | *This step builds the Zero Trust policies and procedures for your Zero Trust initiative.*<br><br>The Zero Trust policies and procedures balance agility with sustainability and meet **governance, risk, and compliance (GRC)** needs.<br><br>All policies and procedures should be guided by the *Zero Trust* mantra and assume compromise, enforce least privilege, and explicitly validate trust.<br><br>The policies and procedures support the following:<br><br>• Classifying assets and identities<br><br>• Using security zones<br><br>• Establishing Zero Trust **Identity and Access Management (IAM)** by covering digital identity and adaptive access management<br><br>This is normally the area of the risk, compliance, security analyst, and security architecture teams. It is owned by security leadership, results in updates to security, risk, and compliance policies, and translates down to business and technology teams during implementation.<br><br>In a Zero Trust *continuous learning* context, this initiative should also establish learning materials and updates to the governance framework to ensure a *whole-organization* understanding and application of the policies and procedures. |

| Playbook Step | Who | Description |
|---|---|---|
| Stage 3 – Create the architecture and model | | |
| **Establish Zero Trust operations** | • Technology senior leaders (especially security, risk, and compliance)<br><br>• Architects (especially security architects)<br><br>• **Security Operations (SecOps/SOC)**<br><br>• Security posture management<br><br>• Technical engineering and operations<br><br>• Security posture management | *This step builds the operational elements for your Zero Trust initiative.*<br><br>Zero Trust introduces security changes to operations throughout the organization, including the following:<br><br>• **SecOps/SOC modernization**: Zero Trust focuses SecOps on the rapid detection, response, and recovery of business assets anywhere in the world. This focuses on minimizing the time adversaries can access the environment (measured as **mean time to remediate (MTTR)**).<br><br>• **Posture management**: The organization will also establish a posture management function to monitor the overall security exposure (using real-time data from cloud services). These teams will monitor for known risks and actively support technical operations teams (IT, OT, and DevOps) to rapidly mitigate risks before attackers find and exploit them. This continuous compliance function provides **on-demand auditing** for many controls.<br><br>• **Sharing strategic threat intelligence**: Doing so with teams throughout the organization helps inform business risk decisions, architectural changes, technical controls, and technical teamwork prioritization.<br><br>This is a collaborative effort with security architecture, SecOps/SOC, posture management, risk, and compliance teams. It is owned by security leadership and translates to business and technology operations teams during implementation. |

**Table 9.3 – Stage 3 – Create the architecture and model**

Now that we have a clear picture of the strategic roadmap, architecture, and processes, we can plan the implementation.

## Stage 4 – Tailor to the business

This stage aligns and connects those Zero Trust components to all the right places and stakeholders throughout the organization.

The following are the steps in this stage:

1. Determine your product model.
2. Determine the business functions and organizational structure.
3. Determine the organization's business processes.

*Table 9.4* covers these steps in detail:

| Playbook Step | Who | Description |
|---|---|---|
| **Stage 4 – Tailor to the business** | | |
| **Determine your product model** | • Organizational senior leaders (including product and business line leaders)<br><br>• Technology senior leaders (especially security)<br><br>• Security posture management<br><br>• Architects (especially security, business, and enterprise architects)<br><br>• Managers<br><br>• Application and product security | *This step captures the product model of your organization.*<br><br>Businesses sell goods and services, which are collectively known as *products*. This product model helps you understand how Zero Trust addresses three key things associated with a product:<br><br>• **Risk**: As a source of potential loss.<br><br>• **Opportunity**: As a mechanism to increase organizational success. This typically takes the form of growing revenue in existing lines of business or growing new sources of revenue by entering new lines of business or geographies.<br><br>• **Ease of doing business** (in terms of agility and cost).<br><br>This context helps link Zero Trust to the organization's revenue and determine which business functions and processes are impacted, how Zero Trust will integrate and impact them, and how best to measure that impact. This impact will be described in terms of people, organizational structure, business process, and capability.<br><br>This initiative will be led by security leaders, using security architecture, enterprise architecture, and business leaders. |

| Playbook Step | Who | Description |
|---|---|---|
| Stage 4 – Tailor to the business | | |
| **Determine the business functions and organizational structure** | • Organizational senior leaders<br><br>• Technology senior leaders (especially security)<br><br>• Architects (especially security, business, and enterprise)<br><br>• Managers<br><br>• Adjacent/ancillary roles (especially business analysts)<br><br>• Enterprise security integration (deputy CISOs and staff, security [business] analysts) | *This step captures the business functions of your organization that provide the people and structure to deliver the products that the organization provides.*<br><br>Create a high-level assessment of the business functions to understand how Zero Trust will impact business functions and organizational structure.<br><br>Business functions provide the people and structure to deliver the products that the organization provides. Perform a high-level assessment of the business functions to understand how Zero Trust will impact business functions and organizational structure.<br><br>This initiative will be led by security leaders, using business architecture resources. It will also involve mid- and senior-level business and technology leadership acting as sources and validating information. The outcomes of this often include training, reorganization to incorporate Zero Trust as an organizational capability, and establishing procedures and policies. Zero Trust metrics for the capabilities serviced by the business function are also reviewed. |

| Playbook Step | Who | Description |
|---|---|---|
| Stage 4 – Tailor to the business | | |
| **Determine the organization's business processes** | • Organizational senior leaders<br><br>• Technology senior leaders (especially security)<br><br>• Architects (especially security, business, and enterprise)<br><br>• Managers | *This step captures the business processes that deliver the products the organization provides.*<br><br>In this step, you create a high-level assessment of the business processes to understand how Zero Trust will impact business functions and organizational structure.<br><br>It is important to keep the scope of this initial discovery light and broad (an inch deep and a mile wide) so that you don't go into too much detail or over-engineer it. This first overall discovery should give a general sense of how Zero Trust will impact business processes. For example, Zero Trust may enable self-service identity and access management. For an organization such as a mid- to large-sized retailer or bank, this can have a huge impact.<br><br>We will look at the details of these processes in the role-specific playbooks.<br><br>This initiative is led by security leaders, using security and business architecture resources. It will also involve mid- and senior-level business and technology leadership, who act as sources and reviewers of information. Zero Trust implications often include training, reorganization to incorporate Zero Trust as an organizational capability, and establishing procedures and policies. Zero Trust metrics for the capabilities serviced by the business function are also reviewed. |

**Table 9.4 – Stage 4 – Tailor to the business**

Now, we are ready to implement Zero Trust and start the continuous improvement cycle.

## Stage 5 – Implement and improve

This stage builds Zero Trust and makes it real, integrating it with the business processes and the technical estate.

The following are the steps in this stage:

1. Build your reusable components for Zero Trust
2. Establish best practices
3. Implement and improve

*Table 9.5* covers the steps in this stage:

| Playbook Step | Who | Description |
|---|---|---|
| Stage 5 – Implement and improve | | |
| **Build your reusable components for Zero Trust** | • Architects (especially security, business, and enterprise)<br><br>• Managers<br><br>• SecOps<br><br>• Application and product security | This step builds the Zero Trust components and services that get implemented in your production environment. These will be used throughout the organization for many applications and business processes.<br><br>This step uses the MVP technique to rapidly develop and deploy the minimum viable version of each component and maximize learning from real-world feedback and validation.<br><br>These Zero Trust components and services lay the groundwork for the business to adopt Zero Trust using elements such as secure trusted zones, adaptive authentication, and developing "token" services for data centricity.<br><br>We strongly encourage a "configure-before-customizing" approach (to avoid the cost/complexity of a custom solution) and a preference order as follows:<br><br>1. Reuse existing components, if available.<br>2. Buy standard components, if available.<br>3. Build custom components, only if required.<br><br>If building a component is not your core business practice, look for a purchase to fill the need (which can be done quite fast in the **Software-as-a-Service** (**SaaS**) world) and avoid customizations unless they're absolutely required (as they create a long-term burden for your organization to maintain). |

| Playbook Step | Who | Description |
|---|---|---|
| Stage 5 – Implement and improve | | |
| **Establish best practices** | • Architects (especially security, business, and enterprise)<br><br>• Managers<br><br>• SecOps<br><br>• Technical engineering and operations<br><br>• Application and product security | This step establishes repeatable patterns and best practices to guide teams and practitioners, helping them avoid wasted time and effort. |
| **Implement and improve** | Entire organization | This step is when the organization implements the roadmap.<br><br>All roles in the organization participate in this step.<br><br>With the roadmap, governance framework, and cultural, training, and communication plan in place, the organization should start executing the roadmap. Start iterating and measuring in each cycle, improving and evolving as you go based on learnings from the real-world environment.<br><br>This is a continuous process that's executed until the end of the roadmap and leads to an agile approach to continuous improvement.<br><br>Each team should feel empowered to move forward with their responsibilities, so long as they are communicating with other teams. To head off conflict in this rapid innovation model, teams should constantly share what they are planning with other teams, ask for feedback, and listen closely to what other teams are doing. This helps everyone adjust in real time. |

**Table 9.5 – Stage 5 –Implement and improve**

As Zero Trust comes online, the world will be constantly changing, so we need to adopt a continuous improvement approach to continually update it as we operate it.

## Stage 6 – Continuously monitor and evolve

This stage represents the ongoing work to run and continually improve Zero Trust. As Zero Trust capabilities come online and are operationalized, we will be continuously monitoring and improving them to adapt to the continuously changing business, technical, and security landscape. This ensures your organization is agile and can respond to the wide range of threats and opportunities you face.

*Table 9.6* covers the step in this stage:

| Playbook Step | Who | Description |
|---|---|---|
| Stage 6 – Continuously monitor and evolve | | |
| **Operate and improve Zero Trust capabilities** | The entire organization | *This is the ongoing operation and continuous improvement of Zero Trust as the organization implements and integrates Zero Trust capabilities from the roadmap into daily operations and usage.*<br><br>This stage focuses on sustainment and improvement, using metrics at the KPI and OKR levels to track the success of Zero Trust and calibrate and improve the capability.<br><br>Organizations will use the governance framework to monitor and continuously improve Zero Trust.<br><br>This typically includes doing the following:<br><br>• Ensuring people are watching the monitoring systems<br><br>• Addressing "drift" or non-compliance of configuration or processes (and focusing on learning from any deviations)<br><br>• Improving or updating any component in the Zero Trust system (architecture, model, capabilities, integration, and so on) based on the availability of new technology, changes in business requirements, evolution in the attack landscape, or other sources<br><br>• Updating the monitoring systems and metrics to improve visibility regarding Zero Trust |

**Table 9.6 – Step 6 – Continuously monitor and evolve**

This wraps up the six playbook stages that build your Zero Trust capabilities and align security to your business priorities, risks, and operating model. This will set your organization up for success with secure and agile operations.

## Summary

In this chapter, we learned about the six-stage process to building Zero Trust that will be used throughout the playbooks.

We covered the detailed steps of the playbook, who leads each, and who they need to work with throughout the organization. This six-stage process enables you to take Zero Trust from a conceptual state to fully implemented and operational, reducing your organizational risk and enabling operational success.

Next up is the final chapter of this book, *Chapter 10*, *Zero Trust Playbook Roles*, where we'll look at the Zero Trust journey from a role-based perspective.

# Zero Trust Playbook Roles

*"Your career is your business and you are its CEO."*

*– Andy Grove*

Now that we have a clear picture of Zero Trust, the three pillars, and the six-stage playbook journey, let's see how to make this real for each role—from CEOs and board members to technical analysts and engineers.

This chapter looks at the Zero Trust journey from a role-based perspective, which complements the strategic view from the six-stage plan described in the previous chapter. The combination of these perspectives brings a clear three-dimensional view of the Zero Trust journey. This also sets the stage for the rest of the playbook series, with each of the books addressing the journey for a set of related roles.

*What does this mean for me?*

The role-based view is critical for individual professionals, managers, and senior leaders to fully understand Zero Trust. This view provides clarity on how it impacts day-to-day work, informs governance and other organizational planning, and enables effective skills and career planning. The *Role-based approach* section later in this chapter provides additional detail and context about why this role-based view of Zero Trust in the playbook is so critical.

This is the final chapter of the *Zero Trust Introduction and Playbook Overview* book that prepares everyone for the journey. After reading this chapter, we can play our part to implement Zero Trust and start enjoying the benefits of this change!

This chapter includes the following topics:

- Summary of the **role-based approach** used in the playbook
- An **illustrative list of roles** transformed by Zero Trust in security, technology, and business
- A description of the **per-role guidance** provided in the playbook for each role
- **Making it real** using our *Acme Bank* example
- Discussing **What's next in The Zero Trust Playbook Series**

Think of this chapter as the final part of the virtual kickoff meeting introducing Zero Trust. After this book, we will each read the playbook for our role to get specific instructions and guidance tailored to how we support Zero Trust in the organization. This is similar to how large program teams have a big kickoff meeting with all stakeholders and then split up into smaller groups to plan and execute each workstream.

Each playbook that follows includes a group of related roles that are affected by Zero Trust in similar ways (security operations, business and technical leaders, product and application security, and more). Each playbook describes how those roles apply and tailor the overall plan to their jobs and responsibilities. The playbooks also include the use of *Acme* examples to illustrate how to apply the guidance to different industries, sizes, and types of organizations.

Now, let's look at the role-based approach in the playbooks and why this is important to you.

# Role-based approach

*Perceptions filter what you see and change how you act in the world.*

We all understand the world around us through the lens of our individual experiences, our personal identity, and the role we are playing at that moment. We see things differently when we view our role as a friend, sibling, student, teacher, boss, employee, customer, vendor, owner, auditor, or other role. This affects what we see and hear, as well as how we act in any situation.

This is also true of our work—we perceive challenges, solutions, and opportunities through the lens of our professional identity and the role(s) we play within an organization.

For this reason, the *Zero Trust Playbook* provides *role-by-role guidance for business, technology, and security roles* that are impacted by and required to support Zero Trust. Each role in the playbook has an important and unique part to play in Zero Trust, regardless of whether it is fulfilled as an occasional part-time duty, a shared duty among multiple people, or a dedicated team of professionals.

This *role-based approach provides clarity and enables immediate actionability*. Each role puts the relevant context into a familiar language, outlines the tasks personnel need to perform, and provides clear guidance on who in the organization to work with. This prevents wasted effort and confusion from trying to figure out exactly what to do, why it needs to be done, who will do it, and how this is supposed to work.

This section covers the following four key aspects of the role-based approach in the playbook:

- **Integration of roles with the six-stage plan**: Describing how the playbook integrates the role-based approach with the six-stage journey
- **Role-related terminology**: Describing how the playbook defines and uses terminology related to roles
- **Zero Trust affects everyone**: Summarizing how Zero Trust affects every role in an organization

- **Role definition and naming**: Describing how the playbook defines role scope and names, including when they vary from current industry norms

Let's start with how the playbook integrates a role-based approach with the six-stage plan.

## Integration of roles with the six-stage plan

*The playbook integrates this role-centric view with the six-stage plan* to drive speed and clarity throughout the strategy, planning, implementation, operation, and continuous improvement of Zero Trust.

*Figure 10.1* illustrates how a combination of the six-stage plan with per-role guidance provides clarity to all roles in an organization:

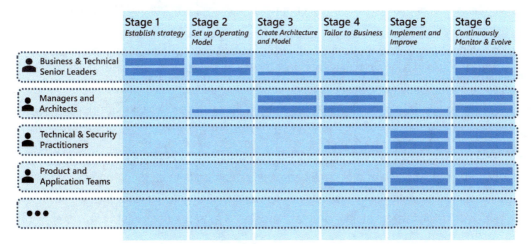

Figure 10.1 – Illustration of how different roles engage at different stages

This diagram shows how **business and technical senior leaders** are heavily involved in the beginning of Zero Trust adoption, setting direction for strategy and culture. This first stage anchors and guides the rest of the work and establishes its importance to the organization.

**Clarity brings agility**. The strategy and culture established in the beginning act as ongoing durable guidelines that empower people, accelerate progress, and increase agility. This clarity empowers people to make local decisions rapidly and confidently in a constantly changing environment that are aligned with Zero Trust and the organization's goals.

In the next stages, **managers and architects** do a lot of the work to plan detailed architectures, models, and processes that tailor Zero Trust to unique business processes.

The Zero Trust capabilities are then implemented by practitioners, including **technical and security practitioners** and **product and application teams**.

All roles help **continuously monitor and evolve Zero Trust**.

Each playbook expands into many more details for each role's involvement. Now, let's clarify some key terminology in this role-based approach.

### Role-related terminology

The playbook uses several terms that have similar but not identical meanings:

- A **discipline** is an area of study that often requires multiple roles and specializations to practice. Some examples of professional disciplines include security operations, architecture, application security, technical leadership, and business leadership.

- A **role** is a collection of tasks that someone performs to enable a capability on an ongoing basis. A role is often assigned to a single person, but multiple people may fulfill the role in a larger organization, or the same person may perform multiple roles in a smaller organization.

- A **role specialization** describes how generally or narrowly tasks are defined for a role. Highly generalized roles span many different tasks while highly specialized roles focus narrowly on a few related tasks. Some roles will always be generalists (such as architects) to drive consistency across many teams in the organization, while others can become more specialized (such as engineers) as the organizational function matures and team size grows.

- *Figure 10.2* illustrates the skill and task profiles of extreme specialists and generalists on this spectrum:

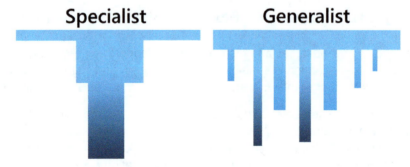

**Figure 10.2 – Task and skill profiles for highly specialized roles versus generalist roles**

Generalist roles (low specialization) perform many types of different tasks, often in smaller organizations where resources are limited. Highly specialized roles perform fewer and similar tasks and are often found in large organizations that require efficiency, scale, and mastery of individual skill sets.

The playbook defines roles in their fully specialized end state (as seen in large organizations) and provides guidance to quickly adapt this to more generalized roles in smaller organizations. The playbook does this by showing the full creation and evolution journey for each role, which is described in the *Role creation and evolution* section later in this chapter.

---

**Notes**

**Stay aware of context and changes**: During a transformation such as Zero Trust, even the most specialized roles must maintain a strong sense of the context around the organization to understand which assumptions are changing and how.

**Shift to capability-centric**: Many roles and specializations are shifting with Zero Trust to a capability-centric focus from a tool-centric or technology-centric definition and scope.

---

Now that we understand the role-based approach, why it's important, and the terminology, let's discuss who is affected by Zero Trust.

## Zero Trust affects everyone

Every role in an organization is affected by Zero Trust—sometimes in small ways and sometimes in large transformative ways. Some illustrative examples include the following:

- Everyone, including frontline workers, must watch carefully for phishing emails and scams from cyber attackers
- Board members and business leaders must integrate security into business and risk discussions.
- Senior technology leaders must build and maintain an agile strategic roadmap that aligns security and technology investments with business priorities and risks
- Technology and security architects and engineers must integrate security into technology designs and security control designs to enable resilience to cybersecurity attacks
- Security operations must find and remove attacker access to business assets using new tools and approaches
- Security and technology managers must update project priorities and processes based on the organization's strategy, risk, and **threat intelligence (TI)**
- Compliance professionals must keep up with a steady flow of new regulatory requirements by using on-demand reporting and by collaborating with teams across the organization

As with digital transformation and cloud transformations, which it usually accompanies, Zero Trust transformation shifts roles into a more agile, informed, and automated approach. This brings out the best of human skills and abilities while computers take on more repetitive and manual tasks, *improving both the daily experience and the effectiveness of security*.

Now, we will take a look at the playbook approach for role definition and naming.

## Role definition and naming

The playbook uses industry-standard terminology and role definitions when possible, including formally defined standards and de facto standards from common practice.

You may encounter new or unfamiliar role terminology in some cases, including the following:

- **New required roles** that don't exist in common practice today. An example of this is **enterprise security integration**, a role focused on aligning security activities and investments with business risk and strategy. This role is critical to Zero Trust as it provides real-time representation for security at business and technology strategy meetings and brings business context to security strategy, planning, and investment decisions.

- **Evolved scope and mission**: Some disciplines and associated role(s) expand or evolve the scope of current roles significantly. Some examples include the following:

  - **Security posture management** evolves from vulnerability management discipline and roles. This change has two main dimensions:

    - The scope of the role increases from only software vulnerabilities to all types of vulnerabilities, including technical operational practices and security configurations

    - The engagement model for the role becomes proactive to assist and engage with technology operations teams on solutions, not just reporting scan results

  - **TI** evolves significantly from a common scope of managing technical **Indicators of Compromise** (**IoCs**) such as file hashes and IP addresses to a full intelligence discipline. This role now analyzes and reports on threat actors, motivations, goals, and what they mean to the organization's business, technology defenses, processes, and more.

  - **Architect alignment** focuses on outcomes rather than technology silos. For example, network and identity architects become access architects who coordinate solutions across all access technologies to ensure a seamless user experience and security posture across the technical estate.

- **Increased specialization of role definitions**: Some roles are defined in greater detail in the playbook than is commonly seen in industry. For example, security operations *Tier 3* analyst roles often perform multiple different jobs of *detection engineering*, *threat hunting*, and *attack simulation* (red and purple teaming). Each of these specializations is defined separately to recognize discrete outcomes, work processes, and skill sets (even if they are performed by a single team or person in some organizations).

## *Industry dynamics and inconsistent terminology*

You may have noticed that role terminology for information security and technology is inconsistent and changes regularly. This is primarily driven by two factors:

- **These industries are still new**: Both technology and security industries have very little history compared to others with centuries or millennia of history, such as building architecture, civil engineering, and others. Many areas of the technology and security industry haven't identified norms and standards, while other areas have had multiple independent standards defined that haven't been fully reconciled.

- **These industries are naturally disruptive**: These industries either generate or manage disruption as a part of their normal value creation. The technology industry primarily creates value by introducing valuable changes to business models and processes of other industries that increase speed, efficiency, and reach (often opening up new markets in the process). The security industry is focused on managing risk arising from the disruptive activities of criminals and governments who are seeking to benefit from the work of existing organizations.

New and changing terminology is often required to develop and validate new concepts and reframe existing concepts in these industries. Because new terminology can be distracting and Zero Trust is designed to manage continuous change, the playbook strives to define any new terminology to be durable across changes to technology, threat landscape, and business models.

---

**Role planning and vendor RBAC models**

Organizations should use the guidance in this playbook as a primary source to design roles rather than basing them on **role-based access control** (**RBAC**) definitions in vendor products such as enterprise identity systems. The vendor definitions are optimized for assigning permissions within a product, while the playbook roles are optimized for driving organizational success and reducing organizational risk.

---

Now, let's review an illustrative list of roles that are key to a Zero Trust transformation.

# Illustrative list of roles

This is an illustrative list of roles impacted by Zero Trust and roles with a clear part to play in the success of Zero Trust, digital, and cloud transformations.

The roles in *Table 6.1* may evolve over time, but only minor limited changes are expected:

| Role Type | Roles |
| --- | --- |
| Organizational Senior Leaders | Member of Board of Directors |
| | **Chief Executive Officer (CEO)** |
| | **Chief Financial Officer (CFO)** |
| | **Chief Operating Officer (COO)** |
| | **Chief Legal Officer (CLO)** |
| | **Chief Privacy Officer (CPO)** |
| | **Chief Risk Officer (CRO)** |
| | Product- and Business-Line Leaders |
| | Communications/Public Relations Director |
| Adjacent / Ancillary Roles | Human Resources |
| | Business Analysts |
| | Internal Readiness/Training |
| | Internal and External Communications |
| Risk and Compliance Roles | Risk Team |
| | Compliance and Audit Team |
| Technology Senior Leaders | **Chief Digital Officer (CDO)** |
| | **Chief Information Officer (CIO)** |
| | **Chief Technology Officer (CTO)** |
| | **Chief Information Security Officer (CISO)** |
| | Enterprise Security Integration |
| | Technology Directors |
| | Security Directors |

| Role Type | Roles |
| --- | --- |
| Architects | Enterprise Architect |
| | Security Architects |
| | Infrastructure Architect |
| | Business Architect |
| | Information Architect |
| | Access Architect |
| | Solution Architect |
| | Software/Application Architects |
| Managers | Technology Manager |
| | Security Manager |
| | **Security Operations** (**SecOps**) Manager |
| | Product Line Manager |
| | Product Owner |
| Security Posture Management | Security Posture Management |
| | Security Governance and Compliance Management |
| | People Security (User Education and Insider Risk) |
| Technical Engineering and Operations | Cloud Engineering and Operations |
| | Endpoint/Productivity |
| | Identity |
| | Infrastructure |
| | Network |
| | Data Security |
| | **Operational Technology** (**OT**) Security |
| | Security Posture Engineering and Operations |

| Role Type | Roles |
|---|---|
| Application and Product Security | Application Team Manager |
| | Software Security Engineer |
| | Software Developer |
| | **Internet of Things (IoT)** Security |
| Security Operations | Triage Analyst |
| | Investigation Analyst |
| | Threat Hunting |
| | Detection Engineering |
| | Attack Simulation (Red and Purple Teaming) |
| | **Incident Management (IM)** |
| | TI |

Table 10.1 – Illustrative list of roles that enable Zero Trust

Now, let's go over the guidance that the playbook provides for each role.

## Per-role guidance

The playbook guidance helps each role navigate the transformation to Zero Trust, manage ongoing Zero Trust operations, and manage the continuous changes to come.

The volume of guidance provided for each role varies by how involved they are with Zero Trust. Security and technology roles are affected by Zero Trust in many ways, while business leaders such as CEOs, CFOs, and board members experience fewer changes (though their actions are critically important to the success of everyone else).

The guidance for each individual role provides clear guidance in these areas:

- Role mission and purpose
- Role creation and evolution
- Key role relationships
- Required skills and knowledge
- Tooling and capabilities

- Zero Trust impact and imperatives for each role
- Playbook stage involvement for each role
- Day in the life of Zero Trust for each role
- Defining and measuring success

## Role mission and purpose

The playbook includes a description of the vital and enduring mission of the role in security and business risk.

This guidance provides a personal north star for people in each role on how to frame their thinking about security risk, business and technology impact, and Zero Trust. This also helps you understand the potential positive impact of creating this role if someone isn't already assigned to do it.

## Role creation and evolution

*We're all the same, but each of us is also unique.*

The playbook describes the typical role specialization journey from the initial creation of a general security function to a team of highly specialized roles within that function.

*This makes the playbook actionable for organizations of all sizes, industries, specializations, and maturity levels*, from the largest global organization to smaller organizations.

This guidance describes who performs tasks when a specialization doesn't exist, when dedicated specializations are usually introduced, how these tasks typically split into deeper specializations as the organization's requirements change, and any role variations and deep specializations related to the role.

You can use this guidance to achieve the following:

- **Adapt the playbook to your organization**: Quickly adapt the playbook guidance to your organization by identifying where you are on this journey of growth and skill specialization
- **Plan for future team growth and specialization** as your requirements change because of revenue, organization size, regulations, mergers, and other factors
- **Plan career and skill development** to keep up with (and get ahead of) skill requirements

*Figure 10.3* provides an illustrative example of the playbook approach to role creation and evolution guidance using security operations:

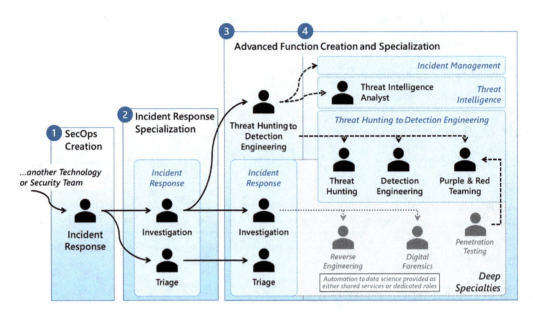

**Figure 10.3 – Typical growth of the path of a security operations team**

In this example, you can see the full journey of the **Security Operations** (**SecOps**) discipline growing from individuals performing part-time tasks to a large specialized team.

SecOps often starts with one or two people from a technical team performing **incident response** (**IR**) tasks on a part-time basis to monitor for attacks and respond to them. Here's an example overview:

- **Stage 1**: As this workload grows and funding is made available, a security operations function is then created to perform *IR* with dedicated resource(s).

- **Stage 2**: As the workload and funding continue to grow, IR often splits into a *triage* analyst role(s) (often called *Tier 1*) that focuses on high-volume attack detections and an *investigation* analyst role(s) (often called *Tier 2*) that focuses on high-complexity investigations.

- **Stages 3 and 4**: As security operations continue to grow, resources are often dedicated to various proactive functions (sometimes called *Tier 3*) focusing on *threat hunting*, *detection engineering*, *TI*, and *attack simulation* (red and purple teaming). This may be a single role that performs multiple specializations (*Stage 3*) or dedicated resources that focus on each of these (*Stage 4*). Additional deep specializations and specializations are also noted in the diagram.

This example shows how the *role creation and evolution* guidance enables you to map these roles to your organizations, regardless of team size or role specialization. People in larger organizations can use this to understand their own roles and those of their colleagues. People in smaller organizations can understand the multiple specializations a role performs and get insight into what to prioritize.

Organizations of all sizes can plan updates to current roles and how to invest in future role specializations as the organization's needs evolve and funding is available. Larger organizations often have dedicated security and technology professionals performing specialized tasks, while smaller businesses, agencies, and non-profit organizations often can't afford to dedicate individuals to every specialization.

> **It's not always about size**
>
> Sometimes, smaller organizations may have increased cybersecurity requirements that other organizations of the same size don't have. Cybersecurity requirements can be driven by the organization's business model, **intellectual property** (**IP**), geographic locations, public profile, and other factors. For example, a financial services organization or an election campaign may face a higher level of cybersecurity threats and risk than a non-profit organization operating with the same number of employees.

As appropriate, the guidance for each role also calls out who typically performs a specialization if a dedicated role isn't present. This doesn't apply to CEOs, of course, but it is ☺ common for IT and technical roles as an organization grows.

> **It's not always a straight line**
>
> Not every team is built in this straightforward linear way—many teams are created as the result of mergers, acquisitions, re-organizations, or other changes.
>
> The playbook uses this linear growth approach because you can adapt it to different situations simply by comparing the size and specialization level of the team and finding the closest overall match.

## Key role relationships

The playbook describes how the role interacts with other roles and specializations on security and Zero Trust topics. It describes the nature of those relationships and key processes and collaboration topics that support that relationship.

This helps individuals in those roles understand who they should reach out to and for what reasons. This also enables intentional and collaborative process planning, team blueprinting, and relationship building. *This can help organizations and individuals overcome the "isolated silo" dynamic where teams don't talk to each other, which creates endless challenges for everyone.*

## Required skills and knowledge

The playbook describes the core competencies of the role that enable individuals to be effective and efficient at performing the role daily.

This guidance helps managers plan and prioritize training and continuing education for their team members. It also enables individuals to plan their career and skill development so that they can continue to contribute and remain valuable.

## Tooling and capabilities for each role

This describes how each role fits into the Zero Trust value chain by describing the role's relationship to Zero Trust capabilities and tooling. This includes the following:

- Identifying the Zero Trust capabilities the role enables

- Identifying the tooling and technology the role depends on

- Describing the impact and importance of automation and **artificial intelligence (AI)** for the role

This guidance enables planning and prioritizing specific technical capabilities for acquisition and process planning, as well as reporting alignment and compliance with standards. This also enables organizations to identify opportunities for automation so that they can effectively plan and prioritize those investments. This guidance also discusses the impact of AI on the role, in terms of classic **machine learning (ML)** models and generative AI such as **large language models (LLMs)** that enable chat or copilot user interfaces.

---

**Standard Zero Trust capabilities**

This section uses standard capability definitions from *The Open Group*'s *Zero Trust Reference Model*. Illustratively, this standard model defines the following Level 1 capabilities:

- **Asset-Centricity (AC-1)**
- **Adaptive Access Control (AAC-1)**
- **Digital Identity (DI-1)**
- **Asset-Centric Protection (ACP-1)**
- **Asset-Centric Security Operations (ACSO-1)**
- **Posture Management (SPM-1)**
- **Zero Trust Governance (ZTG-1)**
- **Security Zones (SZ-1)**
- **Controls Management (CM-1)**

---

## Zero Trust impact and imperatives for each role

This describes what Zero Trust does to the role and what the role does for Zero Trust. This section reduces confusion about *what Zero Trust means for each role*, setting clear expectations about what does and doesn't change with Zero Trust.

This provides clarity on changes related to Zero Trust, *reducing confusion and fear that can cause distractions, missed opportunities, and slowdowns*.

## Playbook-stage involvement for each role

The playbooks describe which roles participate in each step of the six-stage plan, how they participate, and which parts they don't participate in.

This accelerates planning and execution by *setting clear expectations on who is involved and when*. This also helps build teamwork and collaboration because teams and roles know when to work together to deliver a common outcome.

## A day in the life of Zero Trust for each role

The playbook describes specific job tasks and operating modes that make up the role's daily experience of Zero Trust.

Everyone will immediately and clearly understand *how to make Zero Trust real for their role*. This also enables colleagues to work more effectively with the role and managers to better guide people in the role.

Let's take a look at an example.

### A day in the life of an investigation analyst

For example, a *security operations investigation analyst* (sometimes called a *Tier 2 analyst*) operates in these modes:

- **Standard duties**: Duties not related to immediate incidents or monitoring queue
- **On shift**: Monitoring detection queue for new detections
- **On investigation**: Working on a case
- **On investigation**: Engaging deep specializations
- **On investigation**: Documenting investigations

*Figure 10.4* illustrates these investigation analyst modes:

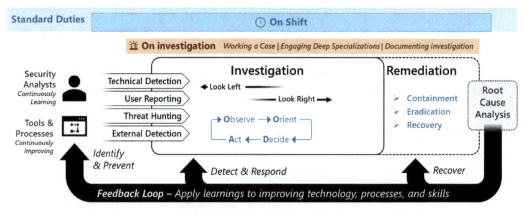

**Figure 10.4 – Operating modes of an investigation analyst**

Just as the playbook helps us understand how Zero Trust impacts the day in the life of the role, it also helps us understand how we define and measure success.

## Defining and measuring success

*Security success is the continuous failure of attackers.*

The playbook describes key role outcomes that enable individual and organizational success, including how to observe and measure those outcomes.

This final type of guidance helps with planning organizational metrics, team metrics, investment prioritization, and individual career objectives.

*Security is hard, and measuring security success can be even harder.* Measuring security success is critically important, but it also comes with significant challenges. You must understand that security investments don't easily or directly align with business outcomes (or attacks). You must also be careful to ensure security metrics drive positive outcomes via learning and don't demotivate people by holding them accountable for outcomes they can't control.

Let's start with why security (and measuring security success) is complex.

### The security alignment paradox

Security is a highly complex discipline, making it both difficult to manage and difficult to measure in simple clear terms. *Figure 10.5* illustrates this complexity:

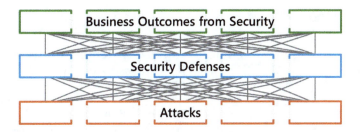

**Figure 10.5 – Conceptual illustration of the security alignment paradox**

Security defenses have *many-to-many* relationships with business outcomes from security— no single defensive measure delivers on a single business outcome, and each of them delivers partially on multiple business outcomes. Similarly, mitigating attacks effectively often requires multiple defensive techniques and can never be 100% effective (which forces us to assume compromise, as we discussed in detail in *Chapter 7, What Zero Trust Success Looks Like*). Security teams must discretely manage attacks, defenses, and risks, and they must map them together with human expertise, processes, frameworks, and technology.

While we wish we could make statements such as *"If we do this defense, we completely block all these attacks and fully remove a business risk,"* they simply wouldn't be true. While security salespeople may be tempted to make implicit or explicit product claims such as this, this kind of promise doesn't hold up in the real world.

### Metrics should not be punitive

The primary focus of metrics should be to drive continuous learning and improvement for individuals, teams, and organizations. We strongly recommend against directly tying any security metrics to personal performance, especially those that can be influenced by external factors.

*Holding people accountable for actions outside their influence or control is not fair, motivating, or productive.*

Many security outcomes are outside the control of the organization. Security outcomes are influenced by well-resourced and highly motivated attackers, security researchers, regulators, vendor/supplier security practices, and others. Additionally, most organizations have a large amount of technical debt in their technical estate that the current staff inherited from their predecessors (such as unmaintainable systems that were designed without security in mind).

Additionally, blaming people undermines the culture of learning, trust, and continuous improvement required for successful Zero Trust, digital, and cloud transformations. When this organizational trust has been undermined, *it is harder to achieve good risk and security outcomes*.

*Figure 10.6* illustrates how unintended consequences result from punitive metrics:

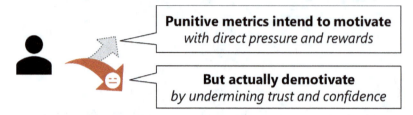

**Punitive metrics intend to motivate**
*with direct pressure and rewards*

**But actually demotivate**
*by undermining trust and confidence*

**Figure 10.6 – Consequences of holding people accountable for factors beyond their control**

Whether your security metrics are improving, degrading, or staying the same, you must *always focus on asking the same three questions*:

- What changed in the external environment?

- What did we do well?

- How can we improve?

> **Objective metrics are a journey**
>
> At the time of writing this book, it is very difficult to measure security objectively and completely. While there is a lot of raw information available on technical systems, the industry is still in the early days of providing consistent security insights based on objective measurements.
>
> While financial disciplines have established standards such as **Generally Accepted Accounting Principles (GAAP)** and **International Financial Reporting Standards (IFRS)**, this does not yet exist for cybersecurity. The industry is maturing fast in this respect, but many gaps still remain in standards and tooling.

The recommended metrics in the playbook are designed explicitly to address these challenges. *We recommend you use the metrics in the playbook to measure security success.*

## Summary of per-role guidance

Collectively, all of this per-role guidance will enable a person in a designated role to be successful in the world of Zero Trust. This will also help other people to more effectively engage with other roles and will also help team managers better guide people on their team.

Now that we understand the guidance for each role, let's take a look at how *Acme Bank* applies the playbook's role-based guidance.

# Making it real

This section shows how our friends at *Acme Bank* (who we met in *Chapter 8, Adoption with the Three-Pillar Model*) formed their top priorities for their roles and teams by applying the *Zero Trust Playbook Series*.

*Acme recognizes that Zero Trust is a long-term initiative but wants Zero Trust now!* Acme is taking an agile approach where each team is getting started immediately on the top priorities while building more detailed and complete plans based on the playbooks. *Acme* expects the teams will have to adjust their priorities and plans as the environment changes and they learn, but they aren't waiting to get started on Zero Trust.

*Acme Bank* held a Zero Trust kickoff meeting with the bank's leadership and other leaders and stakeholders from across technology and security teams. The group discussed business and Zero Trust priorities, identifying top priorities for each team in the bank to get started on immediately. Each team is prioritizing Zero Trust and will provide regular status updates to the group (via the new risk council detailed in this chapter) while continuing to operate the business and continuing to learn.

Each team is also tasked with building more detailed plans for Zero Trust using the playbook, sharing the plans and measurements of success with other teams, and regularly reporting progress through the new risk council.

These are the priority areas for key roles at *Acme Bank*:

- *Acme*'s CEO is focused on supporting Zero Trust with organizational accountability and culture.

  The CEO's top two Zero Trust priorities are as follows:

  - **Accountability and risk management**: Establishing a formal accountability structure and processes to support effective and collaborative decision-making for security risk. This includes the following:

    - **Accountability**: The CEO has tasked the business strategy team with updating organizational scorecards and measurements to reflect that security risk is shared across the organization. *Business leaders will be held accountable for security risk outcomes of decisions, just as they are held accountable for business performance outcomes of decisions.*

    - **Risk management**: The CEO has sponsored the creation of a risk council that provides a process to discuss and manage risk collaboratively across **business units** (**BUs**), technology, compliance, and security stakeholders. This forum will also track the progress against all the top priorities for Zero Trust across business lines and organizational functions listed next.

- **Culture**: The CEO is actively integrating key elements into the organizational culture that are required to enable and support digital and Zero Trust transformations. The CEO has approved funding for an initiative to drive education and enablement of these cultural elements including training programs, performance review process updates, and more. The CEO will also personally model these cultural attributes publicly, regularly speaking on them, and celebrating people's choices that embody these values.

    Cultural elements include the following:

    - **Continuous learning**: Everyone should use a *growth mindset* that focuses on openly admitting mistakes and learning from them (instead of hiding them or finding someone to blame)

    - **Security is everyone's job**: Everyone is a part of keeping the organization's data, systems, customers, and partners safe

    - **Collaboration across roles**: Everyone is empowered to contribute to others' success and to build on the work of others instead of having teams and organizational silos compete with each other

- *Acme*'s CIO and CDO are focused on integrating security into technology strategy and daily operations, including strategic expansion into **peer-to-peer** (P2P) payments.

    The CIO and CDO share these top Zero Trust security priorities:

    - **Security culture and process integration**: The CIO and CDO are making it a top priority to integrate security into the culture and daily processes of technology and development teams. This will include three primary focus areas:

        - **Shifting security left**: The CDO is focused on integrating security into the full development life cycle for new workloads and systems. Security will be integrated at the beginning of the process, starting with requirements definition and design. This will replace the current practice of bringing security in near the end of the process to scan applications for approval. Shifting security left (to earlier in the process) will reduce unplanned delays in delivering capabilities on schedule from last-minute security issues, reduce the cost of fixing security issues late in the process, and reduce organizational risk from attacks.

        - **Security hygiene initiative**: The CIO and CISO are sponsoring a joint initiative to improve the security posture of the organization by applying well-known security best practices (sometimes called *security hygiene*). This will be executed jointly by the CIO's technical teams and the new **posture management** team in the CISO's organization.

        - **Policy and governance**: The CIO and CDO are also requiring every project and architecture to include security requirements before funding will be approved.

- **Zero Trust technologies**: The CIO is prioritizing the implementation of technologies that enable top Zero Trust capabilities. These include adaptive access, asset-centric security operations, and security posture management tools.

- *Acme*'s CISO is focused on building the security strategy and directing its execution.

  The CISO's top two priorities are set out here:

  - **Strategy alignment**: Align and integrate the security strategy with the business and technology strategy. Security leadership will attend all major business technology strategy meetings to integrate and align security with business and technology strategy execution. This will be primarily supported by the CISO's newly hired **enterprise security integration** team, focused on driving risk and strategy integration.

  - **Security strategy implementation**: The CISO is focused on landing the strategy with their team and implementing quick wins to make the strategy real. The CISO has tasked their leadership team with educating each of their teams on Zero Trust and associated cultural changes, sharing the organization's Zero Trust priorities, and getting started on implementing quick wins. The CISO's initial focus areas are as follows:

    - **Security hygiene**: The newly formed **security posture management** team is partnering with multiple technology teams (**infrastructure engineering and operations**, endpoint/productivity **engineering and operations**, and **application and product security** teams) to improve the rigor of security hygiene practices. This will focus on rapidly applying security patches, regularly backing up and rapidly restoring business-critical systems, and applying consistent security configuration baselines across all systems. This will drive an asset-centric approach to cover all assets in all network locations.

    - **Adaptive access**: The CISO is driving a fundamental shift in access control from a network perimeter-centric approach to a risk-based adaptive access approach. This ensures that all user access relies on explicitly validated trust/risk levels instead of on network location. This will be led by the **identity and access** team (detailed later in their section).

    - **Asset-centric security operations**: The CISO is driving a transformation of security operations to enable rapid response for assets regardless of network location. This is led by the **security operations** team (detailed later in their section).

- *Acme*'s architects (**security architects**, **enterprise architects**, and **solution architects**) are focused on providing clear guidance to align technical teams and their work.

  The architects' top two priorities are as follows:

  - **Building a clear vision of the end state**: Provide diagrams and documentation that simply and clearly depict how new and existing components will connect to enable Zero Trust capabilities and outcomes

- **Establish principles, policies, and standards**: Update or create these guidelines and rules that provide clarity on how to achieve that vision to all technical and security teams

- **Apply the architecture vision, principles, policies, and standards**: To implement solutions architectures for business capabilities supporting the provision of *Acme's* goods and services.

- *Acme's* other departments (**Adjacent / Ancillary Roles**) are supporting the development and execution of the security strategy. A few key planned changes include:

  - **Human Resources** is establishing new roles, career paths, and ensuring training materials support the changes.

  - **Business Analysts** are working closely with security and delivery teams to integrate Zero Trust approaches into business strategy planning and processes. They are also weaving Zero Trust into Acme's product offerings as well as their security and trust communications with customers.

  - **Internal Readiness/Training** teams are updating existing training materials and creating new training focused on ensuring all roles have the tailored context they need to support Zero Trust. This includes training for internal employees as well as partners, suppliers, and customers.

  - **Internal and External Communications** teams are updating processes for managing security incidents to communicate with internal employees, customers, and partners. They are integrating Zero Trust into the organization's brand and image communications related to security and trust. They work closely with the Training, Security, Legal, and HR teams to analyze Acme Bank's business operating model and culture  and articulate how continuous learning and improvement will change them.

- *Acme's* **security operations** teams are focused on rapidly shifting the current network perimeter-centric approach to an *asset-centric* approach that is aligned with business priorities and modern technology.

  The SecOps director's top two priorities are as follows:

  - **Aligning with an outcome-focused approach**: Shifting metrics, goals, processes, and culture to focus on organizational risk outcomes instead of the current technology- and tool-centric approach. The SecOps director will be focusing the culture on business risk outcomes, continuous learning, and teamwork (within SecOps and with technology team partners). This will focus first on reducing attacker dwell time with rapid response and recovery for top attacks on any asset in any network location.

  - **Asset-centric tooling**: Updating tools and automation from network perimeter-centric processes to asset-centric **extended detection and response (XDR)** tools that protect systems and data regardless of their geographic or network location. The SecOps team will focus heavily on education and training for identity, endpoint, application, and other technologies to grow the team's skills beyond networking-based approaches.

The team will prioritize the adoption of newer cloud-based tools to reduce overhead and maintenance. This is similar to the productivity team's shift to **Software as a Service (SaaS)** collaboration tools from building and *installing on-premises tooling*.

- *Acme's* **identity and access** team (**access architects**, **identity engineering and operations**, **network engineering and operations**) is focused on shifting current teams and tools to an *adaptive access approach*.

  The **identity and access director**'s top two priorities are these:

  - **Adaptive access capabilities**: The team will architect, design, and implement technical capabilities that explicitly validate user and device trust before approving access requests. This will focus first on validating strong user authentication (**multi-factor authentication (MFA)**, behavior analytics, and TI) and validating device integrity (security hygiene is applied and the device is not compromised by malware). This will ensure that user access control is strong whether they are inside or outside the traditional network perimeter.

  - **Access strategy unification**: The network and identity teams will work with the access architect to create a unified and integrated strategy for all access control. This will guide and govern access controls across networks, identity, applications, IT operating systems, IoT devices, OT environments, and more. This will replace the current disparate strategies that created many inadvertent gaps, overlaps, and seams that frustrate users, slow down process execution, and provide opportunities for attackers to exploit.

- **Infrastructure**: *Acme's* IT engineering and operations teams are focused on integrating security and Zero Trust natively into their processes for designing and operating common infrastructure elements including servers, **virtual machines (VMs)**, containers, networks, storage, and more.

  The **infrastructure director**'s top two priorities are as follows:

  - **Security integration**: Integrating security into the team's workflows, processes, and culture instead of the current approach of *"security is the security team's job"* (and working to avoid and/or deprioritize security):

    - **Security hygiene and posture management**: The infrastructure teams are key to the joint security posture initiative that was sponsored by the CIO and CISO. These teams design and execute technical elements for improving, sustaining, and monitoring security posture across *Acme's* on-premises and multi-cloud infrastructure. This includes rapidly applying security updates to the infrastructure, ensuring infrastructure follows the secure baseline, backing up critical systems, and validating restore processes. These teams will also be adopting the new adaptive access capabilities to increase security for infrastructure management and access.

- **Cloud workload security**: These teams are also taking advantage of the cloud adoption process by integrating security into the *Acme* processes for migrating workloads to the cloud and developing workloads directly in the cloud. The infrastructure teams are making security a native part of these processes by establishing secure landing zones for new and migrated workloads. Integrating security earlier in the process (shift left) reduces the cost and difficulty of applying security measures later and reduces security risk.

- **Security automation**: The infrastructure teams will be integrating security into all **Infrastructure as Code** (**IaC**) projects that automate the deployment of infrastructure components. This will reduce the burden of executing security best practices, increase the speed of executing them, and ensure that security is part of new workloads that rely on the new IaC infrastructure automation (which includes most new DevOps/DevSecOps projects).

- **Application and product security**: *Acme* product teams are focused on increasing security for both new and existing applications and services through the full life cycle, from project approval and funding through design, development, operation, and retirement.

  The top two application and product security priorities for Zero Trust are as follows:

  - **Security integration and culture**: Each product and application development team will focus on integrating security into their culture, skilling plans, development processes, and success metrics. This will include the DevOps processes and **Continuous Integration/Continuous Deployment** (**CI/CD**) automation that all *Acme Bank* teams are currently switching to.

  - **Creative destruction**: *Acme* found that legacy capabilities that can't be maintained properly are restricting its business agility and increasing organizational security risk. As part of the digital transformation, *Acme*'s VP of products is sponsoring a process to identify and prioritize legacy systems to be modernized and replaced.

  *Acme* will be reviewing its entire application catalog to find legacy workloads that should be replaced with new business processes, new cloud services, or new custom business applications. This includes applications and services used by customers and internal employees. *Acme* is using the discovery process that's already underway for the cloud migration to build its list.

---

**A different world view of technology assets**

*Acme* is shifting how it views and manages technology assets to mimic processes and criteria it uses for physical assets such as buildings and vehicles. It expects these assets to have a natural lifetime that includes depreciation, required maintenance, and **end-of-life** (**EOL**) management. While *Acme* wants to get as much value as it can from assets, it doesn't want to do so at the expense of business efficiency, market relevancy and reach, regulatory compliance, or a security risk that could cause business disruption, data loss, and more.

This example with our friends at *Acme Bank* illustrates how Zero Trust applies across various roles and how the playbook guides you through coordinating these at all levels. *Acme's* various roles will use the playbooks to form and execute detailed plans for its part in the rapid adoption of Zero Trust.

Now, let's wrap up this chapter and this book so that we can start executing Zero Trust and enjoying the benefits!

## Summary

In this chapter, we learned about the role-based approach of the playbooks in the *Zero Trust Playbook Series*. We reviewed why the role-based approach is important, an illustrative list of roles that are involved and affected, what guidance is provided for each role in the playbook, and how *Acme Bank* is making it real by planning its top priorities.

Each of the role-specific playbooks in the series is built on this foundational framework and goes much deeper—providing role-specific instructions to guide implementation through each playbook stage. Each playbook shows how to apply Zero Trust principles and reference models to each role and to different industries and organizations via the *Acme* examples.

## Book 1 summary

This chapter closes the *Zero Trust Introduction and Playbook Overview* book in the *Zero Trust Playbook Series*.

Throughout this book, we've shown what Zero Trust is, why it's important to organizations, how to structure a Zero Trust transformation, and how roles across the organization work together to implement it and make it real.

Through the chapters of this book, we learned how the *Zero Trust Playbook* modernizes security across your organization:

- *Chapter 1, Zero Trust – This Is the Way*, got us started by introducing Zero Trust, the *Zero Trust Playbook Series*, and answering common questions about Zero Trust.

- *Chapter 2, Reading the Zero Trust Playbook Series*, introduced us to the structure and layout of information in the playbook series and suggested strategies to get what we need from these books quickly.

- *Chapter 3, Zero Trust Is Security for Today's World*, showed us how Zero Trust is designed for the digital age of continuous change we live in and why it's critically important to get right. This chapter also cleared up some common points of confusion around security and Zero Trust.

- *Chapter 4, Standard Zero Trust Capabilities*, described the standard Zero Trust capabilities in the *Zero Trust Reference Model* from *The Open Group* that are referenced throughout the playbooks. These key elements will stay constant as we continuously improve on Zero Trust.

- *Chapter 5, Artificial Intelligence (AI) and Zero Trust*, taught us about AI and how this technology is disrupting business, technology, security, and society at large. We learned about its impacts, limitations, and relationship to Zero Trust, which will be managed through the guidance for each role in the playbooks.

- *Chapter 6, How to Scope, Size, and Start Zero Trust*, answered top questions about planning and getting started with a Zero Trust transformation. We also learned about key terminology changes, as well as common points of confusion from terminology that is used differently by different teams in an organization.

- *Chapter 7, What Zero Trust Success Looks Like*, covered three key success factors for Zero Trust that are embedded into the playbooks: having a clear strategy and plan, managing mindset and culture shifts, and integrating human empathy.

- *Chapter 8, Adoption with the Three-Pillar Model*, laid out the three pillars of the playbook (strategic, operational, and operating model) and showed us how the elements in that model work together to integrate business, technology, and security to create Zero Trust.

- In *Chapter 9, The Zero Trust Six-Stage Plan*, we learned about the six stages to implement the playbook, including a detailed summary of "who does what." This showed us how the playbook brings everyone together to make Zero Trust real.

- In *Chapter 10, Zero Trust Playbook Roles*, we learned about the role-based approach and per-role guidance in the playbooks. This sets us up for success as we move on to the playbook for our role.

As we noted in the beginning, this series blends the best of agile approaches with the best practices of traditional strategic planning, enabling you to be flexible and fast without losing focus on the north star of the longer journey of end-to-end transformation.

> **Go as big as you can**
> We encourage you to start on Zero Trust at the largest scale you can. While you can start anywhere and get quick wins that will reduce security risk and enable the mission, smaller initiatives are limited in impact compared to a full transformation sponsored by organizational leadership.

Now, let's talk about the next books in the series.

# What's next in The Zero Trust Playbook Series

It's time to get started on execution!

As we discussed before, this *Zero Trust introduction and Playbook Overview* book acts as a big program's kickoff meeting with all stakeholders. This book gave us full context of what type of guidance everyone will get—now, the next step is to move on to the role-specific playbook for our individual role (and playbooks for our key colleagues as appropriate). This is like team members breaking into smaller groups in a large program to plan and execute each workstream.

Each playbook focuses on a group of related roles and describes how to execute their part of the six-stage plan. Each playbook provides three types of guidance to make this real and actionable for everyone:

- **Shared context**: This describes the Zero Trust context that applies to all roles in the playbook. For example, the security operations playbook describes the overall function of SecOps in Zero Trust and changes impacting all SecOps roles.

- **Per-role guidance**: This provides per-role guidance for that individual role, as described earlier in this chapter.

- **Making it real**: This shows how to apply the guidance in the real world using different *Acme* organizations on their Zero Trust journey. The *Acme* family of examples show how to apply Zero Trust across IT, OT, and IoT for many different industries. They also map to key industry frameworks and standards appropriate to each role.

Together, this guidance in the playbooks shows you clearly what Zero Trust will look and feel like in your role (and for your colleagues in your team and across the organization). The playbooks enable you to do the following:

- **Apply Zero Trust in the real world** by building and executing your organization's tailored roadmap to guide your journey

- **Plan career and skill development** to keep up with and get ahead of requirements

The role-specific playbooks provide guidance on the wide variety of roles that are impacted by Zero Trust and required to enable Zero Trust, including the following:

- **Business leaders** support and enable the smooth execution of a Zero Trust strategy that reduces risk and enables the organization to rapidly embrace digital business opportunities. The playbooks include role-specific guidance on Zero Trust for CEOs, CFOs, COOs, CLOs, CPOs, **line-of-business** (**LOB**) leaders, board members, and similar roles. The playbooks include guidance on culture, finance, success metrics, organizational risk and governance, and accountability.

- **Technical leaders** build and lead the execution of a Zero Trust strategy that simultaneously reduces risk and enables digital business processes and business agility. Their work forms, directs, and supports specific initiatives to organize and drive the execution of the Zero Trust strategy. The playbooks include role-specific guidance for CISOs, CIOs, CTOs, technical directors, and other technical and security strategy roles.

- **Managers and architects** translate that Zero Trust strategy into specific plans, architectures, and processes, as well as coordinating and enabling the Zero Trust initiatives. The playbooks include role-specific guidance for managers across security, technology, and business groups, enterprise architects, security architects, technology architects, solution architects, and similar roles.

- **Technical and security practitioners** make Zero Trust real by implementing and operating the technology and processes. These roles bring Zero Trust capabilities to life and integrate them into the organization's technical services, components, and operations. The playbooks include role-specific guidance for engineering and operations professionals focused on infrastructure endpoints, network identity endpoints, cloud services, data, OT, and more.

- **Security operations** apply Zero Trust approaches to manage real-time conflicts with attackers. These roles use Zero Trust capabilities for attack detection, response, and recovery using both reactive approaches and proactive approaches (threat hunting, attack simulation, and more). The playbooks include role-specific guidance for triage analysts (aka *Tier 1*), investigation analysts (aka *Tier 2*), threat hunters, detection engineers, attack simulation (red and purple teaming), IM, TI, and more.

- **Product security and application security** roles ensure that security is integrated into the design, implementation, and operation of applications and services. The playbooks include role-specific guidance for software developers, application team managers, software security engineers, IoT security professionals, and more.

The *Zero Trust Futures* book wraps up the series with a focus on the future and what's to come. This last part looks at how Zero Trust accommodates emerging technologies, including evolving forms of AI, IoT, metaverse technology, affective computing, and more.

*The game is afoot—let's get started!*

# Index

# Other Books You May Enjoy

If you enjoyed this book, you may be interested in these other books by Packt:

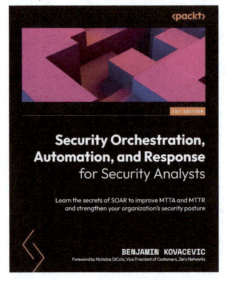

**Security Orchestration, Automation, and Response for Security Analysts**

Benjamin Kovacevic

ISBN: 978-1-80324-291-0

- Get familiarized with and investigate various threat types and attacker techniques
- Analyze email security solution logs and understand email flow and headers
- Practically investigate various Windows threats and attacks
- Analyze web proxy logs to investigate C&C communication attributes
- Reap the general benefits of using the SOAR platform
- Transform manual investigations into automated scenarios
- Learn how to manage known false positives and low-severity incidents for faster resolution
- Explore tips and tricks using various Microsoft Sentinel playbook actions
- Get an overview of tools such as Palo Alto XSOAR, Microsoft Sentinel, and Splunk SOAR

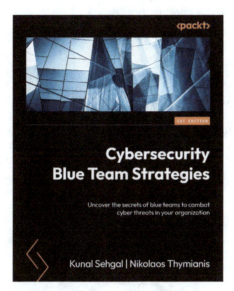

**Cybersecurity Blue Team Strategies**

Kunal Sehgal, Nikolaos Thymianis

ISBN: 978-1-80107-247-2

- Understand blue team operations and its role in safeguarding businesses
- Explore everyday blue team functions and tools used by them
- Become acquainted with risk assessment and management from a blue team perspective
- Discover the making of effective defense strategies and their operations
- Find out what makes a good governance program
- Become familiar with preventive and detective controls for minimizing risk

# Packt is searching for authors like you

If you're interested in becoming an author for Packt, please visit `authors.packtpub.com` and apply today. We have worked with thousands of developers and tech professionals, just like you, to help them share their insight with the global tech community. You can make a general application, apply for a specific hot topic that we are recruiting an author for, or submit your own idea.

# Share Your Thoughts

Now you've finished *Zero Trust Overview and Playbook Introduction*, we'd love to hear your thoughts! Scan the QR code below to go straight to the Amazon review page for this book and share your feedback or leave a review on the site that you purchased it from.

`https://packt.link/r/1800568665`

Your review is important to us and the tech community and will help us make sure we're delivering excellent quality content.

# Download a free PDF copy of this book

Thanks for purchasing this book!

Do you like to read on the go but are unable to carry your print books everywhere?

Is your eBook purchase not compatible with the device of your choice?

Don't worry, now with every Packt book you get a DRM-free PDF version of that book at no cost.

Read anywhere, any place, on any device. Search, copy, and paste code from your favorite technical books directly into your application.

The perks don't stop there, you can get exclusive access to discounts, newsletters, and great free content in your inbox daily

Follow these simple steps to get the benefits:

1. Scan the QR code or visit the link below

https://packt.link/free-ebook/978-1-80056-866-2

2. Submit your proof of purchase
3. That's it! We'll send your free PDF and other benefits to your email directly

www.ingramcontent.com/pod-product-compliance
Lightning Source LLC
LaVergne TN
LVHW081522050326
832903LV00025B/1589